Alcohol and Violence

Alcohol and Violence

The Nature of the Relationship and the Promise of Prevention

Robert Nash Parker and Kevin J. McCaffree

LEXINGTON BOOKS
Lanham • Boulder • New York • Toronto • Plymouth, UK

Published by Lexington Books
A wholly owned subsidiary of The Rowman & Littlefield Publishing Group, Inc.
4501 Forbes Boulevard, Suite 200, Lanham, Maryland 20706
www.rowman.com

10 Thornbury Road, Plymouth PL6 7PP, United Kingdom

British Library Cataloguing in Publication Information Available

Library of Congress Cataloging-in-Publication Data
Parker, Robert Nash.
  Alcohol and violence : the nature of the relationship and the promise of prevention /
Robert Nash Parker and Kevin J. McCaffree.
    p. cm.
  Includes bibliographical references and index.
  ISBN 978-0-7391-8011-2 (cloth : alk. paper)—ISBN 978-0-7391-8012-9 (electronic)
  1. Alcoholism and crime—United States. 2. Violent crimes—United States. 3. Violent
crimes—United States—Prevention. I. McCaffree, Kevin J., 1985– II. Title.
  HV5053.P373 2013
  364.2'4—dc23   2012041480

♾️™ The paper used in this publication meets the minimum requirements of
American National Standard for Information Sciences—Permanence of Paper
for Printed Library Materials, ANSI/NISO Z39.48-1992.

Printed in the United States of America

Contents

Part II: The Promise of Prevention

List of Figures

List of Tables

Robert Nash Parker's Acknowledgments

It is somewhat of an understatement to say that this book has been a long time coming. The senior author recently completed reading a three volume study of the a major historical war in which the author admitted it had taken him five times as long to write about that war as it had taken to fight the war! Although there has been no shooting in connection with the writing or completion of this book, it has taken nearly fifteen years from inception to the completion of this volume in January 2013. Of course, the senior author was not always working full time, part time, or even a little bit on this book during that long period, but as it has often been said in many circumstances, this book and its content were very frequently on my mind and in my thoughts.

The author of the text on the war offered another excuse; he pointed out that there were a lot more people fighting the war then the single author writing about that war. This was true about this book as well; the decision that really facilitated the completion of this book was when the senior author asked Kevin J. McCaffree to join him as a coauthor in the summer of 2011. Kevin has been wonderful to work with, and the two of us have successfully completed a number of projects to date; this book being the most important and, the senior author would suggest, the most successful to date of our collaborations. I (the senior author) am eternally grateful to Kevin for his hard work, creativity, diligence, thoroughness, and his ability to get things done. Truly, although the phrase is so overused, with Kevin's involvement, this book would not have been completed. Many of the chapters in this book existed for several of the last fifteen years in draft form, or in summary, or consisted of an abstract and results submitted to a conference and presented at said conference; what Kevin did in each case, chapter by chapter, was look at what I had produced, update the literature reviews, suggest where new analysis was needed, develop new theoretical arguments or strengthen existing ones, and make revisions. I would then read what he had produced, rewrite, edit, redraw conclusions, cast different light on the results, and conclusions. Kevin would then go over the new product, revise, edit, suggest deletions, and so on, and we would both give a final read and be ready to move to the next chapter. So while there are other authors on some of the chapters (more about which will be said below), who are listed because they made significant and essential contributions to the research reported in the chapters, Kevin and I are responsible for writing this book in its entirety.

Like any honest author, I wish to acknowledge that many others who study alcohol and social behavior have had significant influences on me and on the content of this book. The naming of these individuals and our acknowledgement of their influence in no way results in any responsibility on their part for the content of this work, which remains 100 percent with Kevin and me. First among this group are the "twin" towers of alcohol research, Harold Holder and Robin Room, who were serving as directors of the two NIAAA-funded alcohol research centers in Berkeley, California, when a recently tenured sociologist on his first sabbatical from the University of Iowa, gratefully became a post-doctoral fellow in the then joint training program run by PRC and ARG (Prevention Research Center and Alcohol Research Group, respectively). Each of the directors had significant influence on me, a total "newby" to the field of alcohol research. Harold was a true man of science, and his commitment to the scientific enterprise was inspiring and resonated with my own stance that sociology is a science, and must proceed by the scientific method of theory-driven empirically tested investigations that were continuously adjusted to reflect the results of prior analysis. Harold's passion drove exploration, pursuit of new and creative thinking, and a commitment to achievement that held all who worked at PRC to a very high standard. Harold was encouraging to me directly for the study of alcohol and violence; he directly supported my work on my previous book on the topic, and helped me and others develop some of the research projects that are reported upon in the chapters of this book.

Robin Room is the quintessential scholar, someone driven by ideas and the insatiable need to understand the complex and sometimes surprising relationship between society and alcohol. Robin always has questions; he is, of course, an empirical researcher of the first rate, creative and pioneering in the use of survey research to study drinking patterns and problems, but along with the most useful answers about this relationship, Robin always has questions; are we sure we know what we think we know, and what else might be going on? One of the lessons I learned and continue to learn from Robin is that what appears to be may not be the whole story, and that one should keep peeling the layers of the onion off until the core knowledge is revealed. Robin is also a great recruiting for the field of alcohol research—he is always looking to bring in new folks with new perspectives who can bring new light to old questions, or explore unexplored aspects. Robin's direct influence on this book comes from a question he once put to me after we had attended one of these classic "what is known and not known" up till then about alcohol and various social behaviors; Robin asked me, has anyone done a long-term time series analysis of alcohol and violence in the United States? I said no, not to my knowledge; Robin turned to me, and said, you should do it. The effect of that comment shows directly in several chapters in this book where we have used interrupted time series models as well as other dynamic and over time statistical methods to investigate various aspects of this complex and surprising relationship.

A number of others in the cast of characters in Berkeley at the two centers in the early 1990s when I was there also had an impact on my thinking and my research. Joel Grube, Paul Gruenewald, Roland Moore, Bill Ponicki, Barbara Nygaard, Anita Martin, and others created a great environment for work and fun at the PRC. Paul Gruenewald and Bill Ponicki were fellow conspirators in a growing interest in spatial analysis and mapping as it applied to alcohol and social problems, an influence that is also strongly evident in several of the chapters in this book.

At ARG, the intellectual atmosphere was enlivened by the presence of Cheryl Cherpitel, Connie Weisner, and Tom Greenfield; Andrew Treno, who started as I did as a fellow post doc, was a significant companion in intellectual arms right from the beginning of my exposure and entrance into alcohol research. The seminar, required of pre- and post-doctoral fellows, was no chore for me; it was exciting and stimulating.

Two of the people I met and got to know in this era require additional and special mention here. Maria Alaniz is a coauthor of three of the chapters in this book. These three chapters represent a larger body of work that derives from a research project on which Maria and I were the co-investigators. This project was designed to investigate the link between alcohol, alcohol advertising, and youth violence in communities in northern California. Results from this project have been previously published in several outlets (e.g., Alaniz et al., 1998), but like many multiyear and multifaceted projects, there are often many very interesting and significant results not published in the first rush to get results out into print. One of the advantages of persistence is that we have finally published much of the very exciting results we produced in that project. Maria was a wonderful collaborator; we shared a common viewpoint, worrying about various aspects of the project, commiserating about the problems we ran into, sharing the triumphs, and so on. After I left PRC in 1996, I keep sending emails to Maria saying, I am working on this or that aspect of the data we collected, but I am sure she had her doubts—but she never expressed those, instead encouraging me and offering her support. Now, with the completion of this book, I can finally claim the fulfillment of that collaboration began in 1993. Without Maria's hard work and collaboration, some of the best and most exciting parts of this book would not exist.

One of the coauthors listed on chapter 1, Robert F. Saltz, also deserves additional comment here. Bob Saltz and I were pretty much instant friends during my year as a post-doctoral fellow at PRC, and when I came back in 1991 full time, we just picked up from there. Both trained as sociologists, both with families of Eastern Costal origins, both with experience in New England, we even discovered people in our past in common. Combine that with a taste for Monty Python and other somewhat off-color (or colour supplement? Oh, I see, Kolour supplement) humor, and we would continue to be good friends. Bob is a thinker, first and foremost, but he never takes himself or others too seriously. We wrote a component in the Center grant that allowed me to begin to serious explore the alcohol and violence link with new and creative data collection, work that led to the case control design of the study reported in chapter 1. My time at PRC in general was an exciting time of original research, when I worked with these wonderful people on the "full monty" as it might be called, of research: design a project from conceptualization and theory; write a proposal to get funding for the project, obtain the funds to collect original data, data designed to address the research questions you developed, and then do the analysis to address those questions, and then write up an article and publish it. If this all works correctly, it takes two to three years from start to finish. I guess I did not do things correctly!

This brings me to 1996 when I received this amazing offer from the University of California, Riverside. I really admire all the people who still work at PRC, as they have had to keep succeeding in getting those projects funded, year after year. My insecurities have always been more prominent, so when UC-Riverside offered me a tenured full professor appointment in an excellent Sociology Department, and the directorship of a state-funded research center dealing with crime and justice research, I really felt I had to take it, despite the hardships that commuting would place on me and my life partner, Cecilia L. Ridgeway. However, this brought me into contact with the final two coauthors listed in this book, Valerie Callanan and Deborah Plechner. These were two of first cohort of really good graduate students I have had the pleasure to have worked with at UC-Riverside, and I got both of them involved immediately in this ongoing research on alcohol and violence. I had hoped to help both of their careers to get off to a good start with some joint publications, and their work on chapters 1 and 9 were important and significant. At least here is belated recognition for their dedication and hard work, and my apologies that it took so long.

A few years later I was finally successful in bringing a team to UC-Riverside that would help to put the Presley Center on the cutting edge of research on crime and justice. In 1998 Kirk Williams and Nancy Guerra joined me as senior faculty at the Presley Center. When you work with others in a serious way, as the three of us did to accomplish what we did, you have to compromise your own interests for the common goals. We agreed on a plan to obtain National Center funding, and the hot ticket of the moment was youth violence. We worked for two years writing proposals and getting turned down until we hit the big time—Center grant funding from CDC, which we held through two renewals, amongst distinguished university company—Harvard, Columbia, and Johns Hopkins also held Center designation in the same program. Although I tried to infuse alcohol and violence research into our Center work, there was a lot going on during those years and a lot of work to do to run one of these research Centers, and that took priority. This did delay the book, but my colleagues and I did some amazing things during these years, and Nancy and Kirk are and remain great collaborators and fabulous friends.

Nothing lasts forever, and after two unsuccessful attempts to continue Center funding, Nancy and Kirk received fabulous offers from the University of Delaware, and given the continued deprivations of the University of California, there was little we could do to prevent their loss. However, the end of our collaboration at Presley did create another opportunity for me to refocus on the alcohol and violence book. This created the opportunity, and the collaboration with Kevin created the finished product.

Many other people deserve thanks for their support of me and Kevin during the completion of this project. The two most important people in this category are Donita McCants Carter and Nelda Thomas, the staff at the Presley Center. These two are simply amazing—they master the massive bureaucracy that is the University of California (I like to say that the UC bureaucracy used to be the second worst in the world—and then the Soviet Union fell!), they get things done when we need them, they handle all our emergencies that stem from bad planning and neglect, and they handle all kinds of mechanical and emotional failures that we suffer from. I know they have our back.

The Sociology Department has been a place of good fellowship and support during the past few years, and I especially want to thank Jon Turner, Alexandra Maryianski, Jan Stets, Peter Burke, Tanya Nieri, Bob Hanneman, Rusty Russell, who distracted me with historical novels, and Steve Brint, who has by example shown us all that one can take on important administrative work and still be a productive scholar. I would also like to mention my appreciation for the students in the Crime and Sociolegal Studies core seminar of the Fall 2011 term, who kept Kevin and me both on our toes theoretically, and the students in my first University Honors program ignition seminar, the problem of social order, also in the Fall 2011 term for keeping me honest and inspiring debate. My colleagues on the Honors program steering committee, Nigel Hughes, Sharon Walker, Perry Link, Christine Gailey, Vorris Nunley, and Tom Perring, offered support and encouragement for the scholarly enterprise, and by example of their productivity, inspirational examples for Kevin and me.

Most importantly, and literally without whom nothing would be possible for me, I want to thank Cecilia L. Ridgeway, Lucy Stern Professor of the Social Sciences, and professor, Sociology Department, Stanford University, for her love and encouragement, and for her fierce commitment to the science of sociology. Every idea and method in this book benefited from a discussion with her at some point or another about the theoretical and scientific merits of the concept and its application. The example of accomplishment and commitment to the enterprise of knowledge has been and continues to be my guiding star in my professional and personal life. I would also like to thank her mother, Jaqueline Ridgeway, PhD in English from UC-Riverside, who has extended her hospitality to me in inexhaustive quantities, and engaged me in stimulating discussions, and since my mother died in 2010 (and before), has fully adopted me as her own. She also has been a never failing supporter of the enterprise of UCR and its promise, and her enthusiasm for the campus has many times re-invigorated my own optimism of what is possible at UCR, this book being but one of many research, teaching, and service examples.

In many ways I view this book as the ultimate statement of my view about the role of alcohol and violence and the possibilities for interrupting this connection that is all too common in our society. It has been a great career; not quite over, but I am happy with this statement as the summary of my research career, and recognizing that there is not much time left in my career, I offer this to the researchers, scholars, practitioners, prevention specialists, the victims of alcohol-related violence and yes, the offenders, all of whom I sincerely hope can find something useful herein.

Kevin J. McCaffree's Acknowledgments

There are those who have directly influenced the creation of this book and those whose influence has been more indirect. An exhaustive list of either would be not only arduous, but quite likely impossible, so I'll concede ahead of time that the "thank you" list which follows is necessarily anemic.

I'm honored to be in the position to congratulate and thank our various collaborating chapter authors, chief among them the lead-author of this book, Robert Nash Parker. It is an unhelpful fiction that graduate school teaches through books and isolated contemplation. The majority of what I carry with me as a day-to-day scholar I've gleaned through observing great researchers. Humans are the great mimics among primates, and I've been arrestingly lucky to learn to do my job from those with both passionate and ethically uncompromising research orientations. Rob, the world of public policy, criminology, and quantitative research is better for having heard your voice and the fog of my own professional insecurities has begun to slowly dissipate in response to this realization.

I would like also to thank Nelda Thomas and Donita McCants-Carter, our faithful and hardworking partners at the Presley Center for Crime and Justice Studies who are always ready and able to help with whatever glitch comes up. I'd be simply forgetful not to also thank the Department of Sociology at UC Riverside for all of their help and guidance, if not directly in the making of this book, then in the indirect encouragement I've been given throughout my tenure (so far) in graduate school. Chief among these influences, and profoundly valuable to me and my development as a scholar, are Robert Nash Parker, Jonathan H. Turner, Jan E. Stets, Peter Burke, Stephen K. Sanderson, and Alexandra Maryanski among others. I'm also the fabulously lucky beneficiary of dizzyingly intelligent peers in graduate school who continuously improve my own thinking: Matt Dunn, Tony Roberts, Stanton Gagel, and the rest, you know who you are.

It is personally important to me that I disabuse the reader of the idea that I've made it here, as a coauthor of an important book in this arena of social science, just by virtue of learning the methods of scholarly inquiry. On the contrary, I owe my very love of knowledge to some who've never set foot inside a research institute or lab. My mother and father, Patricia and Stephen, are consistent sources of a fiery encouragement that scalds my fears and pushes me to achieve that which I had once thought was not possible. I've been lucky as well to learn from the strong women in my life; I won't list names (okay, just one, Anondah), but to these women I owe, in part, my attitude and direction in life. Your strength and resilience is an inspiration that reaches far beyond you.

Above all, I'd like to carve out an enduring "thank you," that I wish to stand above all others: my Great-Aunt Ruthie, the woman who handed me my first book at age three or four entitled, "Stories for Kevin"; the woman who thought it necessary to tickle my creativity and intrigue my imaginings as a small child and who is now a few days over ninety. You are with me every day, and you, first above all, taught me to pour fuel on the creative fires that so desperately need cultivation. Ruthie, this book is for you.

Introduction

The existence of a link between alcohol and violence has been acknowledged and discussed in the scientific literature and elsewhere at least since the middle of the twentieth century. Marvin Wolfgang's landmark study of homicides in the City of Philadelphia between 1948 and 1952 (Wolfgang, 1958) was one of the first systematic examinations of the connection between alcohol use and violent incidents, but curiously this aspect of Wolfgang's research was ignored by most students of homicide in the next several decades. Wolfgang's approach was replicated in a number of cities in the United States, but little or no attention was paid to the examination of alcohol and its relationship to homicide (Pettigrew & Spier, 1962; Pokorny, 1965; Voss & Hepburn, 1968; Hepburn & Voss, 1970; Bean & Cushing, 1971; Boudouris, 1971).

Why was this the case? Perhaps the police in other cities were not as sensitive to the role that alcohol seemed to play in homicide, or perhaps the link between the two was considered so mundane that it did not need to be discussed by officers in other places in the United States. Perhaps it had something to do with the role of alcohol in US society; after all, the history of alcohol as a "bad boy" in public policy had been thoroughly and completely mandated in the repeal of Prohibition more than twenty-five years before Wolfgang's research.

The post–World War II era in the United States was one of prosperity and increasing alcohol consumption. Overall consumption between 1950 and 1970 increased some 24 percent and consumption of spirits, the alcoholic beverage of choice of the WW II generation, increased 44 percent during these two decades (NIAAA, 2007). The literature on the impact of Prohibition had begun to suggest that this attempt to legislate morality, a moral campaign by moral entrepreneurs (Gusfield, 1986; Ammerman et al., 1999), was a disastrous mistake from all perspectives, moral, civil, criminal, political, and medical. This notion that Prohibition had been a universal

1

failure became entrenched in the official lore of academia, government agencies tasked to investigate the relationship between alcohol and health, and among the public in general. To question this established dogma was to be labeled, a "Neo-Prohibitionist" or a "Puritanical Moralist," both of which the senior author has been labeled by the alcohol industry and their apologists among social scientists who study addiction and alcohol.

The accepted wisdom concerning Prohibition and its impact was logically extended to the alcohol and violence relationship by suggesting that since Prohibition had caused more rather than less violence, that consumption of alcohol was not a factor in violence (e.g., Peralta & Cruz, 2006). The nadir of this argument in many ways was the publication in 1981 of James Collins's edited volume, *Drinking and Crime: Perspectives on the Relationship between Alcohol Consumption and Criminal Behavior* (Guilford Press); and a subsequent review by Collins published in a 1989 chapter entitled, "Alcohol and Violence: Less Than Meets the Eye" (Wiener & Wolfgang, 1989: 49–67). The edited volume was a collection of studies meant to show that the alcohol and violence relationship was less than it seemed—a causal chain linking alcohol and violence, it was argued, was not supported by the hard evidence of scientific research. For example, Pernanen (1981: 1–69) in a long and confusing chapter repeatedly emphasized that the relationship between alcohol and crime is likely to be spurious. He described three different types of spurious models that might account for the apparently false relationship and called data like Wolfgang's (1958) "coincidence figures" (1981: 61) in a not so subtle attempt to undermine any sense of scientific validity. Yet Pernanen's own attempts to explicate a reasonable theory of alcohol and crime fell flat.

Greenberg (1981: 70–109) presented a long litany of methodological mistakes made by those attempting to investigate this relationship, including poor measurement, inadequate sampling, lack of appropriate controls, and the failure to investigate this relationship across subgroups and contrasting contexts (1981: 71). Most areas of social science can be assessed for bad research, and a great deal is found, but the reader is drawn to the conclusion that this research area is somehow particularly bad. Collins (1981: 152–206) himself offers a smoke screen to the alcohol violence relationship by examining whether or not "career" criminals have their careers in crime caused by alcohol. This is a very red herring, as most experts find that the notion of a "career" criminal is problematic at best and baseless at worst, but, nevertheless, Collins concludes that, "It does not appear that alcohol is a causal or precipitating factor in the origin of criminal careers" (1981: 199). Indeed, Collins cites no evidence that anyone ever had such an hypothesis in the first place; his chapter simply presents research on drinking patterns over the life course, the literature on career criminals, and then states the obvious fact that there seems to be no connection.

Collins's own explicit attempt to undermine the idea that alcohol might be a cause of violence is interesting in the degree to which, despite having edited and written what he did in the 1981 volume, he makes all the mistakes that he identifies as undermining the evidence for such a relationship in the article, "Alcohol and Interpersonal Violence: Less Than Meets the Eye," (1989: 49–67). For example, Collins (1981: 313) argues strongly against the use of incarcerated samples, as does Greenberg (1981: 79–80) in the same volume. However, Collins in 1989 cited prison studies as a major source of data to undermine a causal relationship between alcohol and violence (1989: 54–56). Collins further argues that alcohol is not a cause of violence as some respondents in surveys use a deviance disavowal approach to justify their behavior (1989: 59). This happens in situations where offenders drink, commit violent offenses, and then claim that they drank in order to give themselves an excuse for their behavior (McCaghy, 1968; Mosher, 1983). Such a conclusion gives primacy to the individual subject as an authority who is assumed to fully understand why he behaves the way he does, a level of self-insight probably preciously uncommon among most people most of the time. It also privileges post hoc explanations, rather than the sequence of events that led to the violent crime. As far as Collins is concerned, it looks like prison studies are criticized when they show a connection between alcohol and violence, and used as evidence against such a relationship when the data are less conclusive.

Collins and Greenberg are right that prison studies give a potentially biased view of the role of alcohol in crime. There are a number of reasons for this that neither of these reviews discusses. For example, it may be that subjects in prison studies show higher levels of involvement of both drugs and alcohol (Goldstein's studies of substance use and crime among prisoners are also subject to the same critique, e.g., Goldstein, 1985; see also Parker & Auerhahn, 1998) because in the period right before the inmate was caught for the offense that led to their current imprisonment was an increased period of substance use; careful prison studies ask about the period prior to current incarceration. It also may be the case that incarcerated prisoners do not fully understand the causal factors that resulted in their incarceration. Like the criminal justice system in the United States, in which eyewitness testimony is privileged despite the fact that it is the most unreliable type of evidence available in the system (see Fradella, 2006), social science often privileges the self-reports of respondents or subjects, despite the fact that people do not always completely understand their motivations or actions.

Fortunately, a great deal of new scholarship on the alcohol and violence relationship that does not rely on incarcerated samples has been published in the last two decades, and it is much more likely now than it might have been during the 1980s when Collins and colleagues published their reviews to find many researchers and social scientists who are willing to conclude that alcohol plays a causal role in the genesis of interpersonal violence. For example, Lipsey et al. (1997) came to much stronger conclusions after sifting through the alcohol and violence literature than did Collins (1989). An issue of the National Institute on Alcohol Abuse and Alcoholism's (NIAAA) peer refereed journal, *Alcohol Research and Health* (2001, no. 1), contains a number of papers in which pathways of alcohol to violence and causal relationships are discussed. In its most recent decade-spanning report to the US Congress in 2000 titled "Alcohol and Health," the NIAAA states: ". . . the convergence of environmental studies on the basic finding that alcohol availability and violence are positively related, taken together with the results of individual-level studies suggesting a relationship between alcohol consumption and violence, has increased the scientific community's confidence that alcohol availability plays a causal role in the generation of violence. However, additional research is needed to determine how alcohol availability interacts with other factors in the causal process leading to violence" (2000: 61).

This report stood in stark contrast to a 1990 NIAAA report to Congress indicating that the evidence was unclear, inconclusive, that is was presumptive to argue for a causal role for alcohol in violence, and, finally that, "It should be noted, however, that alcohol's presence in a violent event does not indicate that the drug caused the event" (NIAAA 1990: 307). A decade of research into the link between alcohol and violence provided more and more evidence of a causal connection and indicated the robustness of the finding. However, the 10th report to Congress had the right idea to call for more research investigating how, under what conditions, using what measurement strategies, at what level of aggregation, in what culture, and in what time frame, alcohol contributed as a cause of violence. This book is one answer to this challenge, and it reflects work that we and a number of colleagues and students have done during the seventeen years since the publication of *Alcohol and Homicide: A Deadly Combination of Two American Traditions* (Parker & Rebhun, 1995).

There is one additional idea that needs to be introduced before discussing the content of this volume in more detail. During the last two decades a new approach has come to take its place among public health, social science, and substance abuse researchers based on the idea that if one could understand the causes of problems like alcohol abuse, crime, traffic accidents, infectious disease transmission, and so on, it would be possible to design research studies that would attempt to intervene in the causal chain and thereby prevent the negative outcome in question. This is not really a new idea, but the recognition of its importance is. One indicator is that the Society for Prevention Research, founded in 1991 with nineteen members, organized its 20th Annual meeting in 2012 in Washington, DC, now with 800 members. Nor was this an isolated development. C. Ray Jeffrey's book, *Crime Prevention through Environmental Design*, was published in 1971 (Sage Publications). The basic idea behind these intellectual movements and related ones in other fields is that in order to reduce the harmful consequences of certain behaviors, it may be more effective to alter aspects of the environment—physical, social, political, economic—that either encourage, allow, or inhibit the behaviors that produce the negative outcomes. Environments can be altered, and this change can have a significant impact on the individual's ability to engage in potentially dangerous behaviors.

Thus the concept of environmental prevention: change the environment in which people interact, and you can change the nature of that interaction without having to change people's attitudes, opinions, and desires. For example, the American Medical Association website for environmental prevention as applied to alcohol policy states, "Environmental prevention uses policy interventions to create an alcohol environment that supports healthy, safe behavior" (AMA, 2002). Chapter 6 will provide a review of the environmental prevention literature of the last twenty years with a special focus on alcohol prevention efforts. Indeed, environmental prevention is the underlying notion of the second half of this book: we argue that city official and political leaders can employ alcohol policy in an environmental prevention mode to help reduce and prevent much of the alcohol-related violence that is detailed in the first part of the book.

PART I: THE NATURE OF THE RELATIONSHIP

This book will showcase the strong causal nature of the relationship between alcohol and violence. In the first section, five original research studies are presented in separate chapters that test the range and scope of this relationship. In chapter 1, we explore the relationship between crime victimization, injury, and alcohol. Although much of the focus of previous conceptual and empirical work has been on the role of alcohol as a cause of violence, alcohol can and does contribute to victimization in a number of ways as well. One of the assumptions made by many readers is that for alcohol to have an impact on violence, either the victim or the offender had to have been drinking prior to the event. In a case-control design, with representative samples of victims and non-victims from a medium-sized California community, the study discussed in chapter 1 examines the role that victim drinking plays in the risk of violent crime victimization and injury. Do the circumstances of victimization or injury differ when one has been drinking immediately prior to the victimization? Do victims and non-victims differ in terms of victimization-related drinking, regular drinking patterns, or both? In one of the best measured tests of routine activity theory to date, can routine alcohol-related behavior be considered a risk factor for violence victimization and injury? The results presented in this chapter demonstrate the power of this approach, and indicate that both the general drinking pattern and the specific drinking activity associated with the violent victimization (compared to comparable drinking events among the non-victims) are part of the set of risk factors that lead to violence.

Chapter 2 deals with what is perhaps the most promising area for understanding the alcohol and violence relationship, and the place with the greatest potential for prevention, a space that lies between the individual and the large scale level of the state or nation where policy debates and legislation have typically occurred in the past. In this chapter the results of a study of alcohol availability and youth violence, measured at what we term the "micro-aggregate" level of analysis, are presented. Three small communities in Northern California were examined at the US Census Bureau Block Group level, the smallest unit within the Census data for which consistent data on race, ethnicity, and income can be obtained. Designed to be between four and eight city blocks, with a corresponding population of between 400 and 1800, the block group is small enough to imagine social interaction taking place, but large enough to generalize across units. Why examine youth violence and its relationship to alcohol? The fact that all fifty states in the United States have passed a twenty-one-year-old drinking age does not necessarily mean that youth are no longer able to obtain alcohol. In fact, a study of two similar California communities revealed that youth were successful at buying alcohol somewhere between 30 and 80 percent of the time (Grube, 1997). Is it the case that increased availability of alcohol sold in convenience stores, grocery stores, and even liquor stores is indicative of greater access to alcohol by under-age youth? If this were the case we would expect higher rates of youth violence in block groups with greater retail availability of alcohol, which is one of the main findings reported in this chapter for two of the three cities we examined.

The impact of advertising, a very controversial subject, fraught with ideological, commercial, and moral conflicts and controversies, is examined in chapter 3. Is there a connection between the content of advertising and violence? If so, why would such a relationship exist? In one of the three cities analyzed in chapter 2, we further examined the content of alcohol advertising in each and every place where alcohol was sold in that community. Using trained coders with a 95 percent inter-coder reliability rating, we measured the overall density of ads in each block group, the density of ads that were clearly targeted at specific ethnic groups, and the density of ads that contained images that were obviously exploitative and demeaning to women. These latter ads almost always used Latina models in provocative, sexual, and commodifying positions, with little or no clothing and with a clear message: sex and female adoration come with the use of this alcohol product. The analysis shows that ads with this latter type of content have a significant impact, net of other factors, on the sexual crimes committed against both Latina and non-Latina girls in these same block groups. Though somewhat limited in scope, such findings pose a powerful challenge to the alcohol industry's claims that advertising is only about getting adults to shift brands. With this in mind, we suggest some powerful local tools for regulating the alcohol and violence relationship.

In chapter 4, a two-wave study of the onset of violence and alcohol use is conducted with a sample of elementary school children in California. One of the most controversial areas in the causal versus spurious debate on the alcohol violence relationship has been in the early childhood and adolescent development of violence and alcohol abuse. One major set of studies has consistently found that violence tends to occur prior to the onset of alcohol use among children and younger adolescents, suggesting that at least developmentally, the relationship is either spurious or the causal arrow runs from violence to alcohol abuse (e.g., White et al., 1987; 1993). However, all of these findings have been from one major clinical data set in one location—not from a representative sample, and there has been no replication in other areas with more diverse populations.

Chapter 4, then, reports on a study of late elementary school children in which, across two waves of longitudinal data, we find that early experience of aggression and victimization leads to more favorable attitudes toward violence and aggression over time. However, there is no direct relationship between experiencing violence and alcohol or drug use. In the second wave, however, attitudes supporting the legitimacy of violence do lead to alcohol and drug use. In addition, alcohol and drug use lead to greater aggression and violence in wave 2. These findings are suggestive of a complex reciprocal relationship between aggression, alcohol and drug use, and development that is not fully understood given the current scientific data available for this crucial period of a child's development and growth.

In 1990 Rosemary Gartner published an article specifying and testing what remains today the most comprehensive theoretically driven model of homicide and gender differences among eighteen advanced democratic/industrialized nations of North America, Europe, and Asia. In 1998, the senior author published an article which extended Gartner's original analysis by "adding booze" to the Gartner model, that is, deriving hypotheses about the impact of alcohol on male and female homicide victimization in seventeen of the eighteen nations studied by Gartner covering the same 1950 through 1980 time frame. The findings reported in the latter paper were extraordinary because they showed that alcohol had an impact on both male and female homicide victimization, but that these effects were additive to Gartner's model and were part of interaction effects with Gartner's original concepts. In other words, adding alcohol to the statistical model as a direct cause of violence did little to undermine Gartner's original findings that material context, integrative context, demographic patterns of work and the age structure, and the culture of violence in a society are significant predictors of homicide victimization for women and men. The addition of the alcohol variable also showed some additional differences between the predictors of male and female homicide victimization, and chapter 5, the final examination hereof the nature of the relationship between alcohol and violence, extends this analysis to the year 1995. Given the changing nature of violence during the 1980s and 1990s, especially in the United States, do Gartner's findings hold up? Do the alcohol impacts found in the earlier study persist through an additional fifteen years of data? The results of this chapter show that Gartner's original model has some robustness and that some of the impact that drinking styles and consumption have on male and female homicides results in some differences in predictions of the original model.

PART II: THE PROMISE OF PREVENTION

The relatively new field of environmental prevention is described and reviewed in chapter 6. There are many examples in everyday life of environmental prevention, and in the last decade of the twentieth century the science began to catch up to the practice in this area. It is so often the case that efforts to change the behavior of individuals are found to be difficult if not impossible, especially with regard to addictive behaviors. But what if local officials and others with political influence were to change the environment in such a way that the individual no longer had any choice but to go along? There are many examples of environmental prevention working "magically" where numerous attempts at individual persuasion have failed. One famous example linking alcohol and violence is the case of the infamous bleachers at Fenway Park, the Red Sox's baseball stadium in Boston. Fans would drink too much beer and get into fights by the end of the game. Team officials tried a number of individually oriented prevention strategies: limiting the number of beers each fan could buy; raising the price to discourage individuals; shrinking the size of the cups sold and none of this had an impact on the rate at which drunken fights would break out. Finally, an environmental approach was used: the beer sales windows simply shut after about half the game was over. This environmental strategy worked, and the drunken brawls disappeared from this section of the stands. Environmental prevention has recently shown effectiveness in public health, crime prevention, and in reducing drunk driving and other alcohol related incidents, and there is extant evidence to suggest that alcohol-caused violence can be reduced or increased by changes in the environment. The following four chapters are carefully designed scientific studies which provide empirical evidence of the power of environmental prevention with regard to alcohol-related violence.

The greatest social experiment of the second half of the twentieth century took place between 1976 and 1988. This experiment was a national effort, led by the federal government and such grass roots organizations as MADD (Mothers against Drunk Driving), to raise the minimum age for purchase of alcohol from eighteen to twenty-one, so that now we have a uniform legal lower age limit in all fifty states. During the various national and state debates, no evidence was produced to indicate that concern over youth violence was one of the motivating factors that led to this great social experiment. However, given the theoretical arguments and empirical evidence presented here and elsewhere, it is of great scientific and policy interest to ask, what effects did the raising of the minimum age have on youth violence? In a pooled cross sectional time series model, in which it is possible to account for both state to state variation and over-time state/nation trends, the impact of the minimum drinking age is estimated in the context of the most comprehensive model in this literature. The findings presented in chapter 7 show that minimum age increases had significant effects on reducing crime, especially in the early part of the period 1972 to 1992, and that factors such as taxation, alcohol consumption, alcohol regulation, and William Julius Wilson's concept of urban minority concentration also contribute significantly to a full understanding of youth homicide. This chapter also examines race and gender differences with some surprising results. These results from chapter 7 demonstrate on a national level the power of alcohol-related environmental change to impact violence in important ways.

There is much conventional wisdom and so-called common sense behind the conclusion that America's national experiment with alcohol prohibition was a colossal failure, what with increased criminal violence around smuggling, fantastic increases in illegal production, and speakeasies on every corner in urban areas. Chapter 8 presents hard empirical evidence challenging this view, especially with regard to public health and everyday interpersonal violence. If national prohibition was not a total failure, is it the case that prohibition, as a violence prevention tool for some communities under some circumstances, might be effective today? In the early 1990s the town of Barrow, Alaska, undertook a natural experiment to see if prohibition could work in a modern yet completely isolated Native American/American community. Previously published research based on this set of occurrences, in which the town voted to ban all alcohol, including possession, voted to lift the ban twelve months later, voted to re-impose the ban six months later, and to revoke the ban six months after that, examined some of the public health impact of prohibition; this chapter examines the impact of this experiment on criminal assault. Similar to the findings published in the *Journal of the American Medical Association* in 1997 by Arva Chiu, Pedro Perez, and this book's senior author, the imposition of prohibition had an instantaneous and huge impact on assaults, resulting in a drop of nearly 90 percent of assaults in this community of seven thousand people. When the ban on alcohol was lifted, assaults in one month increased to a rate higher than the average monthly rate based on twelve months of data prior to the imposition of prohibition, and gradually returned to the pre-prohibition average. The second time prohibition was imposed the results were almost identical, and when the prohibitory ban was lifted yet again, assaults increased dramatically. Is prohibition the solution to violence? No, not for the vast majority of communities. However, these results show that for isolated communities with a concern for public health and safety, prohibition in the twenty-first century may be a viable option.

Sometimes the real world is inhospitable to the researcher trying to gain a better understanding of the behavior observed, and sometimes you get really lucky! Recall that in chapter 2 the results from a three community study in Northern California were presented, showing a general and replicable impact of alcohol availability on youth violence over time and across space using geospatial statistical models to correct for the kinds of problems such data engender. In one of those cities, Union City, California, a small suburban community located between San Jose and Oakland on the east side of the San Francisco Bay, science got lucky. Uninfluenced by the fact that a three-year research project on youth violence and alcohol availability was using their community as a site, the City Council decided at the end of year two of the study (1994) to make a major zoning policy change which resulted in the closing of a number of alcohol outlets in five mixed-use residential retail neighborhoods. The change was to revoke the exceptions to the zoning for certain commercial uses and this resulted in a number of retail businesses—not just alcohol outlets—closing. The result was yet another natural experiment the results of which, reported in chapter 9, clearly show that when the outlets were closed, subsequent significant drops in youth violence occurred. These results provide yet another example of the causal effects of alcohol on violence, and the potential to use alcohol control as a policy lever for violence reduction and prevention.

As is the case with several of the chapters in this book, the three communities participating in the "Community Trials Project," funded by NIAAA in the early to mid-1990s, did not explicitly identify alcohol-related violence as a goal of the multiple coordinated interventions launched in these three cities (Ocean Side and Salinas, California, and Florence, South Carolina). However, the initiatives as a whole were designed to reduce consumption and limit availability of alcohol in the communities involved. Thus it is legitimate to ask if these interventions had an impact on rates of violence in these communities. Using interrupted time series statistical models, chapter 10 reports the results, which show significant effects of these interventions in one of the communities; like reductions in the minimum drinking age, alcohol control polices do not necessarily have to be directly aimed at violence in order to reduce violence in the community. The evidence in this study and all of those presented here shows that because there is a causal link between alcohol and violence, adjusting alcohol policy necessarily results in changes in violence.

The research presented in this book provides numerous examples of violence declining as a result of alcohol policy changes. These changes are often cases of enforcement of existing regulations and re-application of existing policies that are neither expensive nor controversial at the local level. Chapter 11, the concluding chapter of the book, not only provides a summary of the findings of the previously discussed research but describes in some detail a set of interventions, policy changes, and practices that would result in reduced rates of violence in communities across the United States. This is the promise that alcohol policy and regulation has for preventing and reducing violence in our cities and communities.

I

THE NATURE OF THE RELATIONSHIP

1

Alcohol and the Risk of Violent Victimization and Injury

Robert Nash Parker, Kevin J. McCaffree,
Valarie Callanan, and Robert F. Saltz

INTRODUCTION

Although there has been a great deal of research in criminology on the causes of assault and robbery, the impact of alcohol has been largely ignored. Though Parker's (1991) review of thirty studies on robbery and assault did not yield one study that dealt with the role of alcohol, things have improved somewhat in the intervening two decades. As with all shifts in thought, the identification and elaboration of the alcohol variable is due in large part to the concerted efforts of a number of researchers.

Today, alcohol consumption is a slightly more common variable entered into models dealing with crimes like robbery and assault in America (e.g., see Scribner et al., 1995; Costanza et al., 2001; Nielsen & Martinez, 2003; Zhu et al., 2004) and the alcohol variable is also not uncommon in the international literature on alcohol and violence (e.g., in the Carribean—Pierce & Kuhns, 2011, or in Australia—Stevenson et al., 1999). Nevertheless, and despite the promising increase in studies taking alcohol's effect on violence into account, the variable of alcohol (both in terms of consumption and availability) is still relatively downplayed in the criminological literature. So-called harder drugs always seem to steal for themselves the lion's share of criminological and media attention (Miller et al., 2006) despite, as it turns out, alcohol being biochemically perhaps the "hardest" and most socially dangerous drug of all (Nutt et al., 2007).

Prior to the early 1990s, the causes of robbery and assault were assumed to lie, not in the use and availability of alcohol, but in poverty (Smith & Bennett, 1985; Sampson, 1987; Smith & Jarjoura, 1987), economic inequality (Carroll & Jackson, 1983; Golden & Messner, 1987), and various lifestyles/routine activities (Cohen & Felson, 1979; Cohen et al., 1981; Hindelang, 1987; Miethe et al., 1987; Sampson & Wooldredge, 1988; Maxfield, 1989). Economic inequality and poverty in general are substantial, consistent, and frequently demonstrated causal factors in human violence. This chapter neither denies this fact nor attempts a new interpretation of these findings. What is examined here is, rather, one important example of the impact of the lifestyle/routine activities that people engage in and how these can facilitate acts of violence. Lifestyles and routine activities, of course, always and of necessity occur in certain ecologies and in certain social structural arrangements with characteristics (such as poverty) that feedback on and influence the daily activities of the people living there.

Routine activity theory (Cohen & Felson, 1979) is one of the most cited and substantiated general theories of crime in contemporary sociological criminology. This ecological/environmental theory specifies three intersecting conditions common to the occurrence of crime: motivated offenders, suitable targets, and a lack of capable guardians. Cohen and Felson write,

> Each successfully completed violation minimally requires an offender with both criminal inclinations and the ability to carry out those inclinations, a person or object providing a suitable target for the offender, and absence of guardians capable of preventing violations. We emphasize that the lack of any one of these elements normally is sufficient to prevent such violations from occurring. [. . .] This ecological analysis of direct contact predatory violations is intended to be more than metaphorical. In the context of such violations, people, gaining and losing sustenance, struggle among themselves for property, safety, territorial hegemony, sexual outlet, physical control, and sometimes for survival itself. The inter-dependence between offenders and victims can be viewed as a predatory relationship between functionally dissimilar individuals or groups. (Cohen & Felson, 1979: 590)

Routine activity theory also borrows heavily from Hawley's (1959) concepts of rhythm, tempo, and the timing of daily movements and activities of individuals and groups. As people go about their daily lives, the patterns along the dimensions of rhythm, tempo, and timing are important in understanding risk of victimization (Cohen & Felson, 1979). As the rhythm, tempo, and timing of daily activities vary across time, space, and across types of people and groups, the exact nature of the convergence of offenders, victims, and guardianship will vary as will vulnerability to victimization. The probabilistic nature of criminal victimization can be seen in this combination; for example, if effective guardianship exists (i.e., police presence), it will not matter how motivated the offender is, nor how vulnerable the potential victim.

Routine activity theory is still, over thirty years after its formal introduction, a frequently used theoretical framework. This theory, of course, has also benefited from the requisite theoretical and conceptual tinkering common to successful, general theories. Marcus Felson, for example, in 1986 added the rather essential concept of *handlers*, or those guardians in charge of watching over or monitoring potential offenders. This important emphasis on social control comes from a theoretical synthesis of both routine activity theory and Travis Hirschi's (1969) control theory, which was developed after Cohen and Felson's initial 1979 publication (Felson, 1995).

Other important theoretical developments include a synthesis of routine activity theory with rational choice theory, emphasizing that the lifestyles people live (including the motivations of both victims and offenders) are oftentimes the result of informal social calculations designed to maximize perceived benefit and minimize perceived costs (Clark & Felson, 1993). Most recently, Chan et al. (2011) proposed an integrated theoretical model merging routine activity theory with social learning theory (Akers, 1985; Akers et al., 2006) in an attempt to understand the motivations of sexually violent offenders. Despite such theoretical cross-pollination, the general tenets of routine activity theory have been used to explain a variety of phenomena such as victimization among high school students (Henson et al., 2010; Popp & Peguero, 2011), victimization over the internet (Marcum et al., 2010), sexualized murder (Chan et al., 2011), self-control and assault (Franklin, 2011), and even seasonal temperature, time of day, and property crime (Cohn & Rotton, 2000).

This chapter examines a very specific routine activity, drinking behavior, to assess its effect on the probability of criminal victimization. Consumption of alcohol in the context of social events and personal enjoyment is a ubiquitous human habit cross-culturally and especially in America, where the habitual consumption of spirits goes back to the founding of the nation (Parker & Rebhun, 1995).

From the routine activity framework, a number of hypotheses can be derived to explore why alcohol may play an important role in victimization. First, the degree to which people engage in behaviors that place them in locations where alcohol is commonly available (i.e., bars), may place them at higher risk of criminal victimization. For example, going out to eat at a restaurant where alcohol is served, meeting friends at a local bar or tavern, or going to dance at a club or disco increases exposure to victimization. This is the basic tenet of the routine activity perspective; one of the most common indicators used to study the impact of routine behavior on the risk of victimization is whether or not a person leaves home to pursue leisure activities at night. Alcohol clearly has an important role in the routine activity framework, because people who do not leave their homes in order to drink are not exposed to increased risk outside the home. This is supported by evidence which shows that locations which sell alcohol are the settings for many of the violent crime victimizations known to police departments (Sherman et al., 1989; Murray & Roncek, 2008).

So why might going out for drinks elevate one's risk of victimization? First, risk is increased independent of whether or not an individual consumes alcohol, because merely being in locations where alcohol is served means one is more likely to experience exposure to motivated offenders, a reduction of capable guardianship (because proximate others are drinking), and an increase in vulnerability (because alcohol relaxes inhibitions).

Second, routine activity theory suggests that consumption of alcohol increases "vulnerability," and thus, increases the risk of victimization. One's self-control is diminished with alcohol intake and, moreover, proximate others who are also drinking have reduced capacity for self-control, which further increases vulnerability. Alcohol consumption by the victim, independent of that of the offender, would therefore have an important role in victimization because it makes one a better (i.e., more vulnerable) target for offenders. Thus, it is possible to explain the role of alcohol in victimization without using more complex and controversial arguments concerning the role of alcohol in aggression, disinhibition, and behavior of the offender (see Room & Collins, 1983; Pernanen, 1989).

Third, many practical and logistical reasons exist for studying the role of alcohol in victimization. Oftentimes in criminological research, distinguishing between the "victim" and the "offender" in a violent incident is somewhat arbitrary, and is usually dependent on which participant suffers the most serious outcome and/or injury (Lauritsen et al., 1991). This is largely due to the fact that the person most injured in a violent conflict is most likely to receive hospital/medical treatment as the "victim" of an attack, regardless of the patient's actual role in the altercation—much research on acute alcohol consumption and injury rely on hospital self-reports raising the issue of self-selection bias in the sample (e.g., Vinson et al., 2003; Watt et al., 2004).

Furthermore, with the exceptions of several important studies on alcohol and homicide (Wolfgang, 1958; Gerson, 1978; Goodman et al., 1986; Welte & Abel, 1989; Gerson & Preston, 1989; Skog, 1989 and, more recently, Parker et al., 2011), and alcohol and suicide (Brent et al., 1987; Hlady & Middaugh, 1988; Welte et al., 1988; Skog, 1989; and, more recently, Sher et al., 2008; Bossarte & Swahn, 2011) research on alcohol and injuries in America has primarily focused on "unintentional" injury, rather than potentially severe "intentional" injury typified by violent crime such as robbery and assault.

For example, Anda et al. (1988) examined alcohol's effect on fatal injuries resulting from a number of unintentional causes, while a well-done review by Cherpitel et al. (2004) focused only on consumption and subsequent injury without disaggregating the sample into victims of criminal violence and victims of unintentional injury. Elmer and Lin (1985) studied the impact of intoxication on the likelihood of severe trauma-related injuries becoming fatal, and Haberman (1987) and Howland and Hingson (1987; 1988) investigated the connection between alcohol and injuries sustained in a number of accidental situations such as falls, drownings, and automobile crashes.

Other analyses (e.g., Vinson et al., 2003; Watt et al., 2004) that mention the role of alcohol in violence and intentional injury often mention such a relationship only in passing, or as a matter of course, without digging deeper into the connection between acute intoxication, emergency room injury, and criminal violence. Of those studies examining intentional injury, many focus on injuries of relatively low severity. For example, almost 75 percent of the alcohol-related injuries analyzed by Treno et al. (2001) focused on sprains, bruises, cuts, and other injuries of relatively low severity. The most recent, inclusive, and systematic literature review of alcohol-related injury (Taylor et al., 2010) took into account four distinct injury groups; among them, intentional injury. Despite the fact that intentional injury produced the highest odds ratios for intoxication relative to the other groups, no analysis of crime-specific injury was offered.

Clearly, we would gain a better understanding of violent victimization and injury sustained if we study alcohol consumption by both victim and offender as well as within the context of specific criminal acts. However, a number of practical and ethical reasons prevent researchers from collecting data on alcohol consumption of "offenders." For example, when injured individuals seek treatment (sometimes in hospitals and emergency rooms) it is not usually known at the time of treatment who the actual offender in the altercation was. Moreover, in the majority of cases, the "offender" remains unknown—in 2009, police agencies were only able to clear 28 percent of robberies and 57 percent of aggravated assaults (Sakiyama et al., 2010). If he or she is known, the "offender" is often in custody, and therefore unavailable for study. Even if the "offender" was available for interviewing immediately after the criminal event, the "offender" is only an alleged offender, thus study of this potential subject raises serious ethical concerns.

Studying victims of criminal violence is also more desirable on scientific grounds. For example, the manner in which the causal relationship between alcohol and violent crime was originally conceptualized involved the way in which alcohol consumption caused the offender to violently attack the victim (Pernanen, 1976, 1981, 1989; Collins, 1981; Room & Collins, 1983; Murdoch et al., 1990). More recent research on acute intoxication and aggression borrows from the individual trait-variable literature in psychology especially as regards trait-aggressiveness (Eckhardt & Crane, 2008; Giancola, 2004). Other research includes laboratory studies on acute intoxication and behavioral responses to stress and frustration (Pederson et al., 2002; Godlaski & Giancola, 2009). Still other studies have investigated alcohol expectancy effects (Begue et al., 2009) as well as the biphasic structure of intoxication by splitting the analysis of drinking episodes into pre-consumption social-psychological expectancy states and the social and neurobiological state of consumption (Moss & Albery, 2009). Still, this laboratory work does not get at actual victimization and criminality. The few studies which have used comparison groups often make comparisons only among prisoners or suspects, leading only to conclusions about the role of alcohol across types of crime, and not about the causal role of alcohol in violence across a more representative population. These studies also suffer from sample selection bias (Berk, 1983), in which the fact that an offender is drinking is likely to influence whether or not the offender is arrested, as well as the seriousness of the violence committed in the act of offending. Utilizing such samples artificially inflates the impact of alcohol.

Rather, as Collins (1983) suggested, a focus on the victim and alcohol consumption may be more efficacious than the traditional concern with the offender. He writes,

> When attempts at causal understanding focus on the offense event or the process of violent interaction, alcohol use is one of the factors that appears to have explanatory potential. That explanatory potential, however, might be manifested in the drinking behavior of the victims rather than in the effects of alcohol on the offender. (Collins, 1983: 7)

There is some evidence to support such a strategy. In a study cited by Collins (1989), Gottfredson (1984) analyzed data from the British Crime Survey and found that drinkers were three times more likely to be victimized than nondrinkers, even when controlling for other important predictors of victimization, such as age and area of residence. One study compared alcohol use by both victims and non-victims of crime and found that "binge drinkers" were at a significantly greater risk of being violently victimized (robbed or assaulted) compared to those who did not binge drink, or drink at all (Callanan et al., 1997). Alcohol use has also been linked to sexual victimization (Gidycz, 2007) and violent (stabbing, shooting, attempted stabbing/shooting, etc.) victimization (Thompson et al., 2008).

One of the problems associated with specifying the relationship between alcohol consumption and victimization is that many people who go out at night to pursue leisure activities do not purposely set out to consume alcohol. Rather, alcohol consumption is incidental to their leisure—a glass of wine at dinner, or beers with friends, for example. In such cases it can be argued that any association between alcohol and victimization is spurious. Nevertheless, if the presence of alcohol in any amount, or over and above certain levels, is associated with higher risk of violent victimization and injury independent of other specific routine activities, the importance of alcohol in understanding victimization would be clearly demonstrated.

Though the general routine activity theory framework has received much empirical support, a large review of empirical studies employing the theory reveals that it has, to date, suffered from a lack of precise indicators (Spano & Frielich, 2009). Spano and Frielich conclude in their review that support for routine activities theory remains both abundant and somewhat vague: "In short, guardianship is a protective factor while target attractiveness, deviant lifestyles, and exposure to potential offenders are risk factors for victimization and criminality" (2009: 312).

The best predictors of violence used thus far in routine activity theory frameworks measure essentially overlapping constructs such as parental involvement (as a proxy measure for the presence of capable guardians), structured versus unstructured activities, and participation in deviant or risky lifestyles (e.g., Schreck & Fisher, 2004; Gover, 2004; Spano & Nagy, 2005; Jackson et al., 2006). Other studies have employed measures such as whether or not individuals go out at night for leisure activities on a routine basis (Miethe, et al., 1987; Maxfield, 1987), or they measure the number of nights per week that individuals engage in this behavior (Sampson & Wooldredge, 1987), as both are, again, used as proxy measures of a lack of capable guardianship. Many studies have also employed measures based on household structure to serve as proxies for routine activities outside of the home.

Though many studies using routine activity theory have demonstrated links between a lack of capable guardianship, offenders, and violence, few if any of these studies feature a specific focus on routine drinking behaviors. Clearly, our understanding of alcohol and violent crime victimization would be greatly improved with more precise indicators to measure routine alcohol-related activity. What makes alcohol consumption a unique variable within the routine activities theory framework is that it isolates a specific behavior. Variables within routine activity theory can be global (i.e., broad, for example, when one leaves the house and where one goes) or specific (i.e., specific to what one *does* once they've left the house or arrived at their preferred destination). Measures of alcohol consumption, of course, do not necessarily tell us *where* people were when they drank, but it does tell us *that they were drinking*. Essential to any analyses of lifestyle and routine activity is both (1) where people engage in the activity/lifestyle (place), and (2) what they did there (behavior). While many indicators of lifestyle and activity are global and general, specific behavioral measures such as alcohol consumption provide more fine-grained tests of lifestyle and routine activity.

The design utilized in this study addresses some of the shortcomings of previous research, and may result in significant progress toward the establishment of a causal model of alcohol's role in violent victimization. In order to adequately assess the role that alcohol plays in the risk of victimization, this study was designed to 1) collect specific alcohol-use data from both non-victims and victims of robbery and assault, and 2) combine the victim data with a representative sample of non-victims from the same community over the same time period so that a group of "controls" could be established and compared to the "cases" represented by the respondents in the victim survey. This study design is important because previous studies of victimization have not included adequate measures of alcohol use on the part of victims, thus restricting our ability to assess the contribution of alcohol to the risk of victimization. In addition, few studies allow for the comparison of these respondents to a sample of respondents from the same community who have not been victims of violent crime. Even though some studies show that alcohol is present among a majority of victims of violent crime (see Murdoch et al., 1990: 1068–1069 for enumeration), we cannot assess the role of alcohol in victimization until we can compare alcohol-consuming victims to those who drink alcohol but have not been victimized.

Specifically, the role of alcohol, both in terms of presence versus absence, as well as the level of consumption, are examined in this chapter with regard to violent criminal victimization by analyzing victims of robbery and victims of assault.

STUDY BACKGROUND

Information from victims was collected from Salinas, California, a city which had approximately 120,000 residents in 1993, the time of the study reported here. Salinas was an ideal site for this study for two reasons; first, as the primary economic and service center for a large surrounding agricultural area, it is a relatively "self-contained" community and not a "bedroom community" or suburb in a larger urban community. This is important because it allows for a consistent determination of the population at risk of violent victimization. Second, US- and Mexican-born Latinos comprised about 50 percent of the city's population when these data were collected in 1993. This provided an opportunity to gather data on Latino victimization patterns, a topic that has not been investigated thoroughly.

In 1990,[1] the city of Salinas had a population of 108,777. Today, Salinas is home to over 150,000 people (150,441 in 2010). Importantly, the rate of population growth between 1990 and 2000 was around 30 percent representing a large influx of immigrants from Mexico. In fact, a full 35 percent of the population of Salinas in 1995 (53,016 people) were foreign born with an astounding 85.6 percent of these foreign-born people hailing from Mexico by the year 2000. To put things into a more national perspective, the state of California, easily one of the most diverse states in the union, had a Hispanic population of 32.4 percent in the year 2000. Salinas, by comparison, had a Hispanic population of 64.1 percent in 2000.

As was mentioned above, the data for this study was collected in Salinas in 1993. These census statistics indicate that the temporal context within which this study took place was an especially turbulent time, in terms of population demographics and population demographic change. Much of the population growth in Salinas during this time period was due to Mexican immigration. The context within which immigration occurs, of any nationality, is an inherently unstable one. Put simply, leaving one country and starting a new life wholesale in another is potentially economically precarious, especially given the consideration that social networks in the new country of residence may, for obvious reasons, be poorly developed (and not to mention the sociological specters of racism and ethnocentrism). Immigrants, as a consequence, may have trouble securing employment, healthcare, and housing (Crowley et al., 2006; Jimenez, 2008). This disadvantage is also tragic because it affects young Mexican immigrant elementary school students, as well—such young people are much more likely to go to economically disadvantaged schools (Crosnoe, 2005). Undocumented immigrant families suffer most of all—a recent study by Hall et al. (2010) shows that though documented Mexican immigrants (of both sexes) already make quite a bit less than non-Latino whites, *undocumented* immigrants make 17 percent less than even documented immigrants.

It is relevant, then, that these data were collected during one of the most demographically interesting times in the history of Salinas. The large growth of the immigrant population in Salinas during the 1990s occurred in a social context marred by poverty and disadvantage. For example, in 2000, the proportion of owner-occupied housing in Salinas sat at 50 percent while the national average came in at just above 66 percent. Salinas also had a family poverty rate of nearly 13 percent in 2000 compared to the national average of 9 percent. Though the median household income in Salinas was actually higher than the national median ($43,720 vs. $41,994), this is explained away by the fact that more people were living together in Salinas per household—the average household in Salinas contained about four people in 2000 compared to only about three people per household in America generally. Tellingly, when *per capita* or *family* income is assessed instead of *household* income, the figures regain their familiar disparity—median family income in Salinas was slightly less than $45,000 (per capita was 14,495), compared to the national median of slightly over $50,000 (and over 21,587 per capita). The reality of immigration, structural disadvantage, and income inequality in Salinas during the time this study was conducted will prove to be important factors in interpreting the results of this study.

DATA COLLECTION

Victims were identified from Salinas Police Department records on robberies and assaults that occurred during 1993 in Salinas, California. Victims were first contacted by mail, offered an incentive to participate in the survey, and given an opportunity to respond by mail with their informed consent. Those who did not respond by mail were contacted by telephone; potential respondents were given the opportunity to give informed consent either over the telephone or by mail. After obtaining informed consent, all participants were interviewed by telephone for approximately twenty-five to forty-five minutes in either English or Spanish. Interview questions explored the details of the victimization event, the circumstances surrounding the event, including any activities, drug and alcohol use, and movements that occurred during the hours prior to the event. Respondents were asked about their initial response to the victimization, any subsequent changes in routine activities, and the extent of the injury from the incident. Additionally, respondents were asked about specific and general patterns of alcohol and other drug use, expectancies concerning alcohol use, and demographic information. The overall response rate was 62 percent; of the 423 completed interviews, 288 were victims of assault and 135 were victims of robbery.

The non-victim sample used as a comparison group was obtained from a random-digit-dial general survey of 1,393 Salinas households conducted during the same year that the victims were identified—1993. The data were collected as part of the general monitoring survey of the "Community Trials" (Harold D. Holder, PhD, principal investigator), funded by grants from NIAAA and CSAP. This survey included a wide variety of alcohol and other drug use, and related injury topics. Specifically, an identical set of items concerning drug and alcohol use was used in both surveys, along with matched questions on a number of other dimensions. In order to ascertain whether patterns of alcohol and other drug use is linked to the risk of victimization, both the victim and non-victim data files were merged along their common variables.

VARIABLES AND VARIABLE MEASUREMENT

A baseline model was built using variables suggested from the victimization literature: situational effects such as place of victimization, time of day, number of bystanders, number of perpetrators, and the relationship between victim and offender; offender characteristics such as gender and victim's perception of alcohol use by the perpetrator; and socio-demographic characteristics of the victim such as ethnicity, education, employment, income, and immigrant status. Alcohol use by the victim was explored in various logistic regression models to determine its relative significance on the probability of being a victim of robbery versus assault, the probability of being injured, and the probability of sustaining serious injury from the violent victimization.

The dependent variable, victimization, was dichotomized as either victim or non-victim. The dichotomized independent variables are gender (female = 0), marital status (married = 1), Latino (non-Latino = 0), foreign born (foreign born = 1) and full-time employment (defined as thirty-five hours per week or more with less than full-time being coded as 0). Income and education were measured as categorical variables. Since these models explore the effects of binge drinking on the probability of victimization, alcohol intake is measured as at least one setting/situation in the twenty-eight days prior to the victimization in which the victim had consumed nine or more alcoholic beverages. This measure was also dichotomized (nine drinks or more = 1).

The second dependent variable, type of victimization, was dichotomized as robbery (n = 135) or assault (n = 288). The third dependent variable, injury, was dichotomized injured (n = 254) or not injured (n = 168). The type of injuries sustained ranged from a scrape to gunshot and stab wounds. These injuries were dichotomized as serious (gunshot wound, stab wound, broken bones; n = 87) or non-serious (cut, scrape, bruise, etc.; n = 116) to form the fourth dependent variable. Placement of injury as serious or non-serious was cross-validated by the type of medical treatment sought, if any. The vast majority of serious injuries resulted in hospital emergency room or acute care admissions, although one victim of a gunshot wound did not seek medical treatment.

The first independent variable, place of victimization, was dummy coded into four variables: work, home, public space (park, street, parking lot, etc.), and other (bar, car, and store); home was the omitted variable. Time of day was dichotomized into nighttime (8 p.m. to 5 a.m.) and daytime (nighttime = 1). Whether the victim was alone was dichotomized (alone = 1); as was the number of perpetrators (more than one perpetrator = 1). Perpetrator characteristics were also dichotomized: gender (male = 1), and alcohol use (perpetrator had been drinking = 1).

Routine activities of the victim included the highest number of drinks in one setting in the previous month that the subject had consumed, whether or not the victim had been drinking prior to the victimization (yes = 1), the number of nights out after 5:30 p.m. in the previous month, and whether the victim had been victimized during the previous six months (yes = 1). Dichotomized socio-demographic variables are gender (female = 1), ethnicity (white = 0, Latino = 1), marital status (married, or living with someone = 1), foreign born, and foreign-born Latino (yes = 1 for both variables). Other socio-demographic variables are age, family income, and education; all are treated as interval data. Additionally, two models which include the interaction term of being foreign born and Latino on the probability of assault and robbery are also examined. Previous research on drinking behavior of Mexican

Americans has revealed that individuals born in Mexico who live in the United States often continue the "festival" style of drinking common in Mexico, typified by heavy, but relatively infrequent, "binge" drinking (Gilbert & Cervantes, 1986). However, both foreign-born and US-born Mexican Americans exhibit riskier drinking styles if they initiate drinking in a US context (Strunin et al., 2007; Neff et al., 1987). Clearly, given the ethnic and immigrant makeup of the sample, model specification may be greatly improved by examining the effects of foreign-born Latino status on the risk of victimization.

STATISTICAL ANALYSIS AND RESULTS

Logistic regression was performed on separate models using the same baseline model (with minor modifications) of the effects of the variables outlined above on the probability of robbery versus assault, the probability of being injured versus not injured (compared across robbery and assault), and the probability of the victim sustaining a serious versus non-serious injury.

Table 1.1 presents the logistic regression estimates for the probability of violent crime victimization. A number of individual characteristics proved to be significant predictors of the probability of being victimized. Age, marital status, ethnicity, and income are associated with lower risk of victimization. Specifically, being older, married, Latino, and having higher income significantly reduced the risk of victimization. On the other hand, being foreign born, and having at least one drinking binge in the twenty-eight days prior to being victimized significantly increased the risk of victimization. However, these results do not hold for predicting the probability of robbery. Although age and income have similar effects on the probability of being a robbery victim as they do for being an assault victim or victim in general, marital status, and more importantly, at least one serious drinking episode, are not significant predictors.

Additionally, a number of situational effects are significant predictors of the probability of being robbed compared to being assaulted. Being in a public space such as a street or parking lot or being alone increases the probability of being robbed by more than two times compared to the probability of being assaulted. The presence of multiple offenders also increased the risk of robbery compared to assault. Results also indicated that older individuals were at a greater risk of being robbed versus assaulted compared to younger individuals. Last, results showed that foreign-born individuals had a much lower risk of being robbed compared to individuals born in the United States.

Importantly, individual characteristics such as income, education, marital status and gender had no statistically significant impact on the probability of type of violent victimization, although women and foreign-born Latinos appear to have a slightly higher risk of being robbed rather than assaulted compared to men and Latinos born in the United States. It is also important to note that going out at night after 5:30 p.m. did not increase one's risk of being robbed compared to assaulted, nor does prior victimization. Most importantly, use of alcohol by the victim (both routine drinking behavior and alcohol use before the event) did not increase the odds of being robbed versus assaulted (see table 1.1).

Table 1.2 presents the logistic regression estimates for the probability of being injured from the violent victimization. The baseline model is compared across robbery and assault victims. Interestingly, the place where the victimization occurred and being alone did not predict the likelihood of being injured for either type of victimization. However, simply being familiar with the perpetrator (perhaps through prior acquaintances) increased the risk of being injured for both robbery and assault. Age decreased the risk of injury for both types of victimization, although it had a much stronger effect on injury from assault. Gender of the perpetrator was significant in predicting injury for assault victims, but not for robbery victims; the probability of injury was lower for assault victims if the offender was female. Again, ethnicity and immigrant status were important in violent victimizations. Specifically, compared to whites, Latinos were at a significantly greater risk of being injured from an assault. However, being a foreign-born Latino actually reduced the risk of injury during robbery.

It appears that the risk of injury is greater for assault victims if the violence occurs at work, in a bar, or in a store, compared to victims who were assaulted in their own or someone else's home. Last, and most importantly, alcohol use by the victim prior to the event plays a very significant role in increasing the risk of injury during a robbery. In fact, the log odds show that alcohol use by the victim prior to being robbed increases the risk of injury by twenty-six times compared to victims who did not drink at all prior to the event. Interestingly, alcohol use by the victim did not predict injury for assault victims.

Table 1.3 presents the logistic regression results for the probability of being seriously injured. A control for type of violent victimization is included in the model. The only variables which impact the probability of sustaining a serious injury versus a non-serious injury are situational effects and perpetrator characteristics. Specifically, robbery victims were at a much lower risk of serious injury than were assault victims and those victimized at work were much less likely to sustain serious injury than those victimized at home. Those who were alone when victimized are twice as likely to sustain serious versus non-serious injury compared to those who are not alone during the violent victimization. Being victimized by more than one perpetrator and victimized by a male offender also significantly increased the risk of sustaining serious injury. Interestingly, none of the individual characteristics seemed to significantly impact the probability of serious injury, although age did appear to slightly lower the risk. Last, alcohol use by both the victim and the perpetrator did not impact the risk of serious injury.

The final analysis looked at the effect of the interaction of being Latino and being foreign born (a foreign-born Latino) on the probability of being victimized. Foreign-born Latino was dichotomized (foreign-born Latino = 1). Again, the effects

Table 1.1. Effects on the Log-Odds of the Probability of Being a Victim of Violence (N = 423; Non-victims N = 1400) and Robbed (n = 135) vs. Assaulted (n = 288)

Variables	Effect	S.E.	Sig.	Exp(B)	Effect	S.E.	Sig.	Exp(B)
Situation Effects								
Place of Victimization[a]:								
Work					-.6162	.5256	.2410	—
Public Space					.9555	.3553	.0072	2.599
Other					-.1898	.3771	.6625	—
Night (8 p.m. to 5 a.m.)					.0973	.2623	.6159	—
Victimized Alone					.9215	.2578	.0004	2.5131
Victim Knew Perpetrator					-.1286	.1862	.4899	—
More Than One Perpetrator					1.0565	.2987	.0004	2.8763
Perpetrator Characteristics								
Gender (Male=1)					.5959	.4134	.1495	—
Perpetrator Drinking					-.0517	.2580	.8412	—
Victim Characteristics								
Drinking Behavior:								
Drinks in Previous Month	.089	.033	.007	1.093	.0026	.0322	.9364	—
Drank Before Victimization					-.3352	.4289	.4345	—
# Nights Out Aft. 5:30 p.m.					-.0166	.0153	.2769	—
Victim in Prev. 6 Months					-.1105	.3221	.7315	—
Demographics								
Gender (Female=1)	-.244	.188	1.678	—	.4979	.3130	.1086	—
Age	-.052	.007	.000	.949	.0237	.0115	.0398	1.0240
Latino	-2.874	.426	.000	.056	.2171	.4342	.6080	—
Foreign Born	3.782	.633	.000	43.918	-1.6888	.8678	.0517	.1847
Foreign-Born Latino	-6.442	1.263	.000	.002	1.4626	.9232	.1131	—
Education	-.229	.087	.008	.795	-.0166	.0164	.3111	—
Family Income	-.249	.043	.000	.779	-.0659	.0533	.2159	—
Marital Status (Married=1)	-.697	.198	.000	.498	.2500	.2542	.3254	—

Victim Model: X^2 =598.462, df = 10, Class. = 86.10; Rob/Asslt Model: X^2 = 414.143, df = 21, Classification = 75.38

[a] Omitted variable is victimization at home; in Victim Models, predictors of victim experience missing

Table 1.2.   Effects on the Probability of Being Injured from Victimization

Variables	Robbery Victims[a] $X^2_{17}=140.264$ Effect	Standard Error	Assault Victims $X^2_{21}=299.756$ Effect	Standard Error
Situation Effects				
Place of Victimization[b]:				
Work	—	—	.4279	.5023
Public Space	−.4796	.6454	.0263	.4658
Otherc	.6869	.7225	.8550*	.3235
Nighttime (8 p.m. to 5 a.m.)	−.2788	.4671	−.4652	.3236
Alone When Victimized	.2793	.4546	.3337	.3500
Victim Knew Perpetrator	.7448*	.4852	.4168*	.2122
Number of Perpetrators	.9135	.5238	.5510	.3814
Perpetrator Characteristics				
Gender (Male=1)	—	—	−1.0831*	.4593
Perpetrator Had Been				
Drinking	.7448	.4852	.1828	.3047
Victim Characteristics				
Drinking Behavior:				
# Drinks in Previous Month	−.1055	.0683	.0165	.0354
Drank Before Victimization	3.2627**	1.2948	.6470	.5390
No. of Nights Out After 5:30				
p.m.	−.0071	.0265	.0200	.0242
Victimized in Previous 6				
Months	.7240	.6352	.2490	.3658
Demographics				
Gender (Female=1)	−.3447	.5388	−.2936	.3552
Age	.0407*	.0172	.0671***	.0180
Latino	1.0049	.7347	1.4000**	.3916
Foreign Born	—	—	.3517	.7497
Foreign-Born Latino	−1.3600*	.6678	−1.0333	.8471
Education	−.0169	.0387	.0799	.0610
Family Income	—	—	−.0697	.0591
Marital Status (Married=1)	−.3111	.4303	−.2577	.3048

Notes:

[a] Foreign born and gender of perpetrator are omitted from the robbery model due to small cell counts; family income is not included because the missing data represents more than 10 percent of the model n, education is used as a proxy.

[b] Omitted category is victimization at home

[c] workplace victimization is collapsed into other victimization category due to small cell counts in workplace victimization

*p < .05; **p < .01, ***p < .001

of being older, married, Latino, and having higher income significantly reduced the probability of victimization, whereas being foreign born and engaging in at least one serious drinking episode twenty-eight days prior to the assault significantly increased the chances of victimization. Additionally, being a foreign-born Latino significantly increased the probability of assault.

Adding the interaction variable to the model predicting the probability of robbery produced interesting results. Being older, Latino, and having a higher income significantly reduced the probability of robbery for both models. Additionally, foreign-born status significantly increased the risk of robbery, as did being a foreign-born Latino. However, the results for binge drinking differed across models. Specifically, having at least one drinking episode with nine or more drinks twenty-eight days prior to the victimization did not have an effect unless foreign-born Latino was added to the model. However, it should be noted, that the effect was not quite statistically significant (p = .0576), although it is close enough to warrant discussion.

DISCUSSION AND CONCLUSION

These results suggest that routine activities and alcohol use may be important variables to consider in understanding the dynamics of violent crimes such as robbery and assault. Routine activities appear important in determining the type of violent victimization. For example, components of the basic routine activity model, that is, lack of capable guardianship (being alone), and suitable target (being in a public space), appear to strongly influence the risk of robbery. Compared to assault, these types of violent victimizations also appear to more often involve strangers and more than one perpetrator.

Interestingly, people in this study were significantly less likely to be injured during the course of a robbery if they were a foreign-born Latino. In other words, there seems to be a *protective effect* of being a foreign-born Latino in this sample. It is at least reasonable to suppose that this protective effect might have arisen from the vibrant immigrant Mexican culture in Salinas. Though foreign-born Latinos in Salinas were victimized by robbery at slightly higher rates, they may have been spared from harm during the course of the robbery, perhaps because they shared the same ethnicity (and quite possibly, the same immigrant background) with the perpetrator. Equally interesting is how this apparent protective operated for assault. Though foreign-born Latinos were more likely to be assaulted, as they were to be robbed, they were, again, significantly less likely to be injured during the event, but this effect did not hold for American-born Latinos. This finding perhaps suggests, again, that the immigrant culture in Salinas had something akin to a protective effect on injury from victimization.

Alcohol use by both the victim and the offender did not play a key role in determining the risk for type of victimization. However, alcohol use by the victim played

Table 1.3. Effects on the Log-Odds of the Probability of Being Seriously Injured from Victimization

Variables	Effect	Standard Error	Significance	Exp(B)
Situation Effects				
Robbery	−8.578*	.4279	.0450	.4241
Place of Victimization[a]:				
Work	−3.0476*	.9802	.0019	.0475
Public Space	−.6737	.5682	.2357	—
Other	−.0010	.4810	.9983	—
Nighttime (8 p.m. to 5 a.m.)	−.2172	.4107	.5969	—
Was Alone When Victimized	.7760*	.3833	.0456	2.1512
Victim Knew Perpetrator	−.3808	.2733	.1635	—
More Than One Perpetrator	1.0151*	.4921	.0391	2.7603
Perpetrator Characteristics				
Gender (Male=1)	.9081	.5042	.0717	2.4795
Perpetrator Had Been Drinking	−.3928	.3651	.2819	—
Victim Characteristics				
Drinking Behavior:				
No. of Drinks in Previous Month	.0576	.0419	.1694	—
Drank Before Victimization	3733	.5023	.4574	—
No. of Nights Out After 5:30 p.m.	.0412	.0313	.1871	—
Victimized in Previous 6 Months	.1079	.4218	.7982	—
Demographics				
Gender (Female=1)	−.3230	.4488	.4717	—
Age	−.0289	.0167	.0833	—
Latino	.3440	.6531	.5984	—
Foreign Born	.2552	.9370	.7853	—
Foreign-Born Latino	−.3900	1.0478	.7097	—
Education	−.0469	.0406	.2480	—
Family Income	−.0331	.0763	.6638	—
Marital Status (Married=1)	.3730	.3690	.3121	—

Model X^2 = 211.125, df = 22, Classification = 74.86

[a] Omitted category is victimization at home

a very significant role in determining whether the victim was injured during the robbery, whereas situational effects were not as significant. It appears that alcohol use by the victim did not increase one's odds of being a "suitable target," but it certainly did increase the risk of being injured during robbery. However, alcohol use did not increase the risk of sustaining serious injury, whereas situational factors played an important role. Namely, being alone, being victimized by more than one offender, and being victimized by a male, all significantly increased the risk of serious injury, for both robbery and assault. Although not shown, one interesting analysis examined the relationship of bystander(s) to the victim and found that strangers, acquaintances, co-workers, or relatives have no impact on reducing the risk of being seriously injured compared to those that were alone during victimization.

Clearly, routine activities, including drinking behaviors, and offender characteristics are important in understanding violent criminal victimizations. Alcohol does not appear to impact the risk of *type of* violent victimization, but *any* alcohol use by the victim prior to the victimization did significantly increase the risk of being injured. Importantly, we found (in models not shown) that the level of consumption does not increase the odds of being injured over that of just drinking any alcohol prior to victimization. Last, alcohol use does not appear to impact the risk of serious injury; rather, other components, such as capable guardianship, reduce the risk of being seriously injured.

In short, by measuring a key concept in the routine activity theory of victimization more precisely, significant new information about the role of alcohol-related behavior on victimization and injury has been discovered, and in particular, new information about the way in which alcohol-related behavior impacts Latino populations of Mexican and US origins has been discovered. Such new findings can help to inform policymakers and others about how to use alcohol policy to better prevent violent victimization.

NOTE

1. All data here is from the US Census Bureau: www.census.gov.

2

Alcohol Availability and Violence among Mexican American Youth

Robert Nash Parker, Kevin J. McCaffree, and Maria Luisa Alaniz

The United States has the largest Hispanic population of any non-Spanish-language-dominant country in the world.[1] Hispanics represent the fastest-growing minority group in the country and will reach a projected nationwide population of nearly 133 million by 2050—nearly a third of the nation's total predicted population. The total Latino population of the United States in 2010 stands at 50.5 million, having increased from 35.3 million in 2000. Among Hispanics, the Mexican origin population increased the most since the 2000 census—from 20.6 million in 2000 to 31.8 million in 2010. California is home to most of these people, with 27.8 percent of the entire nation's population residing in this state.

Despite this growing population, from 2008 to 2009, the poverty rate among Hispanic people grew from 23 percent to 25 percent, a rate not statistically distinct from that of African Americans. According to the Pew Hispanic Center, more Hispanic children live in poverty than any other ethnic group; 6.1 million in 2010. This dismal number marks the first time in United States history that the largest group of poor children are non-white.[2] In 2009, Hispanic youths were the ethnic population most likely to drop out of high school (with a drop-out rate of 17.6 percent).[3]

Despite these alarming statistics, relatively little attention has been spent on Mexican American youth violence and the role of alcohol. Additionally, there is good reason to believe that minorities are often targeted by the alcohol industry, as outlet density is unusually high in these communities—especially Mexican American communities (Alaniz, 1998).

Relatively little research has been done in this area, but there are some important studies worth mentioning. US-born Latinos tend to consume more alcohol than their immigrant counterparts, though the reasons for this remain largely unknown (De La Rosa et al., 2011). There may, as well, be important gender differences regarding the effects of acculturation and place of birth (Alaniz et al., 1999). Evidence also indicates that, among Hispanic youth, those who feel more firmly planted in both their American and Hispanic cultures are less likely to abuse alcohol (Losoya et al., 2008). Tempering these results, however, Ehlers et al. (2009) find that acculturation stress in Mexican youth predicts not only alcohol dependence but also substance dependence more broadly. The effects of assimilation are likely very complex, of course. In fact, Warner et al. (2010) found that assimilation measures did *not* predict alcohol use for immigrant or US-born Mexican adolescents. Acculturation effects may also be most stressful and most risky for Mexican youth with a previous history of alcohol use (Guilamo-Ramos et al., 2004). On the other hand, though parental monitoring, in general, has little to no effect on Mexican youth drinking, parental permissiveness regarding drug use norms has a significant impact on drug use among Mexican American youth (Voisine, 2008). As expected (given their age), Mexican adolescents tend to be most influenced by their peers regarding alcohol use (Parsai, 2009).

Despite this important research, few if any studies have examined the role of alcohol outlet density and crime among Mexican youth at or near the start of the Hispanic population explosion of the last twenty years. According to the US Census Bureau, the Latino population in the United States grew 57.9 percent from 1990 to 2000 and a subsequent 43 percent from 2000 to 2010. A review of the literature published in 1986 by Gilbert and Cervantes lamented the alarming dearth of research on Mexican American youth drinking prior to this period of growth. Gilbert and Cervantes (1986) examine a lot of potential indicators of alcohol misuse, but do not take outlet density into account. Estrada, Rabow, and Watts (1982), meanwhile, found that sibling and parental drinking is the greatest contributing factor in Mexican American youth alcohol consumption. Additionally, Watts and Rabow (1983) concluded that, "there is a growing body of evidence to indicate that [alcohol] availability, in and of itself, may well be contributing to the etiological generation of alcohol problems." Their study of 213 California cities found that there is a higher concentration of alcohol outlets in low-income and ethnic-minority neighborhoods. Despite these promising studies in the 1980s, and with a scant few important exceptions (e.g., Alaniz et al., 1998), little is known about the role of alcohol outlet density in Mexican American youth violence during the heart of the Hispanic population boom of the 1990s.

STUDY BACKGROUND

The purpose of this study was to examine the relationship between alcohol availability, measured by alcohol outlet density, and Mexican youth violence during the 1990s in three Northern California cities. This analysis uses data from another study, "Alcohol Outlet Density and Mexican American Youth Violence," which was funded by the California Wellness Foundation (CWF), and conducted in three northern California cities from 1993 to 1996. This study was itself a follow-up to a larger project that was funded by the National Institutes on Health—National Institutes on Alcohol Abuse and Alcoholism (NIAAA). This larger NIAAA project included an ethnographic component, as well as a residential telephone survey.

The research team that collected these data consisted of bilingual (English/ Spanish) Latino college graduates. During the course of recording data for the ethnographic component of the study, researchers noted certain patterns of interest in the cities under investigation. It appeared as though high densities of alcohol outlets were interacting with ethnically targeted advertising (including alcohol sponsorship of ethnic parties and festivals), to exacerbate alcohol-related problems (such as drunken driving and violence) in the more ethnically segregated areas of the cities.

Additionally, public health and safety advocates in the communities under study made specific requests for social-scientific data that could assist them in combating alcohol-related social problems. They felt that, at the time, they were not being taken seriously by public health and enforcement agencies because they had only anecdotal reports linking alcohol consumption with community violence. In order to explore these concerns and gather empirical data to support (or refute) them, a research proposal was submitted to the California Wellness Foundation. We received funding to conduct a community-based study over a three-year time span (1992–1994). Data from this study were used for the current analysis.

The three Northern California cities included in this analysis were Gilroy, Union City, and Redwood City (the largest). All three cities are manageably small and include high proportions of Mexican residents. Gilroy (site 1), in contrast to large, urban Redwood City, is a rural area in South Monterey County with a population of 21,688. About 46 percent of Gilroy's population is ethnically Mexican and the city itself is situated in close geographical proximity to several migrant farm-worker housing centers; garlic is a major crop produced by farmers in Gilroy.

The second site used for this study was Union City, also in California. Union City is part of a "tri-city" area in the San Francisco East Bay which includes Hayward to the north and Fremont to the south. This city was selected because of its largely suburban population, and should therefore serve to balance findings across urban Redwood City and rural Gilroy. Though Union City does have a commercial strip, the surrounding environment is largely residential. At the time of data collection, Union City had a population of 53,762 and a Mexican population of around 24 percent. Lastly, Redwood City (site 3; located just south of San Francisco) had a mostly urban population of just over 66,000 people, 23 percent of which were ethnically Mexican.

DATA COLLECTION AND CODING

We sought a unit of analysis that could provide us with as close an approximation to the neighborhood as possible while still allowing us to control for the variety of other compelling causes and predictors of violence. It was determined that the US Census geographic unit called the "block group," made up of about four city blocks or their equivalent (including anywhere from 200 to about 2,000 people), would be the best unit of analysis. This is a relatively small geographical unit, providing for a detailed analysis. US Census data from the year 1990 were used in this study.

In order to ascertain whether or not outlet density had an independent effect on anti-social behavior among Mexican youth, we controlled for variables that have received empirical and theoretical support in previous research on the causes and correlates of violence. Reviews of the violence causation literature and the alcohol and violence literature (e.g., Parker, 1993; Parker & Rebhun, 1995; Pratt & Cullen, 2005) suggested that variables representing poverty, family structure, and racial/ethnic composition are important at a minimum to include in any analysis of violence.

Outlet density data was initially obtained from the California Alcohol and Beverage Control (ABC) agency which provided us with a listing of the addresses for all outlets in the three communities of interest to us. Field workers verified these addresses and corrected some. We then contacted city police departments in each of the three communities and received victimization data for everyone between the ages of fifteen and twenty-four. The California Wellness Foundation considered youth to be ages fifteen to twenty-four; Centers for Disease Control often use a similar definition.

Police were asked to provide data on violent crime including robbery, rape, assault, sexual assault, and homicide. All information obtained from police departments, and analyzed in this report, are from 1993.

Our next task was to link the census data on social and economic characteristics of each block group (a total of 114) with the addresses for outlets and crimes. Using available Geographic Information Systems (GIS) software and procedures, a technique referred to in the GIS literature as "geocoding" was used to locate each outlet and violent crime in a block group. Using maps developed by the Census Bureau, GIS software can pinpoint a street address in a larger geographic unit, such as a block group, with the aid of an "address locator" included in the software. We were able to use this address locator to "geocode" 98 percent of the crimes reported and virtually all of the alcohol outlets in these three communities.

Having the data properly "geocoded," we were then able to compare rates of youth violent crime and outlet density, and we measured the latter in terms of both on-site alcohol consumption outlets (such as bars and restaurants) and off-site consumption outlets (such as liquor, grocery, and convenience stores). To correct for the problem of spatial auto-correlation, special software was developed to provide unbiased estimates of statistical significance for observed effects in the presence of spatially auto-correlated error (Ponicki & Gruenewald, 1997).

RESULTS

Table 2.1 summarizes the results of the quantitative assessment of the relationship between alcohol outlet density and Mexican youth violence, measured as rates per 1,000 people in the population for each block group in the three cities examined. The table reports significance tests for the impact of each variable, net of the others, on youth violence. Ordinary least squares (OLS) regression results are presented for the first equation (as the spatially adjusted generalized least squares did not converge) for on-site outlets in the city of Gilroy (site 1). This result occurred most likely because of the small number of units (14) in the site 1 equations. The remainder of the columns of table 2.1 presents spatially adjusted generalized least squares results, with asterisks denoting statistically significant effects.

With the exception of off-premise outlet density in Redwood City (site 3), all of the effects for outlet density are statistically significant, with these models adjusted for the effects of spatial auto-correlation. Particularly important are the results in the final three columns of table 2.1, in which the data from all three sites are combined and the overall model is tested. Here, the results show that outlet density of both the on-premise and off-premise types is a significant predictor of youth violence, controlling for the other variables in the equations.

Further, these overall results show that the percent of workers who are working professionals in a block group has a negative effect on youth violence, suggesting support for the notion that local economic role models and opportunities are important for the prevention of youth involvement in violence (Crutchfield et al., 1982; Parker & Reckdenwald, 2008; Hurd et al., 2009). In addition, divorce had a significant positive net effect on Mexican youth violence, as predicted (e.g., Sampson, 1987). Although the effects of poverty are significant in the on-premise equation for site 2, and percent Latino is significant in the off-premise equation for the city of Gilroy (site 1), in general, the other variables in the model do not consistently predict youth violence rates once outlet density, professional employment, and divorce rates are taken into account.

DISCUSSION

This study establishes a link during the key period of Mexican American population growth of the 1990s between alcohol outlet density and Mexican American youth violence in three northern California cities. Few studies have examined the link between alcohol outlets and Mexican youth crime during the Latino population boom of the 1990s in California. This relationship between outlet density and crime during the '90s is likely a result of increased alcohol consumption by youth. Once intoxicated, situational disinhibition may encourage impulsivity and risk taking, eventually culminating in anti-social violence in some cases.

Selective disinhibition is a theory of alcohol-induced violence advanced by Parker and Rebhun (Parker & Rebhun, 1995; see also Parker, 1993) that emphasizes the respective roles of environment and context in influencing alcohol-related behavior. Within this theory, active constraint operates when an individual effortfully engages in self-regulation and self-control, regardless of the norms or expectations of the setting. The chemical effects of ethanol (the intoxicating ingredient in alcohol) on the brain serve to disinhibit parts of the brain associated with judgment and impulsivity, thus potentially reducing one's ability to invoke active constraint (Pihl et al., 1993;

Table 2.1. Regression Models of Youth Violent Crime

Model Type:	OLS	GLS	GLS	GLS	GLS	GLS	GLS	GLS	GLS	GLS
Predictors	site 1	site 1	site 2	site 2	site 3	site 3	all sites	all sites	all sites	all sites
constant	-0.01	-1.99	0.20	2.62	1.52	1.36	2.00*	1.41	1.92	1.29
on-premise outlet density	5.14*	...	14.34*	...	1.68*	...	6.58*	...	5.89*	...
off-premise outlet density	...	4.42*	...	21.44*	...	0.75	...	9.88*	...	9.27*
% professionals	0.31	2.04*	-0.27	-2.34*	-1.68*	-1.96*	-1.40	-2.40*	-1.67*	-2.68*
% divorced	-0.60	-1.07	0.51	-1.88	0.76	3.81*	-1.57	4.45*	-1.37	4.28
% in poverty	0.87	0.24	0.76	1.04	-0.81	-0.71	0.05	-0.54	-0.25	-0.78
% African-American	...	...	-0.20	0.98	0.02	0.67	-0.13	-0.41	0.40	0.01
% Latino	1.60	3.43*	0.01	-1.90	0.07	-0.11	-0.29	-0.40	-0.59	-0.75
total population	-1.66*	-0.98	0.76	-0.52	0.35	0.08	0.27	0.52	-0.01	0.36
Site 1	...	...	...	...	...	...	...	...	1.68	1.53
Site 3	...	...	...	...	...	...	...	...	0.57	0.70

Table contains Upton and Fingleton's t-statistic for b^(UF).
Significant predictors are in bold type and marked with an asterisk (*).

Barclay, 2008). Passive constraints, on the other hand, are situational norms that may deter or prohibit anti-social behavior. Clearly, on-site alcohol establishments such as restaurants provide more passive constraints, than a city park or an unsupervised house party. Situations, therefore, in which both active and passive constraints are operating are unlikely to produce antisocial violence.

These findings are consequently somewhat surprising and dire. As expected, off-site alcohol establishments were associated with increases in youth violence in each city except Redwood City (site 3). On the other hand, all on-site establishments were signiticant predictors of violence as well, indicating that perhaps the organizational norms of such establishments were too permissive regarding passive constraints against violent acting-out. Alternatively, young people may become intoxicated in on-site establishments before moving their social engagements to more normatively permissive locations such as house parties. Regardless, unregulated off-site establishments may provide easy youth access to alcohol (through "shoulder tap methods" or simply through illegal underage sales). Once the alcohol is purchased, it can be consumed in parks or in houses where passive constraints against violent behavior may be reduced.

This relationship between outlet density and crime may also occur because large numbers of youth are attracted to certain locations where alcohol outlets dominate and define the environment perhaps serving as sites for drug sales, gang-related behavior, and sexual solicitation. All of these processes are likely operating, but it would appear that alcohol outlet concentration may be a significant leverage point around which more effective anti-violence public policy can be made. This is crucially important given the racially and ethnically targeted nature of many alcohol advertisements (see chapter 3 of this volume for more on the impact of advertising on violence).

Therefore, cities and towns should consider ways to prevent further outlet concentrations as well as ways to reduce current concentrations. Such regulation would act as one among many means to combat rates of youth violence in the United States today. Furthermore, detailed qualitative research on the possible links between outlet density and youth violence are needed. However, regardless of the ways in which the abuse of alcohol can cause social harm, alcohol outlet control policies may be one of the few effective and reasonably painless alternatives for youth violence prevention available to communities.

NOTES

1. Unless otherwise noted, all city demographic statistics can be found at the US Census Bureau: www.census.gov.

2. http://pewhispanic.org/.

3. US Department of Education, National Center for Education Statistics. (2011). *The Condition of Education 2011.*

3

Sexual Violence, Alcohol, and Advertising

Robert Nash Parker, Kevin J. McCaffree, Maria Luisa Alaniz, and Randi J. Cartmill

INTRODUCTION

This chapter deals with the content of alcohol advertising and its impact on sexual violence in Latino communities. Calling this topic controversial substantially understates the situation. As our focus here is particularly on youth, the controversy is heightened, if possible. First, the position of the alcohol industry is that their advertisements are not designed to recruit new drinkers from among youth, but rather to attract established drinkers to the brand name reflected in the advertisement. Second, the advertisements we shall examine here are ostensibly designed to focus attention on a product, in this case alcohol, rather than having the effect, as we will claim, of influencing sexual relationships between young men and youth women. Finally, if one accepts the growing and substantial body of evidence that alcohol availability and consumption have effects on violence, how can we distinguish the independent impact of advertisements for alcohol displayed in and around alcohol outlets from the effects of alcohol availability and, indirectly, alcohol consumption itself?

This chapter addresses all of these issues and provides a set of theoretical and empirical answers that we shall argue demonstrate that a relationship between sexist and demeaning (to women) advertising content and the rate of sexual victimization of young Latinas is not only plausible but in fact exists, at least in one California community. If this relationship exists in one community (a community that, while distinct, has a great deal in common with many other communities in California and elsewhere), we may reasonably presume that it exists in other communities. If so, we provide the basis for a prevention intervention policy directed at the content of alcohol advertising that can survive constitutional challenges and may result in reduced sexual victimization of youth.

THEORETICAL ISSUES

Research on the causes of sexual assault provides a number of important dimensions that can be part of the explanation for a relationship between advertising content and sexual assault, particularly linked to alcohol. In general, peer attitudes toward sexual aggression are a common causal factor for sexual assault (Schwartz & DeKeseredy, 1997; Boswell et al., 1996; Stein, 2007; Thompson et al., 2011). In addition, the link between sexual activity, sexual availability, and alcohol use on the part of women in male peer group culture is often cited as an important factor in sexual assault and date or acquaintance rape (Schwartz & Dekeseredy, 1997; Beck et al., 1995; Messman-Moore et al., 2008; Testa & Livingston, 2009). In addition, male peer groups provide a context for learning rape myths and rape techniques (Ellis, 1989; Schwartz & DeKeseredy, 1997; Suarez & Gadalla, 2010). Thus, male peer group socialization, a context extremely important and influential among youth, brings together a number of elements found in previous research to influence sexual assault. The explicit sexual nature of some of the alcohol advertisements displayed in alcohol outlets provide an explicit link between alcohol and sexual availability.

A second important issue examined in this chapter is ethnic targeting in alcohol advertising. In the media in general there is an absence of people of color and particularly Latinos. Children growing up in Latino communities oftentimes may not see themselves and their culture represented in the school curricula or in movies or television programs, but they frequently see their culture perverted in ethnically targeted alcohol advertisements. These advertisements are more concentrated in Latino communities than are similar advertisements in white neighborhoods (Alaniz, 1998; Center on Alcohol Marketing and Youth, 2003). In addition, the use of cultural and historical symbols and Spanish language makes these advertisements even more appealing to young Latinos looking for representation in the media and for an identity amidst the dominant Anglo culture (Alaniz & Wilks, 1995; Watts & Rabow, 1983). The sexually suggestive content and portrayal of Latina models in these advertisements makes it clear that the intended targets of these advertisements are young Latinos.

Can the impact of advertisements on violence, which appear in and around alcohol outlets, be distinguished from the impact of the outlets themselves? This is a reasonable question especially in light of the accumulating evidence concerning the relationship between alcohol availability and violence (Alaniz et al., 1998; Parker & Rebhun, 1995; Parker, 1995; Scribner et al., 1995; Chiu et al., 1997; Livingston, 2008; Mckinney et al., 2009; Parker et al., 2011a; Parker et al., 2011b). As part of a larger study of youth violence, alcohol availability, and ethnic targeting (see Alaniz et al., 1998; Alaniz & Wilks, 1995) we undertook a study of advertising content in and around alcohol outlets in three California cities. We developed an observation protocol to capture the nature and content of all visible advertising in every alcohol outlet in these three communities, one of which was the focus of the research to be discussed below. Research assistants were trained to identify content in a consistent manner, including cultural and historical icons and the sexual content and nature of the participants portrayed.

Among the things we discovered in collecting these data is that the distribution of advertising in outlets, especially advertising with sexist and demeaning content, is not identical to the distribution of outlets. In other words, all outlets do not display these sexualized ads with the same frequency, but rather they are concentrated in some outlets in some neighborhoods. Figure 3.1 shows the distribution of alcohol outlets per 1,000 residents in units of analysis created by the US Census Bureau called "block groups."

These usually consist of between four and eight city blocks or their equivalent, and they vary in terms of population for this community between 200 and 1,850 people. Figure 3.2 contains the same units of analysis, but the data displayed is the density of sexist and demeaning advertisements containing Latino models. Although these two variables are correlated, they are not identical, thus creating the possibility at least that we can measure their impact on youth violence in general and sexual victimization in particular separately.

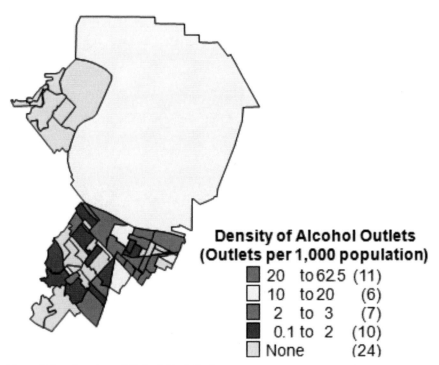

Density of Alcohol Outlets
(Outlets per 1,000 population)

■ 20 to 62.5	(11)
☐ 10 to 20	(6)
■ 2 to 3	(7)
■ 0.1 to 2	(10)
☐ None	(24)

Figure 3.1.   Courtesy of Robert Nash Parker.

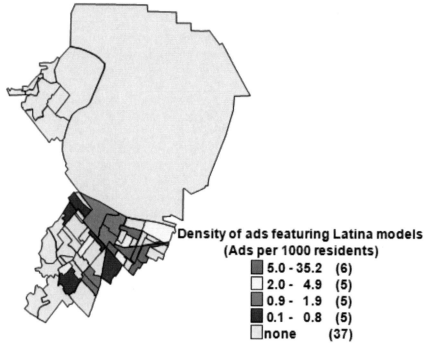

Figure 3.2.   Courtesy of Robert Nash Parker.

ETHNIC TARGETING AND THE
CONTENT OF ALCOHOL ADVERTISING

In general, ethnic targeting is accomplished through three major strategies: (1) the use of Spanish language in the ads, (2) the use of cultural and/or historical symbols or objects, and (3) the use of Latina models. Figures 3.3 and 3.4 are two examples of ads typically found in outlets in Latino neighborhoods, in which the Mexican commemoration of the Battle of Puebla, May 5, 1862, becomes an opportunity to drink.

In figure 3.4, the same holiday is appropriated this time with Spanish language featured prominently. Historical and cultural symbols are also appropriated, as is illustrated by figure 3.5. In this ad the sacred Mayan pyramid, El Castillo, at Chi Chen Itza in Yucatan, Mexico, is turned into a giant blender for margaritas.

Although there are certainly targeted ads developed by the alcohol industry for mainstream American holidays such as Independence Day or Memorial Day, the absence of the recognition of holidays, cultural symbols, and icons important to Latinos in the United States is striking in the mainstream media. In these targeted ads, however, Mexican traditions and history are celebrated and appropriated in combination with alcohol. We simply do not see the Washington Monument turned

Figure 3.3.   Courtesy of Robert Nash Parker.

Figure 3.4.   Courtesy of Robert Nash Parker.

Figure 3.5.   Courtesy of Robert Nash Parker.

into a giant martini glass, or the Lincoln Memorial serving as the base for a giant pitcher of beer.

Even more disturbing for their content and their frequency are ads that exploit attractive and provocatively dressed Latina models to advertise alcohol. These types of ads, in which Latina models depicted in sexist and commodified poses, constituted over 50 percent of the ads in outlets in Latino neighborhoods and less than 20 percent of the ads in outlets in non-Latino neighborhoods. Figures 3.6 and 3.7 are historical photos of women combatants in the 1910 Revolution in Mexico. They are referred to as "Soldaderas" and are inspirational figures for young Mexican girls and for women in general.

Figure 3.8 displays the degrading and sexist image the alcohol industry has constructed on the basis of the Soldaderas. This advertisement was displayed in a convenience store that also sells soda and candy to children, yet there are some communities in which this poster would be judged to be nearly pornographic in content, if it were not an advertisement for a legal product. This type of ad is clearly aimed at young, male Latino drinkers, both under and over the legal drinking age of twenty-one. Figure 3.9 invites the viewer to, "Enter the Rhythm" (translation of the Spanish phrase displayed in the ad). Young males are also interested in cars, motorcycles, and other forms of transportation, and these images are combined with sexual availability and alcohol in figures 3.10 and 3.11.

Figure 3.6. Courtesy of Gustavo Casasola, *Biografía ilustrada del general Francisco Villa, 1878–1966*, Editorial G. Casasola, 1969.

Figure 3.7. Courtesy of El Paso, Texas City Library, Border Heritage Collection.

Figure 3.8. Courtesy of Robert Nash Parker.

Figure 3.9. Courtesy of Robert Nash Parker.

Figures 3.12 through 3.15 show, even more directly, the association between sexual availability, alcohol, and ethnic targeting. Latina models are shown in various stages of undress, or in sexually revealing costumes, and in three of the four scenes the Latina model has been consuming alcohol. It would be surprising if these advertisements did not have any impact on the sexual interactions of some young Hispanic males and females given the targeted audience of young males who, almost by definition, have a strong interest in both alcohol and sexual behavior.

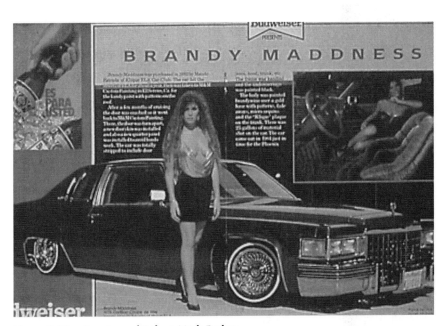

Figure 3.10. Courtesy of Robert Nash Parker.

Figure 3.11.   Courtesy of Robert Nash Parker.

Figure 3.12. Courtesy of Robert Nash Parker.

Figure 3.13. Courtesy of Robert Nash Parker.

Figure 3.14. Courtesy of Robert Nash Parker.

Figure 3.15.   Courtesy of Robert Nash Parker.

VIOLENCE AND SEXUAL VIOLENCE

Figure 3.16 shows the distribution of violence in the same community for which alcohol outlets and alcohol advertisements featuring Latina models were displayed previously. Here the rate of violence in which the victim was female and between the ages of twelve and eighteen inclusive is given. Violence included homicides, rapes, robberies, and assaults reported to the police during 1993. Figure 3.16 displays the enormous variation of the rates of violence in one community, ranging from a high of over 500 per 1,000 female juvenile residents of the block group to the eleven block groups in which no violent crimes against female juveniles were committed.

Figure 3.17 shows the distribution of sexual crimes against female juveniles in 1993, and although they show a similar range of variation to overall violence against female juveniles, sexual crimes, including rape and sexual assault, are more concentrated. Figures 3.18 and 3.19 show the same distributions for violence and sexual violence but with Latinas as victims. These maps show similar properties to those for all female juveniles, with enormous variation and even greater concentration brought about by the relative segregation of housing by ethnicity typical of most American cities.

The descriptive empirical data presented thus far show that the rates of violence and sexual violence against females in general and Latinas in particular vary across

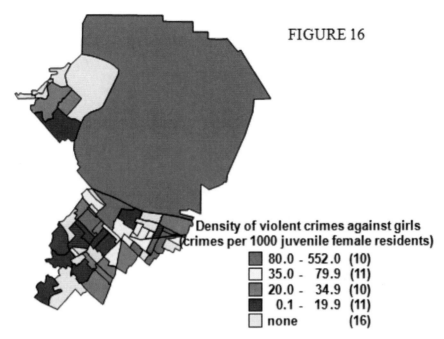

FIGURE 16

Density of violent crimes against girls
(crimes per 1000 juvenile female residents)
- 80.0 - 552.0 (10)
- 35.0 - 79.9 (11)
- 20.0 - 34.9 (10)
- 0.1 - 19.9 (11)
- none (16)

Figure 3.16.   Courtesy of Robert Nash Parker.

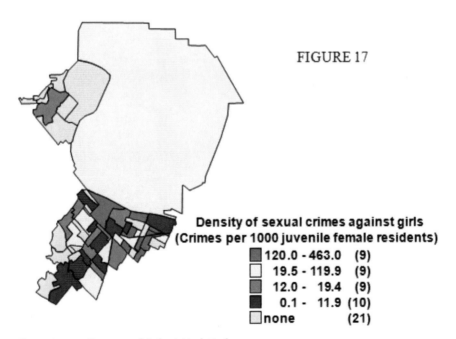

FIGURE 17

Density of sexual crimes against girls
(Crimes per 1000 juvenile female residents)
- 120.0 - 463.0 (9)
- 19.5 - 119.9 (9)
- 12.0 - 19.4 (9)
- 0.1 - 11.9 (10)
- none (21)

Figure 3.17.   Courtesy of Robert Nash Parker.

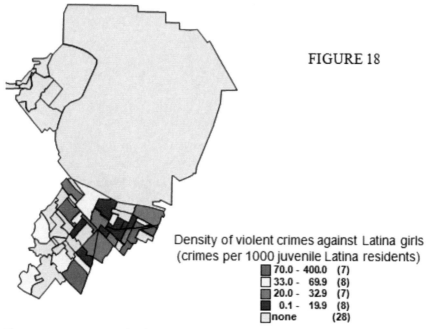

FIGURE 18

Density of violent crimes against Latina girls
(crimes per 1000 juvenile Latina residents)
- 70.0 - 400.0 (7)
- 33.0 - 69.9 (8)
- 20.0 - 32.9 (7)
- 0.1 - 19.9 (8)
- none (28)

Figure 3.18.   Courtesy of Robert Nash Parker.

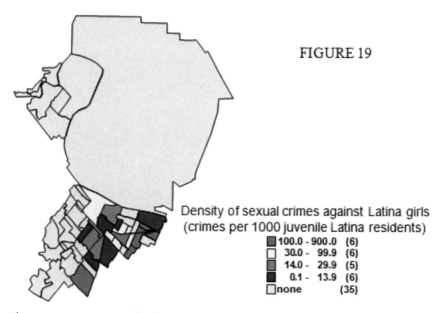

FIGURE 19

Density of sexual crimes against Latina girls
(crimes per 1000 juvenile Latina residents)
- 100.0 - 900.0 (6)
- 30.0 - 99.9 (6)
- 14.0 - 29.9 (5)
- 0.1 - 13.9 (6)
- none (35)

Figure 3.19.   Courtesy of Robert Nash Parker.

block groups in this community. In addition, alcohol outlets and sexualized advertising are not identically distributed in a community. Further, we have suggested that this advertising is targeted toward young male Latino residents of this community, and that the content of the ads links sexual behavior, sexual availability, and alcohol closely together. Now, we can turn to a consideration of the empirical relationship, if any, between the density of such ads and sexual violence against Latinas.

ADVERTISING AND SEXUAL VIOLENCE

The major research question we address here is whether or not there is an empirical relationship between the density of sexualized advertisements for alcohol featuring Latina models and variation in the density and geographic distribution of actual sexual violence against Latinas. If the advertisements featured in figures 3.8 to 3.15 are increasing the likelihood, net of other factors, that sexual violence will occur, the density of such ads should have a significant relationship with the rate of sexual violence net of these other factors.

As we have argued that the ads are linked to male peer group culture, including beliefs about alcohol use by females and the implications this has for sexual availability and sexual willingness, ad density should not impact other types of violence against female juveniles, but should specifically impact sexual violence. Given the ethnically targeted nature of these ads, the impact should also be stronger on sexual violence against Latinas as compared with that against female juveniles of other ethnic groups. These arguments taken together lead to a set of specific predictions concerning the impact of these ads:

1. There should be no significant net relationship between ad density and overall rates of violence against female juveniles.
2. There should be a significant net effect of these ads on sexual violence against female juveniles.
3. There should be a stronger net effect of these ads on sexual violence against Latina juveniles as compared with female juveniles in general.

In addition, the following predictions derive from descriptive data presented earlier concerning the independence of outlet density and ad density:

1. The impact of alcohol outlet density on violence against female juveniles should be independent of the impact of ad density.
2. Outlet density should have stronger effects on violence against female juveniles than it does on sexual violence against female juveniles.

The model we use to test these predictions is based on that used previously by Alaniz et al. (1998). Although that analysis was focused on the issue of immigration and violence, Alaniz et al. (1998: 158–167) describe a comprehensive model with which to analyze the relationship between alcohol outlet density and youth violence in a Latino context. In order to account for a variety of influences on violence and sexual violence, we control for several social and economic characteristics found to be important in previous empirical studies. These data are taken from the 1990 US Census; the data on violent and sexually violent offenses was obtained from local law enforcement agencies in this community and are from the year 1993.

To control for population size, particularly the population of potential offenders, we control for the percent of the population that are young males between the ages of twelve and twenty-four. Although older males may certainly be potential offenders, given the nature of the advertisements and their targeted audience of young males, use of this age range is appropriate.

To control for the impact of ethnic and racial concentrations of population, which would, for example, increase the likelihood that Latinas would be victimized in a neighborhood simply because there are more Latinas, we include the percent African American and the percent Latino among the total population of the block group. Residential stability has generally been found to predict neighborhood crime rates (Sampson & Raudenbush, 1999; Sampson, 1985). We include a measure of the percent of residents living in the same house or apartment for the previous five years to control for the reduced likelihood of crime due to higher levels of residential stability.

We include two measures of poverty, based on a number of studies that find poverty is the most consistent and persistent predictor of violence (see Parker & Anderson-Facile, 2000, for a review of such studies; see also, Valdez et al., 2007). First, we measure the percent of the block groups' population in extreme poverty, defined as those families making less than $5,000 in income (adjusted for inflation, this works out to less than $9,000 in 2011 dollars). Second, we measured the gender gap in poverty by subtracting the percent of men in poverty from the percent of women in poverty in the block group. This gender gap measures the relative number of women who are economically disadvantaged in relation to men, a potential indicator of greater levels of violence and sexual violence against women (Gartner et al., 1990; Peterson & Bailey, 1992; see Fawole, 2008 for a review).

Family structure also has been seen as an important factor in predicting rates of youth crime; we measure the percent of children in single parent families as an indicator of family disruption, disorganization, and reduced levels of supervision of children (Sampson, 1985; Fagan et al., 1987; Sampson & Wilson, 2005; Apel & Kaukinen, 2008). In addition, the importance of role models (often measured as employed adults) in communities has been discussed in a number of studies (Crutchfield, 1989; Parker, 1993; Parker & Reckdenwald, 2008; Hurd et al., 2009). Consequently, we include in our analysis here the percent of all employed adults in professional occupations as an indicator of this concept.

The unemployment rate is also included here as a measure of social disorganization, one that has been found in previous research to be particularly important as a factor in sexual violence and family violence (Parker & Anderson-Facile, 2000; Lin, 2008; see also Pratt & Cullen, 2005 for a general overview of macro-level predictors of crime). In order to specify the complex relationships between economic conditions and ethnicity, we have also included a measure of the unemployment gap in ethnicity. This concept is measured as the difference between the Latino unemployment rate and the white or Anglo unemployment rate in each block group.

Finally, we include several measures to test our major hypotheses concerning the role of outlet density, ad density, and the density of ads with Latina models. First, we measure outlet density with the number of off-sale outlets in each block group divided by the population. Off-sale outlets such as liquor stores, convenience stores, and grocery stores are sites from which youth are most likely to obtain alcohol. In results not reported here, we used overall outlet density and obtained results which were identical to those reported here.

Second, we measure advertising density as the overall number of alcohol ads in all outlets in each block group divided by the population. We use all outlets as sources because while youth may be most likely to buy alcohol at off-site outlets, they are likely to see the ads in most if not all outlet types. Using ads in all outlets measures exposure to ads more effectively than if off-sale outlet ads alone were utilized. Third, we measure ethnically targeted ad density in a similar manner. We include this measure to rule out the possibility that any association we find between ads featuring Latina models and sexual victimization among Latina youth is spurious because ads targeted to the Latino community in general reflect a concentration of Latino patrons at establishments and nothing more. "Ethnically targeted" ads are those which feature Spanish language, Latino cultural symbols, references to countries of origin such as Mexico, Latin American flags, historical events and festivals, such as Cinco de Mayo, and ads featuring Latino models, male and female (see Alaniz & Wilks, 1995). Finally, we measure the density of ads featuring Latina models as a distinct subcategory of ethnically targeted ads.

We examine four dependent variables in order to explicate our major research hypotheses. In all cases we focus on crime against young females between the ages of ten and eighteen during 1993. First, we distinguish between violent victimizations (non-sexual assault, robbery, mugging, theft with personal contact), and sexual violence (sexual assault, rape, and exposure). Second, we classify the victim according to police records as either Latina or non-Latina, so we have four equations in tables 3.1 and 3.2 below.

STUDY RESULTS

The statistical results of this study are given in tables 3.1 and 3.2, where the former examines the relationship between off-site outlet density, violence, and ethnicity, and the latter presents results concerning the role of advertising in sexual and non-sexual violence against young females.

Results presented in table 3.1 indicate that off-sale outlet density has a significant net effect for non-Latina victimization but not for Latina victimization, regardless of the type of victimization. Poverty has a significant effect on non-sexual victimization among both Latinas and non-Latinas, with the gender gap in poverty having a positive effect in both ethnic groups. Family structure also has a positive effect, but only for non-sexual violent victimization among non-Latinas. Finally, table 3.1 shows that the unemployment rate is a significant predictor of sexual violence for both ethnic groups.

Results in table 3.2 present the findings with the inclusion of the advertising measures, and the inclusion of these variables results in some significant changes in our findings. The inclusion of overall ad density, the density of Latino targeted ads, and the density of ads featuring Latina models results in the effects of outlet density dropping below significance. Although the effects of the gender gap in poverty for non-sexual violent victimizations remains significant in the face of controls for the effects of the advertising indicators in both ethnic groups, unemployment remains significant only for non-Latina sexual victimization. Further, the effect of family structure on non-Latina non-sexual violence also becomes insignificant when the impact of advertising is considered.

Concerning the impact of advertising itself, net of the other factors in the models, neither overall density nor the density of targeted ads have any significant effects in table 3.2. However, the density of ads featuring Latina models has a significant net effect on sexual violence among Latinas, as well as among non-Latinas. Recall that we predicted that if our arguments were correct, we should find that the density of ads featuring sexualized Latina models should have a significant net effect on violent sexual victimizations but not on non-sexual violent victimizations. Results in table 3.2 confirm this prediction, with both significant effects for Latina and non-Latina victims of violent sexual crimes.

In general the results of these analyses are supportive of the notion that advertising content plays a detectable role in the genesis of sexual violence. These effects are net of the ethnic composition of the block group where the victimization occurred, net of the social and economic characteristics of this area, net of population and residential stability, net of race and gender specific measures of poverty and unemployment, and even net of alcohol availability.

The alcohol industry has always maintained that their advertising is aimed at adults and is designed to cause individuals who already drink alcohol to shift from one brand of alcohol to another (Watts & Rebow, 1993; Alaniz & Wilks, 1995; Nelson, 2006; see also Distilled Spirits Council, Code of Responsible Practices, 2009). We have found evidence in this study that the commodifying and demeaning manner in which female Latinas are portrayed in commonly viewed alcohol advertising in one community is linked to the pattern of violent sexual victimization of young females in that community.

Although not all offenders in the violent sexual crimes we examined were under the minimum age of purchase for alcohol, it is very likely that most of the offenders

Table 3.1. Regression Models of Victimization, Girls under Eighteen Years of Age

Independent Variables	Latina Girls, Violent Crime	Latina Girls, Sexual Crime	Non-Latina Girls, Violent Crime	Non-Latina girls, Sexual crime
Constant	91.662 (1.104)	147.895 (1.768)	−96.552 (−0.718)	−132.149 (−0.525)
Total Population	0.003 (0.236)	−0.015 (−1.584)	−0.025 (−1.431)	−0.052 (−1.467)
% Latino	−0.624 (−0.764)	−1.528 (−1.976)	1.501 (1.122)	1.933 (0.753)
% African-American	−4.602 (−1.527)	−3.158 (−1.178)	8.463 (1.696)	−10.868 (−1.112)
Residential Stability	−68.515 (−0.826)	−113.458 (−1.357)	−43.902 (−0.331)	−34.669 (−0.151)
% in Extreme Poverty	156.057 (0.383)	−56.567 (−0.146)	495.274 (0.746)	1168.104 (0.938)
Gender Gap in Poverty	**24.106 (2.878)** *	0.260 (0.032)	**40.237 (2.944)** *	−3.752 (−0.143)
% Single Parent Families	−55.731 (−0.282)	328.957 (1.883)	**698.213 (2.107)** *	1333.078 (1.901)
% in Professional Occupations	−2.168 (−1.104)	−3.111 (−1.580)	−0.724 (−0.228)	−2.008 (−0.340)
Unemployment Rate	1.862 (0.538)	**6.322 (2.039)** *	7.781 (1.356)	**48.619 (4.211)** *
Racial Gap in Unemployment	−0.341 (−0.351)	0.400 (0.456)	0.951 (0.592)	4.518 (1.424)
Off-Sale Outlet Density	2.409 (0.289)	12.648 (−1.657)	**38.353 (2.796)** *	**65.250 (2.472)** *

Value in parenthesis is the T statistic; those in **bold** type and starred are statistically significant.

Table 3.2. Regression Models of Testing the Effect of Targeted Advertising on Victimization of Girls under Eighteen Years of Age

Independent Variables	Latina Girls, Violent Crime	Latina Girls, Sexual Crime	Non-Latina Girls, Violent Crime	Non-Latina Girls, Sexual Crime
Constant	85.067 (0.963)	153.311 (1.902)	-138.382 (-0.993)	-225.138 (-0.910)
Total Population	0.003 (0.277)	-0.015 (-1.759)	-0.023 (-1.261)	-0.044 (-1.312)
% Latino	-0.313 (-0.354)	-0.919 (-1.234)	2.375 (1.643)	4.782 (1.815)
% African-American	-3.541 (-1.018)	-0.080 (-0.030)	11.426 (1.968)	1.798 (0.168)
Residential Stability	-84.088 (-0.886)	-168.469 (-1.931)	-61.162 (-0.435)	-15.286 (-0.068)
% in Extreme Poverty	16.495 (0.036)	-478.757 (-1.209)	87.480 (0.122)	189.157 (0.155)
Gender Gap in Poverty	**26.993 (2.996)** *	5.122 (0.663)	**44.993 (3.120)** *	15.594 (0.610)
% Single Parent Families	-96.217 (-0.423)	319.612 (1.811)	641.565 (1.662)	1048.322 (1.418)
% in Professional Occupations	-1.531 (-0.702)	-2.259 (-1.119)	1.213 (0.349)	2.307 (0.372)
Unemployment Rate	0.336 (0.081)	3.203 (1.016)	5.102 (0.719)	**28.570 (2.112)** *
Racial Gap in Unemployment	-0.422 (-0.420)	0.326 (0.408)	0.611 (0.370)	3.196 (1.063)
Off-Sale Outlet Density	-7.869 (-0.619)	11.903 (-1.160)	19.259 (0.934)	-16.297 (-0.443)
Density of Alcohol Ads	0.036 (0.552)	0.082 (1.529)	0.110 (1.036)	0.166 (0.885)
Density of Targeted Alcohol Ads	-0.000 (-0.102)	-0.005 (-0.818)	-0.006 (-0.487)	-0.011 (-0.473)
Density of Ads with Latina	2.693 (0.804)	**7.295 (2.650)** *	5.122 (0.948)	**26.724 (2.805)** *
Models				

Value in parenthesis is the T statistic; those in **bold** type and starred are statistically significant.

were juveniles (under twenty-one years of age) as well, given the well-known similarities between victims and offenders in criminal victimization (Lauretson et al., 1991). Thus, we argue that this statistical evidence indicates that individuals who are not supposed to be the target of alcohol advertising have not only been influenced by that advertising but influenced in a very specific way by its content. If the sexual content of these ads were not a primary factor in their influence on young male Latinos and non-Latinos in this community, we would not have found the effects only for sexually violent victimizations. Further, if the ads in general, regardless of content, were substitutes for some other unmeasured variable correlated with both ads and sexual violence, we would have seen effects for *all* alcohol ads and not just sexualized ones. Lastly, we argued that if the sexual content of the ads was linked to sexual violence, we should not find effects for non-sexual violence, and the results in table 3.2 show that this prediction was supported by our analyses as well.

Concerning our arguments about the impact of ethnic targeting on violence and sexual violence, once again these results are substantively important. We suggested that ethnic targeting should result in stronger effects of these ads for Latina victims compared to non-Latina victims. One way to examine this question is by comparing the standardized effect of the density of Latina model ads in the equations reported in table 3.2 for Latina and non-Latina sexual violence. Applying the standard formula, we find that the standardized or Beta coefficient for sexist ad density on Latina sexual violence is .480, and the corresponding figure for non-Latina sexual violence is .406 (these coefficients are significantly different from one another at p £ .05). This means that the effect of sexist and demeaning ads featuring Latina models has a stronger effect on sexual violence against Latina girls, just as we predicted above, and as one would expect given the ethnic targeting of these advertisements.

We also hypothesized that any effect of advertising and its content on violence would be independent of the outlets in which alcohol is sold and in which these ads are observed by youth and others in this community. The results are somewhat more mixed with regard to this argument. Although the net effects of Latina model ads on sexual violence were significant in the face of controls for outlet density, we had predicted that outlet density should have significant effects net of advertising. The results in table 3.2 show that this was not the case. Perhaps the lack of power in these data make it difficult to detect distinct effects given that these two concepts are conceptually and empirically correlated. Or perhaps it is possible that this study has uncovered a fundamental mechanism connecting alcohol outlet density and crime—the impact of advertisements. This study provides clear evidence that sexually demeaning advertisements cause both Latina and non-Latina girls to suffer from sexual assaults at a higher rate. Thus, outlet density simply may not affect sexual assault (or not impact it as much) once advertisements are controlled for.

In this study, the first analysis of its kind (to our knowledge), we have found empirical evidence that the specific content of alcohol advertising in alcohol outlets is related to a type of violence in the surrounding neighborhoods that is consistent with the nature of the advertisements' sexualized content. The density of alcohol ads in which Latina models are displayed in demeaning, sexist, and commodifying poses and situations was related to sexually violent victimization of Latina and non-Latina girls net of a wide variety of theoretically and empirically important covariates and causes of such violence. Further, our results show that the density of advertising with this content is *not related* to more general measures of violence in the same neighborhoods.

Though replications of this study are needed, if those results are consistent with what we have found here, as we would expect theoretically, the fact that we have been able to trace a specific advertising content to a specific negative social outcome, sexual violence, is very suggestive for both research and policy. These findings must mark the beginning of a very important policy debate concerning the nature of alcohol advertising and its impact on the communities in which such advertising is placed. A policy based on these results would not limit the industry's right to advertise, or even necessarily limit the density of the ads, but rather focus on their content.

We do not believe that the alcohol industry wishes to sell additional alcohol at the expense of the safety of women and girls in our communities, as the confidence women in particular and people in general have in the safety of their communities is almost certainly related to their willingness to consume alcohol as part of regular leisure activities. We believe that policies can be implemented that enhance both the safety of communities and the economic well-being of the alcohol industry—a "win-win" situation for all concerned.

4

Alcohol, Drugs, Victimization, and Aggression

The Impact of a School-Based Mental Health Intervention on Adolescent Substance Use and Violent Behavior

Robert Nash Parker and Kevin J. McCaffree

INTRODUCTION

In this chapter we examine the relationship between alcohol and other drug use and aggression in elementary school children. Examining the alcohol/drug and violence/ aggression relationship among children in grades 3 through 6, or ages eight through twelve, is a difficult undertaking at best. Children often have muddled understandings of their motivations and the motivations of their significant others. Understanding the reasons people give for their actions and the relationship between these stated reasons and the *actual* causes of behavior are often two very different things. Having said all of this, children may well be more reliable sources of information than one might think. In an article presenting the results of a symposium on alcohol research, Donovan et al. (2004) reported that, overall, young children were indeed reliable reporters of their own alcohol use.

Social research on young people is inherently complex. Given these inherent difficulties, we have taken an interdisciplinary approach to the relationship between drugs, alcohol, and aggression among children. The research for this chapter, then, represents both an extension and a reaffirmation of the advances in understanding of sociology, interpersonal aggression, developmental psychology, and biochemistry that have been made over the last several decades.

The few studies that have investigated substance use among elementary school children have repeatedly shown very little in the way of actual intoxication, addiction, and abuse, which is a very important and positive outcome. For example, in a study of Baltimore youth aged nine to eleven only 4.2 percent had tried alcohol and other drugs in the last year, from a measured baseline of no use (Chilcoat et al., 1995). Donovan et al. (2004) found that among elementary school children in grades 4 to 6, only 5 percent had tried alcohol.

However, studies of aggression and violence in later teenage years often find that early onset and use of alcohol and/or marijuana are significant predictors of later violence, aggression, and victimization (Lier et al., 2009). For example, Grube et al. (1996) find that the onset of drinking—at or before age twelve—is significantly related to adolescent violence and drug use. So despite the relative lack of prevalence of alcohol and drug use among elementary school–aged children, the later negative consequences associated with such early onset of alcohol and drug use make this topic an important one for additional research.

Regardless of whether or not one believes that alcohol's effect on aggression is *direct and causal*, most all scholars agree that the consumption of alcohol in America is a common *precursor* to a variety of aggressive acts including assault, homicide, rape, and suicide (Denson et al., 2011). The cost to American society of alcohol-related criminal aggression is estimated to be at least $205 billion per year and this society-wide impact is twice that of all other drugs combined (Pihl & Sutton, 2009). Though chronic alcohol abuse can result in a variety of health issues (Agarwal & Seitz, 2001), it appears that acute alcohol intoxication is responsible for a lion's share of aggression and violence in American society (Giancola et al., 2010).

Drinking alcohol does not, of course, inevitably lead to violence. Alcohol intoxication is associated, cross-culturally, with a panoply of heterogenous behaviors and this observation has led to the disintegration of a simple theory of "disinhibition" (Begue & Subra, 2008). Neuro-physiologically, alcohol use by both humans and non-human animals produces both an anxiolytic (anxiety-reducing) and also a rewarding, euphoric effect, most likely the result of stimulation to the brain's ventral striatum, a reward circuit associated not only with pleasure from food but from the acquisition of things like money and praise (Gilman et al., 2008).

The popularly invoked neuropsychological construct, "executive cognitive functioning" (a composite of a variety of higher order cognitive abilities such as abstract reasoning, mental flexibility, planning, memory storage, self awareness, and monitoring), is also disrupted by alcohol use and it is this disruption that has been shown, repeatedly, to mediate aggressive acts (Begue & Subra, 2008; Volkow et al., 2008).

Hull (1981) proposed a theory of alcohol's effect on self-awareness in which he argued that alcohol consumption interferes with the brain's ability to maintain states of self-awareness and that it was this effect that prevented individuals from matching their conduct with both self (internal) and societal (external) standards for behavior. Notably, it does not follow from Hull's argument that intoxicated individuals, though less self-aware, will necessarily engage in violent acts or any other act, for that matter.

Hull's thesis has since been generally supported in laboratory studies (e.g., Hull et al., 1983). Additionally, the effect of alcohol on executive cognitive functioning (mentioned above) provides general support for Hull's theory. Much empirical support has also come indirectly by showing consistently that reminding intoxicated individuals of themselves and their actions (via mirrors or video recorders built into experimental laboratory settings—see Bailey et al., 1983 for the earliest of these studies), thus inducing self-awareness, reduces the frequency of subsequent aggressive acts (Ito et al., 1996).

Modern theorizing about alcohol and aggression has absorbed and moved beyond Hull's theory of alcohol and self-awareness. Steele and Josephs (1990) proposed an enduring model of alcohol's effect on cognition—not inconsistent with but certainly more robust than that of Hull's. Steel and Josephs argued that alcohol causes individuals to differentially focus on immediate, attention-grabbing stimuli in a given environment. This theory of alcohol myopia is defined as a "state of shortsightedness in which superficially understood, immediate aspects of experience have a disproportionate influence on behaviors and emotions" (Steele & Josephs, 1990: 923).

A sober individual can, at least in principle, attend to a variety of emotional and situational stimuli and assess a best course of action based on the stimuli most deserving, given a range of motives, of one's attention. Intoxicated subjects, on the other hand, and according to alcohol myopia theory, are stuck in a kind of cognitive tunnel vision responsive only to the most provocative and immediate of concerns. It must be noted that, though alcohol has a myopic effect on attentional capacities, this narrowing of focus can be on both calming as well as instigative cues. In fact, in many laboratory studies, intoxicated subjects must be provoked with an annoying or frustrating stimulus before exhibiting aggressive behavior, indicating that cognitive/emotional states and environment play a very significant role in the alcohol/aggression relationship above and beyond the myopic effects of alcohol on cognition (Begue & Subra, 2008).

In the laboratory, alcohol and aggressiveness have been linked in numerous studies over the past twenty years. Most simply, a direct effect between alcohol and intoxicated aggression has been demonstrated by gathering a group of adult volunteers, splitting them into two groups (control vs. experimental groups) and by giving one group—but not the other—enough alcohol to intoxicate, but not harm, them in a safe, research setting. After one group demonstrates adequate physiological intoxication, a reaction-time game is often played pitting participants against one another. In reality, the participants playing the reaction game aren't actually *playing* at all. Their "competitor" is a preprogrammed computer, hidden in an adjacent room, which has already determined whether or not the participant will win or lose. Each game played by each participant is only a ruse, a trick to get the participant to believe that they are actually engaging in a competitive task with a fellow research volunteer. As it turns out, it's a good thing that intoxicated subjects aren't playing with another human being, because they consistently exhibit greater aggressive responses upon losing (Giancola et al., 2003). This connection between intoxication and aggressiveness holds regardless of individual differences in income, education, or ethnicity.

As might be expected, though, men are typically more at risk of exhibiting intoxicated aggression than women. The apparent relationship between intoxication, aggression, and gender, both culturally and subculturally, has lead researchers to consider the role of culture and setting in producing intoxicated, anti-social behavior. In some respects, what it means to be a young man in emerging adulthood hinges on alcohol use, one's ability to keep up with peers who use and abuse alcohol, and one's ability to act sufficiently masculine or *macho* while intoxicated (Campbell, 2000). In unfamiliar settings, or in settings with loose normative expectations for behavior (i.e., bars, parties, and other relaxed, relatively open gatherings), a sort of "situational disinhibition" may occur. Alcohol use, in other words, sometimes causes aggressive responses and sometimes doesn't because of the varying formal and informal norms (which may act as active or passive constraints on intoxicated aggression) of different situations (Parker & Rebuhn, 1995).

In sum, perhaps the most fundamental and major conclusion of contemporary research into alcohol use and behavior is that, despite a universally human bio-physiological response to ethanol (the intoxicating ingredient in alcoholic beverages), the social/behavioral display that often follows intoxication varies importantly from culture to culture. Following Parker's (1995) theory of selective disinhibition, mentioned briefly above, depending on the normative constraints of the situation, culture, or sub-culture, some intoxicated displays are absolutely unthinkable and seriously discouraged (one might imagine the regrettable situation of a blacked-out family member at a funeral or wedding) while in other situations, cultures, or sub-cultures, intoxicated displays of extreme and colorful disregard are normative and encouraged (imagine behavior at a post-graduation frat party). These various differences in expectations surrounding intoxicated behavior become even more starkly visible when comparing cultures cross-nationally (see Edgerton & MacAndrew, 2003).

Whatever the physiological details of intoxication, it is worth stating explicitly that both alcohol consumption and related social/cultural activities, aggression, and violence are learned behaviors. If researchers are to better understand this relationship and its origins, perhaps the best place to begin such inquiry is in the context of development. As individuals grow and age between five and fifteen, much of the behavioral and social foundation of their adult life is established. Not only is this period of pre to post adolescence the appropriate time frame within which to discover the behavioral and social link, if one exists, between alcohol and aggression, but it may also be the most appropriate place to intervene in the development of this relationship, and to break the link between alcohol and aggression before it becomes an established and dangerous pattern in adulthood.

The situation with drugs other than alcohol is much more difficult to summarize. Parker and Auerhahn (1998) claim that no credible scientific evidence exists in the published literature to justify the claim that drugs such as marijuana, cocaine, amphetamines, or heroin cause aggression and violence. Other researchers disagree with this assessment; as a consequence, the work in this chapter includes a consideration of other drugs as well as alcohol in the study of substance use and aggression.

The data used in this chapter are from a study that attempted, via an intervention program, to prevent the establishment of the link between substance use and aggression beginning in an elementary school setting. Baseline and one wave of post intervention data are analyzed. The major hypothesis is that the intervention, Wellness Mental Health centers (described below), significantly reduced the level of substance use and the occurrence of aggressive behavior and attitudes among the sample of children ages eight through twelve.

STUDY APPROACH

Design

The Wellness Centers were designed to bring together a variety of social services (mental health, police, probation, and family advocacy) in one readily accessible area, and to promote healthy lifestyles among students and their families. Centers provide counseling, group activities, and after-school activities as well as outreach and education. Wellness centers were established in five schools: one elementary school, one middle school, two high schools, and one continuation high school. Control schools were selected for similarity in size and demographics; this chapter reports results from the experimental and control elementary schools.

Sample

All children in grades 3 through 6 at the control and experimental schools were targeted for testing. The working sample consists of 386 children, representing a response rate of approximately 30 percent. Of those children, approximately 157 had data for both pre- and post-test. The sample was divided approximately equally between boys (48.9 percent) and girls (51.1 percent). Ethnicity data were available for 191 students. The ethnic distribution was as follows: 54.5 percent Hispanic; 30.9 percent White; 10.5 percent African American; 2.1 percent Asian. Approximately 17.8 percent of students came from socioeconomically disadvantaged homes (measured by free or reduced lunch status), and 27.2 percent spoke English as a second language.

Procedure

Participants completed the Student Wellness Survey (SWS) in groups ranging in size from ten students to forty. In the first wave of data collection, the SWS consisted of eight scales: the Positive Identity Inventory (Smith & Ozer, unpublished manuscript), which assesses the importance of various long-term goals; items from the Index of Empathy for Children and Adolescents (Bryant, 1982); items from the Coping Scale for Children and Youth (Brodzinsky, Elias, Steiger, Simon, Gill, & Hitt, 1992); items assessing social self-efficacy; items assessing concentration and impulse control; items from the Normative Beliefs About Aggression scale (Huesmann, Guerra, Miller, & Zelli, 1992); and items addressing school violence (taken from the California School Climate and Safety Survey; Furlong & Morrison, 1994) and victimization (taken from the Multidimensional Peer-Victimization Scale; Mynard & Joseph, 2000). In the second wave of data collection, items from the California

Healthy Kids Survey were added to evaluate drug and alcohol usage. Initial assessment was performed in February 2001, with follow-up in October 2001.

Archival data provided by the school district included ethnicity, English language learner/nonlearner status, home language, parent education, socioeconomic status, and standardized achievement scores in reading, math, language, and spelling. Finally, we have the intervention of the Wellness centers, described previously, in roughly 50 percent of the sample of 144 children in grades 3 through 6 for which we have complete data. If these centers are having an impact, it should demonstrate itself in reductions in aggression, victimization, and substance use. Here we measure simply whether the school in question had a wellness center or not.

MODEL SPECIFICATION

The focus of the research being reported here is on the factors that lead to the development of aggressive behaviors and victimization in pre adolescence and the impact of such experiences on substance use and subsequent aggressive and victimization experiences. In addition, we have preliminary data from the wellness centers which allows us to take a first look at the impact of a mental health intervention in the school designed to disrupt such patterns of substance use and aggressive behavior. The heuristic model in figure 4.1 gives a schematic representation of the conceptual framework we examine here.

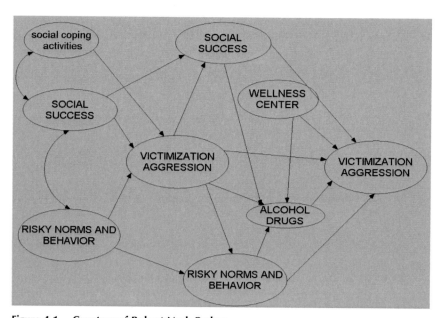

Figure 4.1.   Courtesy of Robert Nash Parker.

Measures of social success, such as empathy for others and social efficacy, should reduce early involvement in aggressive and victim behavior. Empathy will make it difficult for a child to victimize another while self-efficacy, as a form of social capital, should buffer a child from exposure to risk of victimization. On the other hand, some children already display risky behaviors and beliefs early in childhood. In this case, we measure the ability of a child to control impulsive behavior, and we also examine his/her attitudes toward aggressive and violent behaviors. Lack of impulse control should make a child more likely to engage in violence against others and to put themselves in situations where the risk of victimization is higher. Positive attitudes about violence and aggression should also increase the likelihood of both victimization and aggression.

Early experiences of victimization and aggression should in turn influence social success and risky behaviors and attitudes. A child who has been victimized may develop a greater sense of empathy for others so treated, but it is unlikely that social efficacy is enhanced by aggressive behaviors. Rather the opposite is more likely, given that other children will begin to avoid an overly aggressive individual, thus reinforcing a decline in social skills and social capital.

Additionally, early involvement in aggressive and violent behaviors may also compound stress on a preadolescent child that could lead to the development of alcohol and drug use in subsequent years of adolescence. The impact of stress on young people has been investigated at length and though much work remains to be done, some preliminary conclusions may help point the way toward a more comprehensive biosocial understanding of the development of alcohol use and aggression in preadolescence. Alcohol use and abuse can conspire to create stressful environments in a variety of ways, and such environments are always risky for young people to grow up and develop in.

RESULTS

Independent of the effects of ethnicity, income, parental education, and other control variables, those children who had less impulse control were more likely to be aggressive in the first wave of data collection. This relationship held true in the next wave as well. Not surprisingly, those children most likely to be violent in the second wave of interviews were also more impulsive and aggressive in the first wave. If nothing else, this shows the internal validity of this study at the same time that it shows the link between impulsivity and aggression (see table 4.1).

Another finding of interest was that children who sought out assistance from others regarding coping with emotions and feelings were more likely to be aggressive themselves. At first, this may seem counterintuitive—aren't children who seek out help better off than those who do not? Well, only if the children seeking assistance *actually* get help, and only if that help is *actually* effective. Presumably, children who seek out help would benefit from receiving it. After all, there is some evidence that

Table 4.1. Aggression, Alcohol, and Drugs among Elementary School Students

	Aggression Wave 1	Victimization Wave 1	Alcohol Wave 2	Norms re Aggression Wave 2	Impulse Control Wave 2	Victimization Wave 2	Aggression Wave 2
Impulse Control W1	-.306*	-.383*					
Impulse Control W2			-.035		—	-.074*	-.091*
Assistance Coping W1	.059*	.062					
Aggression W1				-.469*			.187*
Victimization W1					-.225*	.421*	.070
Norms re Aggression W2			-.129*			-.026	-.109*

seeking adult guidance is a common response regarding elementary school–aged children and drug use (Huetteman et al., 1992). If they do not receive help or counseling, or do not receive it adequately, they may well be at increased risk of inappropriately attempting to deal with their own negative emotions in isolation, resulting in aggressive acting-out in some children.

But what does it mean to say that aggressive children in this study generally had poorer impulse control or that they were more likely to have sought assistance to help cope with tough feelings? In other words, *why* might these two indicators predict aggression? And what relationship do they have with one another?

Hirschi (1990) has suggested that those people (children or adults) most likely to engage in aggressive behavior are people that literally couldn't have chosen otherwise. Hirschi (1990) argues, in effect, that criminals of all ages suffer from the same disability—low self-control. This "general" theory of crime, though frequently criticized (Pratt & Cullen, 2000), nevertheless highlights an important fact: presumably very few people *want* to harm others and be sequestered in jails and prisons. In order for a person to engage in aggressive behavior that not only breaks the legal and moral code of our culture but also sets up difficult barriers for future achievement (e.g., getting a job, or, in the case of children, doing well in school), there must be some miscalculation going on in the mind of the offender. For Hirschi, this miscalculation is a sort of poorly built mental algorithm, instilled in childhood, which leads the child (and, subsequently, the adult) to see social life as nothing more than a set of opportunities for pleasure and immediate gratification despite the negative social and personal consequences that follow. For Hirschi, proper self-control must be taught during the formative years of a child's life, ideally by the family. Other researchers, with different theoretical orientations, such as Moffit (1993), agree that some sort of psychological deficit may be operating, but disagree as to its source and also as to what constitutes "low self-control" in the first place (does one antisocial act mean the child is troubled? Two acts? Three? How bad does an act have to be? What if the child stops committing these acts once they reach adulthood? Would that mean they learned self-control on their own, contra Hirschi? Or maybe they always had it but, for possibly environmental reasons, didn't think it necessary, or prudent, to use it)?

All things considered, the explanation proposed in this chapter is a heuristic one, one that attempts a reciprocal link between individual brain chemistry and social environment that is emerging from recent research across many disciplines.

Serotonin is a chemical in the brain which help regulates very basic physiological functioning such as body temperature, appetite, emotions/mood, and sleep quality. Its effects on the nervous system are vast. The human body, in an effort to acclimate and adapt to prolonged periods of elevated stress (represented in the body as elevated levels of cortisol, a stress hormone), tapers off, over time, the rate of serotonin transfer in the brain. The effect on the nervous system is significant—depleted levels of serotonin, over time, lead to depressive, anxious, and potentially angry reactive behavior (Ninan, 1999).

Stressful environments (which, in principle, can be multi-causal: poverty, physical abuse, substance use, high crime, unstable emotional connections, etc.) not only expose children to dysfunction, they have the potential to actually restructure the child's neurochemistry such that set points of physiological functioning can be established in one setting (e.g., a troubled home) which may be utterly inappropriate in another setting (e.g., a quiet school classroom). For example, Davies et al. (2009) found that constant parental arguing, when experienced by toddlers, led to elevated levels of cortisol in the bloodstream of these toddlers, along with decreased activity of the sympathetic nervous system. This isn't true only for toddlers, of course, but also for elementary and middle school–aged children (Pendry & Adam, 2007). The potential disconnect between a stressful home life and a relatively secure school environment provides opportunities for some troubled children to act out in ways that are anti-social and inappropriate for the school setting regardless of how "adaptive" such a stress response may be in the home environment the child is most used to.

Put simply, children familiar with stressful environments will develop a tendency to default to a fear response when encountering stress—a fear response that, in young children, is commonly exhibited as aggression and anger (Zucker et al., 2008). Indeed, this "response inhibition" in children is what is often captured in sociological and criminological accounts of poor impulse control. Perhaps most tragic of all, children's emotional reactivity to environmental stress actually creates a feedback loop, where the child's angry (i.e., fearful) responses to stress further tax the child's physiological stress response, thus mediating and exacerbating the impact of external stress (Davies et al., 2009). For these reasons, school-aged children exposed to prolonged environmental stress are at a far greater risk of exhibiting violent behavior as they mature (Singer, 1999; Guerra, 2003).

But why serotonin? Clearly, what occurs in the brain of a child is dependent not only on the chemicals in the brain at that moment, but also the external, environmental stimuli that is provoking and encouraging the distribution of serotonin in the brain. It is well understood in the biological literature that how humans process stress importantly influences their aggressiveness (Craig, 2007). Common alleles (kinds of genes) that help build serotonin pathways in the brain contribute importantly to how well people respond to abusive upbringings and other prolonged stressful encounters. Serotonin specifically operates as a behavior regulator; elevated levels of serotonin neurotransmission in the brain are associated with better impulse control and inhibition (Zuckers-Lucki, 1998).

Additionally, deficits in the body's ability to regulate and synthesize serotonin has been found to influence impulsivity, aggression, and hyperactivity (ADHD). This holds true especially for maltreated children and those exposed to consistent stressors (Zucker et al., 2008). The findings that inform this chapter are consistent with this interpretation. The children in our sample that had less developed impulse control were more likely to be violent in the first wave of data collection. Conversely, children in our study who had high impulse control were less likely to act aggressively and, interestingly, also less likely to be the victims of such attacks. In other words, children with high impulse control were simply less likely *to be involved* in any altercation. This impact of high impulse control held through both waves of data collection.

Children in our study who were most often victimized also exhibited lower levels of impulse control. Consistent victimization, a form of prolonged exposure to a stressful stimulus, can lead to elevated levels of cortisol in the blood, and subsequent drops in serotonin and changes in the regulation of the nervous system. This repeated sequence may well lead to more impulsive, angry/fearful reactivity—precisely the characteristics that may well land that child in a future altercation. As it turns out, this is exactly what the data in our study show. Children that were involved in altercations in the first wave of data collection were more likely to be involved in altercations in the second wave as well. And not just involved in these altercations as victims. Research shows that those children who are victimized are also at an elevated risk of being involved in future altercations—as victim *or* aggressor (Sullivan et al.). A reciprocal relationship, therefore, emerges: one that ties victimization to environmental stress to neuro-chemically mediated impulsivity to future victimization and aggression to future environmental stress. As will be detailed next, once alcohol enters this iterating cycle, the potential for violence soars.

Those children who were most often aggressive were also more likely to develop normative beliefs favoring aggression as an appropriate response in certain situations. Sykes and Matza (1957) explicitly lay out a theory of "neutralization." Neutralization occurs when an otherwise well-intentioned child commits an illegal or improper act and then rationalizes the situation or their own motives so as to "neutralize," or avoid, their responsibility for the incident. This activity, Sykes and Matza concede, is common in children, as most children seek out approval and want to be law-abiders.

These attempts at neutralization, because the child wishes to maintain a positive sense of self, are consequently very successful at convincing the child that what occurred was not his/her fault after all. Rationalizing that an altercation was the other boy's fault, or a consequence of the teacher's meanness, or some other excuse, allows the child to maintain a guilt-free, positive self-image without any of the hang-ups of personal responsibility. Unchecked, Sykes and Matza argue, such attempts at neutralization will become more frequent and more damaging for the child's personal and social life. The results from this study indicating that violent children begin developing beliefs favorable to aggression represents a process of these children developing techniques of neutralization. In fact, Guerra et al. (2003) found that children exposed to community violence were more likely to develop beliefs about people and social situations that were favorable to aggression as well as engage in aggressive fantasizing. Children who reported having more normative beliefs favoring aggression were also more likely to have begun using alcohol in the second wave of data collection.

The development in children of normative beliefs favorable to aggression literally represents the internalization that violence in this or that situation was or is okay. This represents a significant step in the anti-social development of a child's social cognition (Werner & Nixon, 2005). The internalization of such beliefs, usually occurring among children in later waves of data collection both in our study and in others (e.g., Guerra et al., 2003) also had an important effect of encouraging future aggressiveness.

Once these socially at-risk teens are exposed to alcohol, aggression is exacerbated. Alcohol is, after all, easy to obtain and the likelihood of a person drinking increases with age before eventually leveling off. After all, many, if not most, young people get their alcohol from home (Warner & White, 2000). Considering the second wave of data collection, the greater the experience of aggression is early on, the more likely children will be to develop attitudes and norms favorable to violence. This in turn leads to a significant increase in the frequency of alcohol consumption. So while our findings do not support the notion of a direct effect between early violence and victimization and subsequent substance use, in both the case of drugs and alcohol, an indirect effect through aggressive attitudes appears to influence additional substance use. In turn, both frequent drug and alcohol use lead to later experiences with aggressive behavior in the second wave of the data.

Finally, the impact of the Wellness Centers is negligible in these data. Although the impact of Wellness Centers on alcohol use is negative, as expected, it is far from statistical significance and thus of no import. The presence of the Wellness Centers has thus far in these data had little impact on aggressive behavior or victimization.

Though stressful, risky environments abound (many children, of course, are born every year to parents who drink heavily and irresponsibly), children can, themselves, increase the stress in their own environments by engaging in anti-social aggression which, usually, brings sanctions and formal or informal punishments which may further increase the amount of stress in a young person's life. Of particular interest here in terms of the mechanism relating stress to intoxication to aggression is the reciprocal relationship that may exist regarding stress, serotonin, impulsivity, and conduct disorders in children. Whether the stress stems from home life, peers, or the child's own aggressive actions, a child's sensitivity to and physiological ability to produce and regulate serotonin has been implicated in numerous behavioral disorders and there is good reason to believe that alcohol, specifically, may further exacerbate such problems (Pihl & Lemarquand, 1998). While exploring the bio-social mechanisms running from stress to aggression to substance use (and back again), it is always important to keep in mind different levels of analysis from family life, to social status, to psychological disposition, to environmental risk factors, to neurochemistry—all play a role, and all provide part of the overall picture.

Because the work presented here strongly supports the existence of a link between aggressiveness (measured by previous aggressive episodes as well as the degree to which a child harbors beliefs favorable to—or in defense of—aggression) and intoxication, a major relationship of interest in this study was that running from alcohol and drugs to victimization and aggression. Though serotonergic neurotransmitters play a large role in how the body responds to stress, fear, and anger, the role of prevention research must ultimately be a practical and realistic one. After all, smart, scientifically informed social and political policy cannot and should not go around regulating brain chemistry directly. Interventions must be targeted at the level of behavior, community, and culture. Alcohol use among pre-adolescents is a serious risk factor for violent acting-out. The sooner the mechanics of the relationship are understood and its sources explored, the sooner effective developmentally focused strategies can be implemented to curb the twin pitfalls of difficult childhoods and addictive psycho-active substances.

5

Alcohol, Homicide, and Cultural Context

A Cross National Analysis of Gender Specific Victimization

Robert Nash Parker and Kevin J. McCaffree

Note: Substantial portions of the following chapter were originally published in Homicide Studies, 2(1), 6–30, 1998; the definitive final version of that article can be found at: http://hsx.sagepub.com/content/2/1/6.full.pdf+html. © 1998 Sage Publications, Inc.

INTRODUCTION

Past research on homicide in North America has been rich and varied in terms of theoretical approaches, orientation, data sources, methods, and time periods (Sampson, 1986; 1987; Williams & Flewelling, 1988; Parker, 1989; Silverman & Kennedy, 1987; 1988; Balkwell, 1990; Bailey & Peterson, 1989; Bailey, 1990). Recently, some attention has been devoted to the impact of alcohol and drugs on homicide (Parker & Rebhun, 1995; Parker, 1995; Sprunt et al., 1994; Klien et al., 1991; Stevens et al., 2011; Pridemore & Grubesic, 2011), following in the tradition begun by Wolfgang (1958). However, this research is still limited in that it has been based on data and analyses of homicide rates only in the United States during particular time periods (Gartner, 1990: 94; and with important recent exceptions, e.g., see Bye, 2008; Dearden & Payne, 2009). Although European researchers have been more willing to examine the relationship between homicide and alcohol, and more likely to consider variation in this relationship over time, much of the research suffers similarly from the "parochialism" (see Kohn, 1987) of the North American research on homicide (e.g., Hansen, 1985; Linqvist, 1986; Lenke, 1982; 1987; 1990; Skog, 1986).

Beginning in the mid-1980s, criminology saw a resurgence in truly comparative or cross national research on homicide, for example, Krahn et al. (1986), Fiala and LaFree (1988), Messner (1989), and Gartner (1990), although none of these studies considered the role of alcohol in the genesis of homicidal violence. The purpose of this chapter is to present a dynamic international analysis investigating the role of alcohol in homicide, within the context of a well-developed theoretical model of gender-specific homicide victimization (Gartner, 1990).

Given the focus of law enforcement, US federal officials, mass media, and public interest on the connection between illegal drugs and violence, it may seem curious that this chapter focuses *entirely* on the alcohol and homicide relationship. There are two general reasons for the exclusive attention of this study to alcohol, the first of which is based on results from a number of empirical studies of the relationships among violence, alcohol, and other drugs. Despite the beliefs of many officials, professionals, and citizens in the United States, the empirical evidence demonstrates that alcohol is by far the most important "drug" in terms of involvement in homicide and other forms of violence (Abel, 1987; Sprunt et al., 1994; 1995; Wieczorek et al., 1990; Yarvis, 1994; Fendrich et al., 1995; Goldstein et al., 1992; Kuhns, 2011; Darke et al., 2009). For example, National Crime Victim Survey respondents reported in the early '90s that less than 10 percent of the assailants who victimized them were under the influence of drugs, while more than 25 percent of these assailants were perceived as having used alcohol (Bureau of Justice Statistics, 1992a). More recent data is similarly suggestive. Nearly four in ten (36.8 percent) state prisoners arrested for violent offenses report being drunk at the time of the offense (Bureau of Justice Statistics, 2004). Also worth noting is that, among jail inmates, alcohol use was most prevalent during the commission of violent offenses (Bureau of Justice Statistics, 2002). For a good recent analysis not only of the powerful impact of alcohol on violent offending, but of dose-dependent effects (in the predictable direction of more alcohol, more violence), see Felson and Staff (2010). Furthermore, data drawn from urinalysis of individuals arrested for violent offenses have shown that just over 5 percent were under the influence of drugs other than alcohol at the time of arrest (Bureau of Justice Statistics, 1992b). In fact, a recently published review of the toxicology results of over 30,000 homicide victims found that the most prevalent drug in victims' systems other than alcohol was cocaine, found in 11 percent, a comparatively smaller proportion than is typical of alcohol (Kuhns et al., 2009). Studies in general of both homicide offenders and victims have found relatively little involvement of illegal drugs and a great deal of involvement of alcohol (Welte & Abel, 1989; Kratcoski, 1990; Garriott, 1993; Tradiff et al., 1995; see Fagan, 1990; Parker & Auerhahn, 1998; Felson & Staff, 2010; Kuhns, 2011). Wieczorek and colleagues (1990), for example, in an analysis of interviews with nearly two thousand convicted murderers, found that around half of all offenders admitted to being high on alcohol—findings even indicated a heavier period of consumption prior to the homicide itself.

The second reason for the exclusive focus on alcohol and homicide has to do with the cross-national nature of this study. The attention given to illegal drugs, attitudes toward drug users, indeed even the legality of certain drugs themselves varies dramatically across the time and space examined here. The situation with regard to alcohol, however, is relatively stable and comparable across the nation states and time periods examined here. Although there were some minor variations in alcohol regulations in these nations during the post-war 1950 to 1995 time period (i.e., changes in the minimum drinking age in the United States, introduction and removal of "strong" beer in some of the Nordic states), the overall stability of the regulatory framework for alcohol makes the comparative enterprise represented by this study more appropriate.

After a review of Gartner's cross national model of gender–specific homicide, two aspects of the alcohol/homicide relationship are discussed theoretically, and two hypotheses are derived: the first involving alcohol consumption, divorce, and male victimization; the second involving the relationship between divorce, cross national variation in drinking styles, and female victimization. The database required to test these hypotheses and replicate the Gartner model is described, along with the analytic and statistical problems posed by such pooled cross sectional data, as well the appropriate statistical solutions. This chapter concludes with a discussion of the importance of theoretically derived hypotheses, interaction effects, and the importance of cross national research on the relationship of alcohol, gender, and violence.

GARTNER'S FOUR DOMAINS OF HOMICIDE VICTIMIZATION

Gartner (1990: 94–96) organized her model of homicide causation into four sets of structural characteristics, as depicted in figure 5.1. The "material context," in which the concepts of absolute and relative deprivation reside, has a long theoretical and empirical history in homicide research.

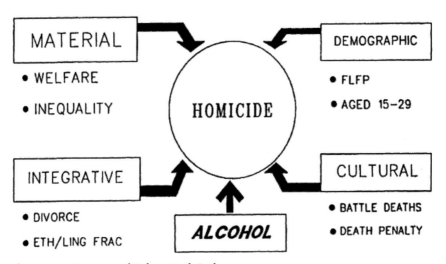

Figure 5.1. Courtesy of Robert Nash Parker

Relative deprivation or inequality has been particularly found to be a significant predictor of homicide rates in cross national studies (Messner, 1982; 1989; Krahn et al., 1986). Absolute deprivation or poverty has also proved to be a consistent predictor of homicide in North American research (Loftin & Hill, 1974; Parker & Smith, 1979; Messner, 1983; Williams, 1984; Messner & Tardiff, 1986; Williams & Flewelling, 1988; Parker, 1989; Pridemore, 2011; but see Messner et al., 2010 for recent contradictory findings). In addition, at least a few studies report that government attempts to alleviate poverty (i.e., take steps toward becoming a "welfare state") result overwhelmingly in reductions in violence and homicide (DeFranzo, 1983; Fiala & La Free, 1988; Savolainen, 2000). Thus for Gartner, *the material domain contains measures of relative deprivation based on income inequality and a summary measure of government efforts to provide a "safety net" for its least advantaged citizens* (1990: 95).

The second domain in Gartner's model is the "integrative context," with the link to homicide based on the notion that greater the degree of social integration among members of a society, the less likely violence will be used as a means of dispute resolution (1990: 95). *Thus, the divorce ratio and a measure of ethnic and linguistic heterogeneity tap the absence of social ties and the therefore reduce the protective impact of social bonds, both formal and informal, leading to higher hypothesized rates of victimization* (Gartner, 1990: 95).

The third domain of the model is the "demographic context" (Gartner, 1990:95). Gartner bases her discussion of the relationship between increasing proportions of young people (the post–World War II "baby boom") and adult women working outside the home in most of the nations under consideration in terms of the routine activity/lifestyle paradigm (e.g., Hindelang et al., 1978; Cohen & Felson, 1979; Sampson, 1987; Gartner et al., 1990), which focuses on the role of daily activities, routine behaviors, and the variation in relative risk of victimization that such routines and behaviors produce. For example, *a greater proportion of women working outside the home* would increase exposure to a larger pool of motivated offenders, and reduce the effectiveness of potential guardians in the family (Cohen et al., 1981). Similarly, *the greater the proportion of young people*, the greater the likelihood of lifestyles and routine activities that involve going out at night, a major indicator of increased risk (see Miethe et al., 1987; Sampson & Wooldredge, 1987; Schwartz & Pitts, 1995).

Finally, Gartner's model includes a domain she labels the "cultural context." This domain is linked to homicide victimization in terms of the legitimation of violence as a viable, useful, and even acceptable means for dispute resolution in a society. Based on both research on the impact of state violence on individuals (e.g., Archer & Gartner, 1984; Bowers, 1984; Landau & Pfefferman, 1988; Williams & Flewelling, 1988) and studies of modeling, habituation, and learning (e.g., Bandura, 1973; Comstock, 1975), *Gartner argues that involvement in wars and the willingness to have capital punishment* as a sanctioned state response to homicide are indicative of a society in which violence is legitimated. In such societies, it is hypothesized that violence will be used at a higher rate in the resolution of individual disputes (1990: 96).

THE FIFTH DOMAIN: ALCOHOL CONTEXT

The final domain included in figure 5.1 is the alcohol context, which is added to Gartner's model in this extension of her research. Figures 5.2 and 5.3 show why, from an empirical perspective, it is reasonable to expect a relationship cross nationally between alcohol and homicide. These graphs depict the relationship, over time, between spirits consumption in pure ethanol equivalent per capita, and the homicide victimization rate for females and males, respectively, in three of the seventeen nations analyzed here.

Certainly the data for the United States and Austria (the two types of dashed lines) show a consistency over time between these two variables. The data for Canada is somewhat less convincing, especially since 1970, when the two trends seem to be operating independent of one another (Smart & Mann, 1987). Although not necessarily conclusive (see Treno et al., 1992; McDowall et al., 1980), these data are indicative of a positive relationship between alcohol and homicide. More recent empirical investigations have strengthened the link between alcohol consumption and violence. In fact, a consensus of research is tying not only alcohol outlet density (Parker et al., 2011a; Zhu et al., 2004) but also the specific *type* of alcoholic beverage—single serve—to elevated rates of homicide and violent crime (Parker et al., 2011b).

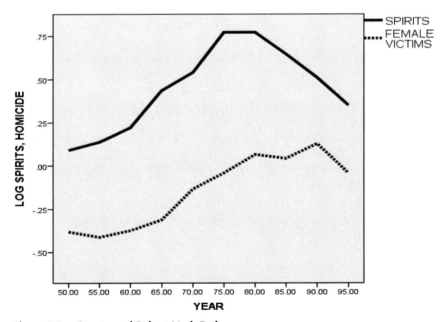

Figure 5.2. Courtesy of Robert Nash Parker.

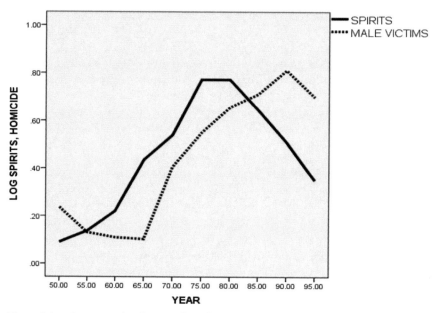

Figure 5.3.   Courtesy of Robert Nash Parker

THE THEORY OF SOCIAL DISINHIBITION

Parker (1993) and Parker and Rebhun (1995) attempt to specifically link alcohol and violence in an overall conceptual model. Parker and Rebhun (1995) describe a social disinhibition approach, which tries to explain why it is that normatively proscribed behavior is "disinhibited" in relatively few cases of alcohol-involved interpersonal disputes. Alcohol selectively disinhibits violence depending on contextual factors such as characteristics of the situation, the actors involved, their relationships to one another, and the impact of bystanders. The theory, briefly discussed in chapter 4, proposes that individuals are constrained from engaging in certain behaviors in a social situation by the norms that they have internalized; however, people do violate norms, and may have conflicting sets of norms to draw on in some situations. It is possible that norms which have the least institutional support are more likely to be disinhibited in a situation, all else being equal (Parker, 1993: 118); this may explain the frequent association between alcohol and spousal violence, noted in the family violence literature (e.g., Stets, 1990).

In order to explain how choices are made between these conflicting normative structures, Parker and Rebhun (1995: 34–35) introduce the concepts of *active and passive constraint*. In potentially violent situations it takes active constraint—a proactive and conscious decision not to use violence to "solve" the dispute—to preclude violence. In some of these cases, alcohol may disinhibit norms that usually prevent or constrain individuals from engaging in violent behavior. Thus, the selective nature of alcohol-related homicide is dependent upon the interaction of an impaired rationality and the nature of the social situation. The nature of the social situation, or the context in which behavior takes place, is of paramount importance in providing passive, or situational, constraint which may determine the outcome of a potentially violent situation (Parker & Rebhun, 1995; see also Wilbanks, 1984).

A test of this particular specification of the theory was reported by Parker (1995). Cross-sectional analysis of US state-level data for five different types of homicide, differentiated by circumstances of crime and/or victim-offender relationship (e.g., robbery homicide; family homicide), showed that the impact of poverty on robbery and other felony homicides was stronger in states with above-average rates of alcohol consumption.

Parker and Rebhun (1995) also report the results of a test of this approach that utilized a longitudinal design. Using city level data, they found that increases in alcohol availability helped to explain increasing homicide in these cities between 1960 and 1980. This study also found some evidence that availability interacted with poverty, routine activities, and a lack of social bonds.

CONSUMPTION, DIVORCE, AND GENDER-SPECIFIC HOMICIDE

Two aspects of alcohol-related activities are considered in this research: consumption and drinking "style" or drinking culture, the latter usually framed in the distinction between "wet" and "dry" drinking styles (Room, 1989). The alcohol-related hypotheses to be specified and tested here argue that consumption and aspects of the wet/dry distinction interact with one of Gartner's factors, divorce, to produce distinct effects on homicide victimization by gender.

Figures 5.2 and 5.3 show that alcohol consumption and homicide victimization of both men and women may be linked. However, the purpose of this chapter is to present a test of a more detailed hypothesis: that the rate of consumption interacts with a nation's divorce rate to raise homicide victimization of men above that predicted by consumption, divorce, and the other factors in Gartner's model. The selection of divorce as a focus for this research is based on a number of reasons. First, divorce has been linked to homicide in a number of previous studies (e.g., Williams & Flewelling, 1988; Parker & Toth, 1990; Dugan et al., 1999; Tcherni, 2011; see also Beaulieu & Messner, 2010 for a detailed discussion). Second, the way in which divorce is hypothesized to affect homicide in Gartner's model, in terms of the weakening of social control and integration, makes divorce a likely candidate for the enhancing effect of alcohol on violence described above. If high divorce rates lead to lower social control and less social integration, homicide becomes a more viable strategy for the solution of interpersonal disputes. Less social control and social integration means that normative prohibitions against violence have less impact on individual behavior. In this situation, alcohol is likely to break down the active constraint required to prevent violence in cases where violence is a potentially successful strategy. Thus consumption is likely to enhance the positive effect divorce rates have on rates of homicide.

Why should the interaction of consumption and divorce affect male homicide victimization more than that of female victimization? First, men as a group consume far more alcohol than women in all of the seventeen nations included in this analysis (Makela et al., 1981, vol. 1: 23), so whatever the impact of consumption, it is likely that men will be affected more than women. Second, rates of violence among men are also substantially higher than those among women; Gartner (1990: 99) reports that for the eighteen nations in her study (seventeen of which are included here), the mean male homicide victimization rate was more than twice the female rate. Therefore, it should be the case that if the consumption/divorce interaction has an impact, it is more likely to be on the male victimization rate.

The wet/dry cultural distinction should have a different sort of relationship with homicide victimization. This distinction has been seen as one which involves both a cluster of distinctive drinking patterns and behaviors and a differing relationship between alcohol and various social problems. In addition, this categorization of societies has been seen as reflecting distinctive social attitudes toward alcohol and its role in society, i.e., the degree to which alcohol and related behaviors and practices are integrated or not into the social and culture framework of a society (Room, 1972; 1989). The dry drinking style is characterized by consumption of spirits, episodic beer drinking, lower overall consumption rates, and more frequent association between consumption and violence. In contrast, the wet drinking style is seen as involving more wine consumption, more frequent and/or regular consumption of moderate or high amounts, higher overall consumption rates, and less association with violence (see Room, 1989: 5–9). In dry nations, drinking is less integrated into regular social interaction, and in wet style nations, drinking is more integrated.

Table 5.1 presents the operationalization of this wet/dry distinction for the seventeen nations included in this analysis. As indicated in table 5.1, the Scandinavian countries have traditionally served as examples of the dry drinking style, while nations such as France, and Italy have been seen as the archetypal wet societies. It becomes very clear early in the exercise of classification, however, that a number of the seventeen nations included here do not easily fit into one of these two categories. It has long been acknowledged that elements of both styles exist in the United States (see Room, 1972), but the same is also true of the other nations in the "mixed" category in table 5.1: the former West Germany had elements of both in its "dryer" Protestant northern section as opposed to its "wetter" Catholic southern section, and the nations of the United Kingdom, as well as both its former North American colonies, certainly exhibit traits of both styles. Canada has clear claim to both styles, being a union between a major former colony of France and of England. These "mixed" tendencies are also reflected in consumption rates of various beverage types, also a factor utilized in this attempt at operationalization.

Table 5.1.   Nations Classified by Drinking Style

DRY	*WET*	*MIXED*
DENMARK	AUSTRIA	CANADA
FINLAND	AUSTRALIA	WEST GERMANY
NETHERLANDS	BELGIUM	IRELAND
NORWAY	FRANCE	ENGLAND AND WALES
SWEDEN	ITALY	UNITED STATES
	NEW ZEALAND	
	SWITZERLAND	

The authors would argue *that it is in these "mixed" nations that the role of alcohol is most pronounced vis-à-vis violence*, despite the traditional assumption that connection between alcohol and violence would be strongest in dry societies. The ambivalent nature of alcohol's place in the social and cultural framework of mixed-style nations (Room, 1976) combines the most problematic aspects of both the wet and dry drinking styles. In these nations alcohol is more integrated in everyday social life than it is in the dry societies, but on the other hand, drinking behaviors include binge drinking less often as well as the more integrated style of regular, consistent consumption. It is precisely this combination of drinking styles that place people at greater risk of alcohol-related violence in these nations, particularly women. Women who are victims of homicide are almost always killed by men (see Silverman & Kennedy, 1987; Browne & Williams, 1989; Kellerman & Mercy, 1992; Campbell et al., 2003), and if the mixed drinking style is one in which problematic drinking behavior is more integrated into regular social life, risk for women would increase.

Divorce is also the focus of this effect, and the prediction is that being in the mixed category on the wet/dry drinking style continuum would lead to an even stronger association between divorce and female homicide victimization. As argued previously, the socially disintegrative impact of divorce on homicide makes it an obvious candidate for the violence-enhancing effect of drinking style. The fact that in mixed nations drinking is more integrated into regular social life indicates that this pattern of drinking is more likely to take place in social settings which include both men and women. Divorce itself may also be a source of conflict between men and women, also producing a situation in which active constraint would be required to keep men from settling their differences with estranged spouses or friends with violence. Yet this is often the situation in which women are killed (Block, 1987; Silverman & Kennedy, 1987; Browne & Williams, 1989; Campbell et al., 2007;

Campbell et al., 2003), in disputes with partners, spouses, and/or former intimates. Thus, a mixed drinking style and higher divorce rates should lead to even higher rates of female homicide victimization.

DATA, RESEARCH DESIGN, AND STATISTICAL METHODS

As indicated in table 5.1, the analysis is conducted with data from seventeen industrialized democracies in North America, Western Europe, and the Pacific Basin. All variables are measured ten times during the post–war 1950–1995 period at five-year intervals, with certain exceptions noted below. The pooled cross section time series design yields ten time periods by seventeen nations, or 170 "cases" for analysis.

Analyzing data structured in this manner introduces several statistical problems that make traditional regression or Ordinary Least Squares (OLS) models unusable. However, the statistical issues raised by such data have been the subject of a great deal of research, and standard solutions to these problems are well documented in the literature (Johnston, 1972: 214–221, 246–249; Stimson, 1985; Maddala, 1971; Mundlak, 1978). Following this literature, as well as the approach used by Gartner (1990: 100), I have estimated the models used here with a modified GLS approach with first order serial correlation. This approach corrects the estimates for both heteroscedasticity and a first order serial dependence, which was consistent with diagnostic results from preliminary analyses. All of the variables have been logged to minimize the impact of skewed distributions.

Measurement

The two dependent variables examined here are the female and male homicide victimization rates per 100,000 people calculated as averages over five annual observations for each five-year period (WHO, 1951–1996). The independent variables include the percent of gross national product (GNP) spent by each nation on welfare and social security expenditures, including both cash payments and in-kind transfers across a number of welfare categories such as old age and disability pensions, unemployment benefits, aid to dependent families and children, public health programs, pre-natal care, and so on (ILO, various years). The GINI index of income inequality, as calculated by Weatherby et al. (1983) for the year 1965, is included, as is the number of divorces per 1,000 marriages (United Nations, 1951–1996) and the ethnic/linguistic fractionalization index presented by Taylor and Hudson (1972), again for the year 1965.

Female labor force participation is measured by the total number of females in the labor force in 1970 (ILO, 1977) divided by the number of households in that year for each nation (United Nations, 1971). Proportion of the population aged fifteen to twenty-nine is available at each time point for each nation (United Nation, 1951–1996), and is calculated as a five-year average similar to how homicide victimization rates were calculated above. A dummy variable equal to 1 if a nation had a death penalty statute in effect at each five-year measurement point and 0 otherwise is included (United Nations, 1985), as is a summary measure that varies only by nation for the number of battle deaths suffered divided by the pre-war population, for each war during the twentieth century (Small & Singer, 1981).

Measurement of Alcohol Indicators

Two aspects of alcohol, consumption and drinking style, are included in this analysis. Consumption is indexed by the liters, in pure alcohol, of spirits consumption per capita at each of the five-year measurement points between 1950 and 1995 inclusive (Produktschap voor Gedistilleerde Dranken, 1988; 1996). This indicator was selected because of its theoretical and empirical association with violence in cross national comparisons (see Room, 1989). The second and third indicators are dummy variables based on the categorization given in table 5.1; wet, which takes the value of 1 if a country is in the "wet" category, and 0 otherwise, and mixed, which takes the value 1 if the country is in the "mixed" category and otherwise.

Finally, there are two interaction terms used in the analysis, in which the log of divorce is multiplied by log spirits consumption in the first case, and by the "mixed" versus wet and dry dummy variable in the second case. These interaction terms are used to test the hypotheses discussed previously with regard to the enhancing impact of spirits consumption on divorce *and* on male victimization as well as the potential effects of combining the impact of drinking style and divorce for female victimization.

RESULTS

Table 5.2 reports the results of four models, two each for female and male homicide victimization, respectively, with the first being a main-effects-only model and the second reporting results from the tests of the interaction hypotheses. The first column of table 5.2 gives the main effects for female victimization, including spirits consumption and the two dummy variables representing the wet, dry, and mixed drinking styles. Table 5.2 shows that the significant predictors of female victimization include the divorce rate, ethnic and linguistic fractionalization, female labor force participation, consumption of pure alcohol (spirits), and the percent of young people in the population. Column 3 of table 5.2 reports the parallel analysis for males. Ethnic and linguistic heterogeneity, along with the proportion of young people in the population and consumption of alcohol all predicted male homicide victimization.

These results differ somewhat from those reported by Gartner (1990: 102). In the case of female victimization, our findings do not replicate statistically significant results for the effects of welfare spending, battle deaths, death penalty, or income

Table 5.2. Homicide Victimization by Gender, with Alcohol Consumption and Drinking Style

Independent Variables	Female Victimization		Male Victimization	
	Main Effects Model	Interaction Model	Main Effects Model	Interaction Model
Welfare Expenditures	−0.002	−0.001	0.013	0.015
Inequality	0.290	0.010	1.556	0.132
Divorce Rate	0.061*	0.047*	0.127	−0.429*
Ethnic/Linguistic Fractionalization	1.341*	1.042*	5.015*	4.815*
Female Labor Force Participation Rate per Household	1.601*	1.601*	1.739	3.193*
Population Aged Fifteen to Twenty-Nine	0.020*	0.020*	0.113*	0.096*
Twentieth-Century Battle Deaths	0.032	0.027	0.147	0.148
Death Penalty Statute	0.075	0.121	0.152	0.101
Spirits Consumption (Pure Alcohol)	0.131*	0.108*	0.291*	−0.285
Wet/Dry Drinking Style, Wet	-0.337	−0.266	−1.806	−01.811
Wet/Dry Drinking Style, Mixed	0.157	−0.017	0.900	0.588
Mixed/Divorce	—	0.135*	—	—
Spirits/Divorce	—	—	—	0.282*
Constant	-0.811*	−0.582	−4.302*	−03.149*
R^2 (overall)	0.527	0.615	0.379	0.423
Rho (AR 1 Model)	0.472	0.443	0.820	0.621

*Unstandardized Coefficient at least 1.6 times Standard Error

inequality. Likewise, for men, the impacts of battle deaths, welfare spending, and income inequality were insignificant.[1] With regard to female victimization, our results do support Gartner's findings of significant effects for ethnic heterogeneity, the divorce rate, and female labor force participation, all of which were associated with increases in victimization for women. Regarding male victimization, as can be seen in column 3 of table 5.2, the only significant main effect shared in common with Gartner (1990: 102) was ethnic heterogeneity.

Columns 2 and 4 of table 5.2 give results for the tests of the interaction hypotheses described previously. Considering the impact of divorce with "mixed" drinking style on female victimization, results in column 2 of table 5.2 for the most part duplicate findings from column 1. Notice, however, that the interaction of divorce with a mixed-drinking cultural context had its own significant effect on increasing homicide, net of the other effects.

Considering the interaction hypothesis advanced for male victimization, column 4 of table 5.2 shows that the divorce by spirits interaction term is also statistically significant, again net of a still significant main effect of divorce and the remaining variables in the model. There is one exception to this main effect of spirits consumption, which is positively and significantly related to male homicide victimization in column 3. Namely, this effect appears significant *only in the main effects model*; this effect is wiped out by an interaction effect of divorce and spirit consumption, as can be seen toward the bottom of column 4. Thus, for both male and female homicide victimization, hypotheses that predicted enhancing effects of consumption and drinking style are largely supported in this analysis.

STUDY FINDINGS IN COMPARISON TO GARTNER (1990)

In general, findings provide mixed support for Gartner's theoretical predictions. Specifically, her predictions regarding the cultural and material context of homicide were not supported. Neither battle deaths nor the existence of a death penalty statute—measures used to replicate Gartner's "cultural context"—were significant in either model for either men or women. Similarly, welfare spending and income inequality—measures of the "material context" of homicide—failed to predict victimization rates for either gender.

It is perplexing that Gartner's "material context" was not predictive of victimization rates in our models given that researchers studying homicide not only agree that poverty is a critical risk factor for increased homicide rates (e.g., Pridemore, 2011), but also that social welfare spending reduces this risk (Savolainen, 2000; Savage et al., 2008; Worrall, 2009). The issue of national welfare spending and homicide is especially salient in the present political climate where cutting government programs designed to provide safety nets for less fortunate and less successful citizens is clearly out of favor among both conservative political leaders and followers. Nevertheless, our findings stand in contrast to Gartner's (1990) regarding welfare spending and homicide, and stand in contrast to findings in many studies, over the last thirty years at least, which point to an important and inverse relationship between social support and homicide rates.

The divorce rate was also associated with both male and female homicide victimizations net of the other predictors in these models. Interestingly, however, the divorce rate failed to predict male homicide victimization in the main effects model, reaching significance only in the interaction model. That is, once a variable measuring the combined effect of spirits consumption and divorce rate is introduced into the model, the main effect of divorce becomes not only significant, but the coefficient is also negative, which is opposite of past empirical findings. Past findings have suggested that the divorce rate tends to increase the rate of homicide offending for men and, given that men tend to kill other men, the theoretical prediction would be that the divorce rate should *increase* male homicide victimization. Indeed, this would be consistent not only with Gartner's (1990) findings, but also with more recent research on divorce and homicide (e.g., Beaulieu & Messner, 2009; Tcherni, 2011). Our findings do, however, indicate an important interaction effect between spirit consumption and divorce. These results, at the least, suggest that divorce by itself may be, though traumatic, not as important in driving up male homicide victimization rates as *both a combination of divorce and substance abuse*. The important point here is that, for both men and women and across all models, spirits consumption had a statistically significant effect on homicide victimization. The lesson here may be that, for men at least, divorce may not drive up victimization rates (or may not drive them up to the same degree) where alcohol use is less prevalent.

Findings do support Gartner's theorized integrative and demographic effects on crime. Gartner (1990) argued that social ties exert a protective effect on individuals as the more people are bonded to one another, and to institutions in society such as the family, the lower the general risk of homicide victimization. It is often harder and more socially costly to victimize strongly bonded individuals than it is to pick out victims on the social fringe. Moreover, social bonds themselves are protective in that valued relationships are a motivation *not* to victimize. Consistent with Gartner (1990), our findings indicate that higher divorce rates, in addition to greater degrees of ethnic/linguistic heterogeneity (fractionalization)—measures of Gartner's "integrative context"—increased the risk of homicide victimization for women. This effect of ethnic/linguistic heterogeneity on homicide victimization held for men as well, a finding consistent with present and past research (Altheimer, 2008).

Our findings also show that increased labor force participation—a measure of Gartner's "demographic context"—is associated with increases in victimization rates for both men and women, though the effect for men shows up only in the interaction model. There may be several reasons for this finding. First, as the number of women working per household increases, so does the rate of female homicide victimization. A routine activity–based (Cohen & Felson, 1979) interpretation concerning a shift in the locus of activities of women to the larger economic and social world and away from the home is a likely explanation for this relationship (Gartner, 1990: 96).

However, it is also likely that some of this relationship is explained by increases in social conflict between men and women related to increased participation of the latter in what was almost exclusively a male domain, the world of work. In fact, evidence from US data suggests that women are at much higher risk than men for being killed in the workplace by former or current intimate partners and close acquaintances. It is also the case, however, that occupations in which women predominate, such as cashiers and retail sales, also have greater workplace homicide risk (see Bachman, 1994; US Department of Labor, 1997). In the United States, workplace homicide accounts for less than 10 percent of the yearly total, and given the much lower rates in most of the nations examined here, comparable data may not be available.

CONCLUSION

This effort to extend Gartner's (1990) model of cross national homicide causation has had mixed success. Though only half of Gartner's proposed contextual factors were supported by this analysis, the newly introduced "alcohol context" was an important predictor across all models. More specifically Gartner's (1990) predicted effects of social integration (divorce rate and ethnic heterogeneity) and demographic variables (population aged fifteen to twenty-nine and labor force participation) were replicated and confirmed, but her findings relating to material well-being (welfare expenditures and inequality) and culture (battle deaths and existence of the death penalty) were not replicated. Importantly, however, the introduction of variables measuring alcohol consumption and drinking style *did consistently* predict homicide victimization rates.

In general, both research on alcohol and research on violence have ignored or at least overlooked the impact of interaction effects. Interaction effects, like the ones explored here, were perhaps tarnished in the scientific history of social research by purely empiricist approaches such as that exemplified in the once popular computer program called the "Automatic Interaction Detector," in which effects were advanced with little or no basis in conceptual and/or theoretical frameworks. This atheoretical approach may have caused researchers to shy away from even considering the possibility of interactions, and yet, as this study demonstrates, new discoveries await research in which interaction effects are logically examined in theoretical analysis and rigorously tested empirically. In the case where typically distinctive conceptual domains are brought together, as in the case of homicide causation and alcohol, and particularly in the case of a behavior such as drinking alcohol, which is engaged in by large numbers of people throughout the world with such differential impacts, interaction effects are very likely the only way in which our understanding of how alcohol is related to complex behaviors like homicide is to be advanced. Perhaps another call is needed for more and fuller investigations into variable interactions, this time beginning with a more prudent approach that involves theory, conceptualization, and empirical relationships; as illustrated here, such an approach is likely to bear considerable fruit in social research.

NOTE

1. There are possibly a number of technical reasons why income inequality was not a significant predictor of homicide, despite Gartner's (1990: 102) analysis finding significance. Our interpretation follows that of Firebaugh (2003), who shows empirically that the world has seen a decline in *between-country* income inequality, along with a rise in *within-country* inequality over the last twenty or so years of economic globalization. Ghose's (2004) analyses of global inequality and trade liberalization from 1981 to 1997, as another example, showed international reductions in income inequality, despite no effect on within-country inequality. Thus, between-nation global inequality seems to have declined over the last twenty to thirty years, which may be why our measure of GINI inequality was insignificant compared with Gartner's (1990) analysis, which was conducted over twenty years ago (for more on this ongoing income inequality debate, see Dowrick & Akmal, 2005, and Wade, 2004).

6

The History, Logic, and Importance of Environmental Crime Prevention

Robert Nash Parker and Kevin J. McCaffree

INTRODUCTION

C. Ray Jeffery, in his book, *Crime Prevention through Environmental Design* (1971), brought to the fore a method of crime-fighting that targeted the ecology directly, instead of the individual. The notion of reducing crime by focusing on the setting, or environment, was a somewhat indirect, theoretically based attack on the usefulness of individual methods such as increased jail or prison terms or educational programs.

In theory, reducing problematic precipitators or triggers in an environment or simply raising the opportunity cost of committing a crime should change the decision-making process of individuals, and reduce the likelihood that a crime will occur. Environmental crime prevention treats individual reason ("free will") and therefore behavior as tethered to, in equal parts and in interlocking ways, genes and ecology. Humans may make seemingly "free," unfettered choices in their daily life, but sociological criminology must concede that these choices are importantly shaped by opportunities, facilitators, peer influences, and normative expectations. Since little can be done on a practical scale genetically at this point to help reduce crime (and it is ethically questionable whether it should be considered at all), the environment, it would seem, holds much of the remaining promise of prevention.

Crime prevention through environmental design, or CPTED, is not meant to be a replacement for more individualistic crime-reducing strategies. Indeed, the assumptions underlying CPTED diverge markedly from those underlying more individualistic strategies. The individual-focused DARE drug-prevention educational program initiated by the Los Angeles Police Department in the early 1980s, for example, has proven nearly or perhaps completely ineffective (Ennett et al., 1994). Unfortunately, most all individual-focused educational programs and interventions tend to be relatively ineffective over the long term despite some evidence of short-term benefits, (see Kelly-Weeder et al., 2011 for a review of policy effectiveness). Also, and perhaps equally important, environmental crime prevention focuses on, at the risk of sounding redundant, *prevention*, that is, acting to manipulate the environment in such a way that preempts deviance and law violation before it occurs. This point of view stands in sharp contrast to a strictly reactive view, which sees crime as something to be considered only after it occurs. CPTED, in being a proactive approach, also, in some cases, may attend to the aesthetic environment, environmental stressors, and fear of crime generally, and increasing quality-of-life variables (employment, income, community efficacy, child-care, etc.) in a given ecology (Clarke, 1995).

But why only short-term effectiveness for intervention and educational (not to mention more punitive) methods like DARE? Put simply, *any* beneficial effects of educational programs on crime and substance abuse reduction will inevitably be undermined if the larger environment is not conducive to legalistic behavior. Individuals can be educated and trained to the nth degree; yet, in an environment filled with criminal opportunities or uncontrolled access to addictive intoxicants, this training will be of marginal utility. Human beings respond to an *environment* and to *other people*. The degree to which an environment and one's peers facilitate and encourage illegal behavior is the degree to which such behavior is likely to occur, and this view is not only supportive of CPTED, but is also a mainstream tenet of major criminological theories (i.e., learning theory [Akers, 2009], routine activities theory [Cohen & Felson, 1979], or rational choice theory [Cornish & Clarke, 2003]). As Robinson (1999) suggests, the term *environment* in CPTED is meant to highlight the outer, ecological environment and not necessarily the inner environment of the individual (which may include cognitive scripts, schemas, and Sutherland-esque definitions). CPTED does not preclude the use of individual-level strategies, it only highlights the shortcomings of such strategies and suggests more enduring and more structural and environmental methods of crime prevention.

Having said all of this, even a brief perusal of most criminological texts reveals an historically persistent individualistic bias in criminology, with more recent manifestations focusing on such allegedly delinquency and crime-explaining concepts such as the "maturity gap" (Moffitt, 1993) or low self-control (Hirschi & Gottfredson, 2001). Despite this persistent individual-level theoretical focus, in the early 1960s Elizabeth Wood (1961), an employee of the Chicago Housing Authority, began openly advocating for the importance of housing and tenement up-keep to improve community safety and cohesion.[1] For Wood, the community environment represented a hub of potentiality, upward mobility, and safety. The degradation of the structures, especially the housing structures of a community, lead therefore to a symbolic and actual degradation of life-chances and security. Wood's efforts at socially redesigning the living quarters of residents included restructuring apartment complexes so as to improve the visibility of units and establishing places for open forums to facilitate residential participation and community building.

C. Ray Jeffery (the acknowledged criminological popularizer of CPTED who will be discussed shortly) himself notes Jane Jacobs (1961) as a major influence on his thinking. Jacobs's focus was explicitly on urban residential crime and hers represented a more narrowed focus on deviance as opposed to quality of life more generally. Jacobs railed against what she saw to be erroneous and ill-advised post–World War II urban planning that eroded community in favor of conceding to transportation-by-automobile. For Jacobs, such planning ultimately cashed out in urban areas choked with mass, unkempt housing structures, and residents, essentially isolated from one another, traveling on foot in their neighborhoods of back alleys and dark, unsupervised streets. Jacobs argued that community safety relied on the eyes and ears of residents and their willingness to take the safety of their community into their own hands. Ultimately, though, the ability of a people to watch over each other was predicated for Jacobs, at least in part, on a neighborhood structure supportive of frequent social interaction, resident visibility, and institutions (community centers, churches) and resources that promote community-level policies targeting problem areas.

Seven years later, in 1968, Schlomo Angel's *Discouraging Crime Through City Planning* put forth the idea that dilapidated or relatively unsupervised environments were criminogenic precisely because they afforded a greater relative proportion of *opportunities* for criminal acts. Areas with low levels of formal (police) and informal (normative or peer sanctioning) social control produce a breakdown in community crime fighting ability, thus opening avenues for crimes easily committed and easily gotten away with. If human beings are rational actors that weigh the costs and potential benefits of their behaviors, as Angel argued they were, than a withering away of norms and supervision will decrease the apparent cost of crime, thus contributing to its overall increase. In Durkheimian terms, the collective conscience is weakened in an area where individuals feel isolated and socio-culturally un-invested. This weakened collective conscience impairs the normative force of prohibitions against deviant or law-violating acts. For Angel, the solution to this problem of isolation and disaffection was to increase or funnel neighborhood activity to areas of high visibility and high levels of social interaction, perhaps near areas of mass transit or shopping. These bustling areas represented places where numerous informal "witnesses" might deter crime that would otherwise occur in back alleys or side streets. Ultimately, Angel contended that increasing visibility and interaction through city planning were the key methods available to policy makers for reducing crime.

C Ray Jeffery would later call Oscar Newman's *Defensible Space* (1972) a formal "operationalization" of Jane Jacobs's work, thus extending environmental prevention thinking explicitly into its second decade. The 1970s would also see the publication of Jeffery's seminal work as well as several major funded studies into urban development, urban planning, and crime.

A "defensible space," Newman (1972) argued, is a space designed and constructed in such a way as to encourage the collective residential pursuit of stability and safety. This was to be accomplished by designing community structures with four basic thoughts in mind: territoriality, surveillance, image, and milieu. Newman suggested that all human beings have an inborn sense of territoriality, not unlike other mammals, which compels them to take ownership of the spaces wherein they live and construct their lives. Though perhaps the reader can detect a hint of Marx's notion of humans' "species being" here, ultimately, Newman wishes to, with Jacobs (1961), highlight the joint inadequacies of post–WW II suburban sprawl and urban concentration. This sense of territoriality and surveillance can be re-ignited in residents, Newman argued, and residents can be made to feel "in-control" of their community. Importantly, this sense of ownership can be architecturally provoked, for example, by building apartment complexes with numerous windows to increase visibility, improving neighborhood street lighting, streamlining roads and alleyways so as to improve function and decrease disuse, and building complexes situated into groups or mini-communities.

Newman's (1972) concepts of image and milieu, on the other hand, speak to the importance of upkeep and aesthetic maintenance of community structures (i.e., removing graffiti, fixing "broken windows") as well as to the importance of proximity to the police and open areas of commerce, such as those discussed by Angel (1968). Newman's work, though perhaps not new in a theoretically strict sense, was a nevertheless pivotal integration, extension, and application of many preexisting scattered ideas about the role of the environment in encouraging or discouraging criminal acts. In fact, within a few years of publication, Newman's influence propelled the Law Enforcement Assistance Administration (LEAA) to fund a multimillion-dollar study of various urban spaces and his principles of crime prevention continue to influence public housing policy to this day (Robinson, 1999).

C. Ray Jeffery's important work, *Crime Prevention Through Environmental Design* (1971), openly attacked more traditional crime-control methods such as retribution or deterrence. Jeffery took a deep approach to the problem of crime, emphasizing that prevention must ultimately see the individual as a physical-chemical organism, determined by epigenetic gene-environment interactions (and proximately, by the brain) to seek rewards and avoid punishments in a given environment presumably teeming with multiple forms of both positive and negative stimuli. For Jeffery, then,

A [proper] CPTED model would be based on ecology, including biological ecology, social ecology, urban geography, psychological learning theory, urban planning, and criminology. It would be based on an individual-brain-environmental model where individuals interact with the physical environment by means of the brain. . . . The brain is the organ of behavior, all behavior is controlled by the brain, and the brain is created by the interaction of the individual with the environment. (Jeffery, 1999)

Briefly, Jeffery identifies three possible models of behavior, the *environment-mind-behavioral* model, the *environment-behavior* model, and the *environment-brain-behavior* model (Jeffery & Zahm, 1993). The first model is based on Descartes' ontology of the mind, commonly called "Cartesian dualism." This position holds that the mind, or the source of subjective thought and conscience, is somehow independent or detached from the physical substance and material of the brain. This is condescendingly sometimes referred to as the "ectoplasm" theory in modern neuroscience because it posits that the stuff of thought is somehow separate and different from the (material) stuff of the brain. Nevertheless, this view of behavior necessarily severs itself off from positing strong environmental influences on behavior. If our thoughts are somehow separated from the material reality of neurons and circuits in the brain, then there simply remains no physical mechanism to transport external, environmental stimuli to cognition and thought (and subsequently, behavior).

Consequently, Jeffery eschews the Cartesian *environment-mind-behavioral* model. The second model of behavior he discusses is that of Pavlov, and B. F. Skinner, among others. This model emphasizes the stimulus-response cycle that encourages the probability of a displayed behavior (Jeffery, 1971). As a behaviorist theory, this *environment-behavior* model ignores internal, subjective cognition and only seeks to establish the objective, observed relationship between the presentation of a stimulus (i.e., a reward or reinforcement) and a predictable, subsequent behavior (i.e., whatever action has been repeatedly paired with the reinforcing stimuli).

Jeffery's theory of behavior draws heavily from the stimulus-response model, but also insists on the importance of a third, more interdisciplinary model. The *environment-brain-behavior* model seeks to integrate work from cognitive psychology and developmental genetics. Jeffery's position is that a true theory of crime would need to trace a path from the genetic predispositions of the individual genome to the material and emotional structure of the environment and back again, constantly, throughout the life course (Jeffery & Zahm, 1993; Jeffery, 1999). This third model represents an evolution of Jeffery's thinking on environmental prevention, and marks a move away from the more "black box" classical behaviorist thinking (which, of course, ignores the subjective individual) of his earlier efforts (Jeffery, 1999; see also, Robinson, 1999).

Jeffery's contribution was a view of crime that fully emphasized individual biology as well as fully emphasizing the causal role of the environment (Jeffery, 1999; Robinson, 1999). Later commentators have helped to flesh out the compatibilities between mainstream criminological theorizing and Jeffery's discipline-hopping insights. Clarke (1989), for example, suggests that CPTED (or "situational crime prevention" as he calls it) is compatible with both opportunity theory/routine activities theory and rational choice theory. Environments, according to Clarke, are essentially interlocking opportunity structures, with some environments and some environmental changes providing numerous and fresh opportunities for crime. This idea, of course, goes back to the beginning of environmental-prevention theorizing (e.g., Wood, 1961). Clarke suggests, however, that even seemingly trivial and relatively unnoticed alterations to an environment can affect the opportunity structure of an environment. Citing work done by Cohen and Felson (1979) within routine activity theory, he shows that an increased prevalence of lightweight electronic goods during the 1960s and 1970s, along with a relative spike in unoccupied homes on account of increased female labor force participation, may well have accounted for the increase in residential burglary during that time period.

Clarke (1989; see also Cornish & Clarke, 2003) also points out that CPTED is compatible with rational choice theorizing, which views the offending individual as someone who makes rational choices (i.e., rational from the point of view of a fallible, enculturated human subject and *not* rational from the point of view of a detached, "objective," context-less calculating machine) in order to obtain sexual, economic, or status-related goals. In some cases, such as the persistent overconsumption of alcohol, rational choice theorists might argue that such potentially dangerous behaviors may be seen by the actors as ends in themselves, in addition to often being related to status and cultural notions of masculinity and toughness. Most significantly, rational choice theory views the criminal as fundamentally self-interested (Clarke, 1989). This is not a commentary on the nature of criminal offenders, as any otherwise law-abiding person can, as well, be tempted with the allure of criminal gain. Rational choice theory therefore targets temptations (or precipitators) in the environment that can sway the scales for a rational actor, and cause him or her to think that the benefit of committing a crime outweighs the cost.

Cornish and Clarke (2003) argue further, within a rational choice paradigm, that what constitutes a precipitating influence will vary by the objective (physical) and subjective (perceptual) environments within which people operate. Social life and interaction shape what people value, as does strategically altering the cost/benefit structure of an environment. As Cornish and Clarke (2003) argue:

> [W]hen [theorists] talk about the power of situations to provoke, what they often have implicitly in mind is not the power of a one-off freely entered setting to precipitate offending, but, rather, that of aversive, long-term inescapable environments and their nested settings and associated aversive cues so to do. Although the provocations concerned are undoubtedly situational ones, then, they are the persistent and repetitive products of ongoing lifestyles which determine both the offender's exposure to them, and his or her perceptions of their significance.

In other words, environmental structure is the ultimate source of situational dynamics. Wortley (2001), for example, argues that at least sixteen kinds of "precipitators" can encourage a crime to occur. Precipitators are various but all can be overcome in certain ways, including decreasing the amount of "triggers" in an environment (i.e., pawn shops that sell guns frivolously), or by increasing the amount of rules in an environment, within reason (i.e., carefully targeted and researched city ordinances with a defined duration and follow-up research/evaluation period).

PUTTING IT ALL TOGETHER: EFFECTIVE ENVIRONMENTAL PREVENTION STRATEGIES

There are at least four important components of any useful attempt to prevent crime environmentally (Clarke, 1997). Firstly, researchers and public officials must determine the situational conditions that are allowing or facilitating crime (generally issues of supervision, construction or regulation, etc.). Next, policy makers and analysts should simply explore (i.e., brainstorm about/investigate past research into) potential opportunity blockers that might impede the commission of the crime. Third, and most important, these different ways of blocking the crime (i.e., passed city ordinances) are most useful when they are cost-effective and reasonable as opposed to utopian and lavish (despite the political sexiness of the latter). Indeed, more workable strategies may be even more successful politically if they can be shown to have a clear long-term benefit to the community by reducing crime-control expenditures. Clarke (1997) points out that, oftentimes, planners seriously underestimate the time and effort (and persistence) it takes to effectively establish and implement environmental prevention strategies. Finally, in order for any progress to be made, the environmental change must be closely monitored and examined for its effectiveness in carefully controlled follow-up studies. A recent study of single-serve beverage sales within a specific Southern California community, for example, led to the passing of a city ordinance which banned the sales of such drinks (which, research showed, increased violent victimization), along with the promise of follow-up research and analysis (Parker et al., 2011a). This type of environmental research and policy implementation, though energy-intensive, provides much promise for long-term crime reduction.

Specifically regarding environmental attempts to address alcohol-related violence, numerous environmental prevention projects have been undertaken with predictably beneficial results. Minimum legal drinking age statutes (MLDA), for example, were swiftly adopted by all fifty states after many states in the 1970s lowered the minimum drinking age to eighteen, nineteen, or twenty. Research on the impact of lowering of the age limit was unequivocal—a lower drinking age meant significantly more car accidents and deaths (Kelly-Weeder, 2011; Wagenaar & Toomey, 2002). After adopting MLDA laws, states also experienced fewer episodes of problem drinking among juveniles *and* adults (Norberg et al., 2009; Kelly-Weeder, 2011), suggesting a general cultural shift away from treating alcohol frivolously, with MLDA regulations as the possible exogenous catalyst (though some recent research would contest this conclusion, e.g., Miron & Tetelbaum, 2009). Other explanations are possible too. Miron and Tetelbaum (2009), for example, place the source of the national impact of MLDA laws on the states that adopted such laws prior to any federal encouragement. Thus, it may be that acceptance of MLDA laws grew organically out of certain receptive environments without any outside encouragement (akin to Oscar Newman's notions of territoriality and taking back a sense of ownership of one's community), whereas in other locations, the law had to be more or less imposed from the top-down federally with presumably less efficaciousness and community commitment.

Some environmental prevention strategies (literally) affect opportunity costs, such as raising taxes on alcoholic beverages. Raising taxes on alcoholic beverages has consistently been found to be a relatively straightforward way to reliably reduce problem drinking (Wagenaar et al., 2009). Additionally, reducing alcohol outlet density itself in a given environment has been shown to reduce violence, especially violence among minorities where outlets and advertising are often concentrated (Al-aniz, 1998; Scribner et al., 2000; Parker et al., 2011b).

Still another effective way to re-mold the environment is to focus on server liability. This approach focuses on changing the environment of those who disseminate alcohol in liquor stores and restaurants. Holding servers and owners of alcohol-serving establishments financially liable for altercations that occur upon over-intoxication (especially if these involve alcohol dissemination to minors) will help create an environment where the costs of apathetic business practice outweigh any potential benefits (Gursoy, 2011). Outside of liquor stores and restaurants, some researchers have even turned their eyes to more environmentally embedded settings where alcohol can be misused, such as informal social gatherings, "hangouts" with older peers, and in the home where parental stashes of alcohol may be plundered (Wagenaar et al., 1993). Though environmental changes targeted at consumption in these more private settings can be difficult, Fletcher and associates (2000), for example, showed that home grocery delivery services, if unmonitored, can be a source of alcohol for underage drinkers. The last established method of reducing alcohol-related crime with environmental changes concerns alcohol advertising. A random sample of fifteen- to twenty-six-year-olds by Snyder and colleagues (2006) indicated that per capita expenditures on alcohol advertising, along with self-reported exposure to advertisements, predicted increased consumption, with more advertising exposure leading to even more drinking. This effect extended to the under twenty-one set as well, indicating an important effect of alcohol advertising on under-age alcohol use. Another, this time longitudinal, study found that non-drinking seventh graders exposed to in-store beer displays were more likely to begin drinking two years later, in the ninth grade (Ellickson et al., 2005). In fact, Smith and Foxcroft's (2009) review of seven cohort studies of over thirteen thousand young people revealed that those who were non-drinkers were significantly more likely to begin drinking if they were exposed to more, rather than fewer, alcohol advertisements.

Environmental prevention strategies are a complement to, and not a replacement for, individual-level interventions. The importance of the environment cannot be overstated with regard to the alcohol/crime relationship. Crime occurs within a specific ecology; often an ecology of unemployment and concentrated poverty (Lee, 2000; Hipp & Yates, 2011) which provides a suite of environmental stressors from the inability to achieve upward mobility, secure health insurance, obtain quality schooling, or feel a sense of safety. Alcohol outlet concentration is also highest in such disadvantaged environments (Duncan et al., 2002). Research consistently confirms that social bonds such as marriage, employment, and education mediate the relationship between alcohol misuse and violence in such disadvantaged areas (e.g., see Valdez et al., 2007). Of course, regardless of environment, individuals will vary in their dispositional traits and their attitudes toward the law and toward crime. Peer groups differ and so do motivations and specific situational circumstances. For these reasons, prevention in sociological criminology must address ways in which environments can be restructured or improved upon regardless of the socio-demographic profile of the community. Certainly, some communities are more "at-risk" than others, given demographic and structural conditions, but any given environment can, in principle, be made safer with well-researched and well-implemented policy directives such as holding servers financially liable for serving intoxicated patrons, or by regulating and restricting the amount of alcohol advertisements in stores.

A fundamental concern of environmental prevention research and policy is the well-being of citizens in their communities. Well-being is, of course, most flagrantly and egregiously violated in cases of rape, robbery, assault, murder, and the like, yet more quiet and basic concerns for safety, comfort, and mobility are also addressed through environmental prevention strategies. Recent research by Marzbali and colleagues (2012), for example, found that environmental crime prevention strategies may even reduce individuals' subjective fear of crime through the effect such strategies have on reducing vicitimization. Far from ignoring the individual, then, environmental prevention strategies deal with the well-being of specific community members indirectly by fortifying and supporting structures in the environment that preemptively deter or prevent behavior associated with violence.

NOTE

1. The following discussion is in various ways indebted to Matthew B. Robinson's *The Theoretical Development of "CPTED": 25 Years of Responses.*

II

THE PROMISE OF PREVENTION

7

The Impact of Raising the Minimum Drinking Age on Youth Homicide

Robert Nash Parker and Kevin J. McCaffree

INTRODUCTION

Between 1976 and 1986, the United States engaged in what could be described as a massive public health–related "natural experiment," when increases in the minimum legal age for purchase of alcoholic beverages were implemented in different states. A number of important studies have addressed the impact of this legal change on alcohol-related outcomes such as consumption by young drinkers, drunk driving by young drivers, and rates of alcohol-involved automobile crash fatalities. In each case, it appears that this experiment has been found to have significant and positive impacts on the public health of the youth population (O'Malley & Wagenaar, 1991; Wagenaar, 1983; Males, 1986; Cook & Tauchen, 1984; DuMouchel et al., 1987; Saffer & Grossman, 1987; Vingilis & DeGenova, 1984; Wagenaar & Toomey, 2002; Kelly-Weeder et al., 2011). An especially important public health outcome, homicide in the youth population, has not been examined in the context of this legal intervention. Although a reduction in youth homicide was not among the anticipated consequences of raising the legal drinking age, there is increasing evidence to suggest a link between alcohol and homicide, and as such, a reduction in alcohol availability to young people (see Parker et al., 2011) might be expected to result in decreases in youth homicide.

It is well known that the United States is one of the most violent societies in the world, boasting higher rates of homicide than any other comparable industrialized nation (National Research Council, 1993; FBI Uniform Crime Report, 2010). Blumstein (1995) attributes much of the increase in homicide rates after 1985 to increases in youth homicide. This conclusion is supported by an analysis of age-specific victimization trends; in the period 1986 to 1994, rates of homicide victimization for persons over twenty-five declined, while rates of youth homicide steadily increased.

The majority of this increase is observed in the younger age categories, with victimization rates for fourteen- to seventeen-year-olds increasing 120 percent, while the corresponding increase for older youths (eighteen to twenty-four) was less than half that (Maguire & Pastore 1997).

These trends indicate that youth homicide is likely a heterogeneous phenomenon, with presumably different etiological factors influencing homicides in different segments of the youth population. This idea has not been lost on researchers of homicide rates in the general population. As Messner and Sampson (1991) and Huff-Corzine et al. (1991) have demonstrated, many of the predictors of homicide operate differentially depending on race. For example, Sampson (1987) finds that economic deprivation, among other predictors, has a greater impact on African American violent victimization than it does on non-African American rates. An examination of race-specific rates of victimization might reveal that among African American youth, poverty has such a strong impact that any additional impact of minimal drinking age laws may be statistically non-significant, while the opposite may be true for non-African Americans.

Careful analysis of the trends in youth homicide rates reveals important differences in the risk of victimization according to gender and race. A recent study, for example, found that improvements in gender equity regarding education, income, and employment have had an important impact on reducing female homicide victimization (Vieraitis et al., 2011). Overall, homicide rates in the general population indicate that males are victimized at a rate nearly four times that of females; in terms of racial disparity, the black-white ratio for homicide victimization is 7:1 (Maguire & Pastore, 1997). In fact, though blacks represent only 13 percent of the national population, they accounted for nearly half of all homicide victims in the United States in 2007 (Violence Policy Center, 2010). Josh Sugarmann, executive director of the Violence Policy Center in Washington, DC, points out the disparity in black homicide rates—36.36 victims per 100,000 in Pennsylvania, 34.82 in Missouri, and 30.89 in Indiana, compared with a national average of only 5.3 per 100,000 for the US population in general (Sugarmann, 2010).

Not only do such differences persist in youth homicide, but differences in the *rate of increase* in the homicide rate for different segments of the youth population also indicate that different factors and processes over time may be involved in the explanation of homicide for different subgroups. For example, among youths aged fourteen to seventeen, the rate of victimization for white males increased 118 percent between 1986 and 1994; for black males in the same age group, the corresponding increase was 171 percent. Increases in victimization rates are much lower in the age group eighteen to twenty-four, but still reflect enormous racial disparity. Between 1986 and 1994, homicide rates for white males aged eighteen to twenty-four increased 28 percent, but the rates for black males in this age group increased 61 percent (Maguire & Pastore, 1997). More recent research shows that these increases in youth homicide and violence for both whites and blacks are likely caused by urban increases in economic disadvantage during the mid-'80s to early '90s (Strom

& MacDonald, 2007; MacDonald & Gover, 2005). Escalations in gang and drug market activity likely also played a role in increasing homicide victimization rates over this period (e.g., see Browne et al., 2010). A look at the trends in female youth homicide victimization further supports the case for examining race- and gender-specific models of homicide victimization. Here, perhaps due to the lower overall probability of a female being the victim of a homicide, the racial differences are even more pronounced. For both age groups fourteen to seventeen and eighteen to twenty-four, rates of white female victimization declined during this period, while for black females aged fourteen to seventeen, the victimization rate increased 61 percent. The homicide rate increased 6 percent for older black female youths (eighteen to twenty-four) during this period (Maguire & Pastore, 1997).

BACKGROUND ON MINIMUM AGE DRINKING LAWS

In the last twenty-five years, there has been a great deal of fluctuation in the laws governing the minimum age at which individuals can legally purchase alcohol. During the period from 1970 to 1975, twenty-nine states lowered the minimum age of purchase for alcohol (Wagenaar, 1983: 3). These decreases can be seen as part of a general re-thinking of the legal status of young people in the United States, largely encouraged by the Vietnam War draft, which resulted not only in a lowering of the minimum purchase age for alcohol, but also in the change of the minimum legal voting age from twenty-one to eighteen. After these changes to minimum purchase laws were made, a body of research began to accumulate that demonstrated increased traffic fatalities after the minimum drinking age was lowered (Douglas et al., 1974; Cucchiaro et al., 1974; Whitehead et al., 1975; Cook & Tauchen, 1982, 1984; Kelly-Weeder et al., 2011; Wagenaar & Toomey, 2002), which gave strength to growing grassroots anti-drunk driving organizations (groups like Mothers Against Drunk Driving or MADD and Students Against Driving Drunk or SADD). In response to this public outcry, states began to reverse the changes made only years before. The first increase in the minimum drinking age occurred in the state of Minnesota in 1976. Other states quickly followed suit, and by 1988, the minimum age of purchase across all US states was twenty-one, due in large part to the passage of federal legislation that required all states to increase the minimum age of purchase for alcohol, or risk losing substantial federal funding dedicated to highway repair and construction.

VIOLENCE AND ACCESS TO ALCOHOL

The relationship between alcohol and homicide is one that has been acknowledged for some time in the research literature on homicide (Wolfgang, 1958; Collins, 1981; National Committee for Injury Prevention and Control, 1989; Office of Substance Abuse Prevention, 1992; Parker, 1993), albeit without much progress in

the area of developing strategies or interventions designed to reduce the rate of homicide (with important exceptions, see Parker et al., 2011a). Despite these problems,
there are a number of possible perspectives from which to derive the expectation of
a relationship between homicide and alcohol (see Pernanen, 1981, 1991; Parker &
Rebhun, 1995; Parker, 1995).

There is evidence that the cognitive effects associated with alcohol may be even
stronger in younger drinkers, due to the inherent cognitive limitations associated
with the developmental stage of adolescence (Leigh, 1987), expectancies surrounding alcohol (George et al., 1988; Corcoran & Thomas, 1991; Brown et al., 1987),
as well as increased vulnerability to both physiological and psychopharmacological
effects, due to limited experience with alcohol (Goode, 1993).

In attempting to explain how it is that while most disputes between individuals in
which alcohol is involved do not result in violence, but that an important minority
of these situations do, one approach that borrows from and expands upon earlier,
biologically based "disinhibition" approaches (see Room & Collins, 1983) is that
of Parker and Rebhun (1995), who advance a social disinhibition approach. This
framework posits that both active and passive constraints operate in the interaction
of individuals in situations constrained by norms proscribing the use of violence as
a means for dispute resolution; the effects of alcohol may act to "disinhibit" active
constraint. Parker and Rebhun suggest that this disinhibition is most likely to occur in those situations in which the normative frameworks prohibiting violence are
weakest, or alternatively, where normative frameworks prohibiting violence coexist
with contradictory norms. Face-value support for this theory can be found in the
frequently noted association between alcohol and spousal violence and homicide
(e.g. Stets, 1990; Blount et al., 1994).

A number of studies link alcohol availability to rates of violence at the community
and societal level (e.g., Chiu, Perez, & Parker, 1997; Alaniz, Cartmill, & Parker,
1997; Parker & Rebhun, 1995). It is therefore expected that states which reduced
alcohol availability to youth would experience decreases in the rates of youth homicide, especially given recent data that alcohol outlet concentration leads to rising
rates of youth homicide (Parker et al., 2011b). It is further expected that decreases
in alcohol availability would be realized differentially by different subgroups of youth
victims, based on the different situational dynamics of violence suggested by the
selective disinhibition framework.

Finally, we must consider the ways in which alcohol availability and consumption
may be linked to homicide on the *victimization* end of this relationship. From this
perspective, alcohol consumption may lead to violent victimization because victims
under the influence may be more vulnerable, and are therefore attractive targets
for potential offenders (Hindelang et. al., 1978; Cohen & Felson, 1979; Sampson,
1987). Thus, from a number of theoretical and conceptual frameworks, a link between homicide and alcohol consumption is likely to exist, and any legal intervention that addresses availability, especially among a subpopulation (young people)
that is often associated with criminal violence (see Gartner & Parker, 1990; Hirschi
& Gottfredson, 1983), will likely have an impact on homicide.

We have attempted to place this analysis within the context of a comprehensive predictive model of homicide, including additional factors known to be relevant in explaining variation in homicide rates. These include demographic factors such as the relative size of the young male population and the degree of poverty in an area. Indeed, prior research has shown poverty to be one of the best and most consistent predictor of homicide rates (Loftin & Hill, 1974; Loftin & Parker, 1985; Parker, 1989; regarding youth homicide see also MacDonald and Gover, 2005; Strom & MacDonald, 2007). We include measures of poverty and inequality in this analysis, to test for differential effects associated with absolute and relative deprivation. Urbanization is also included, as a control variable, as urban areas tend to be characterized by higher rates of homicide than rural areas (Loftin & Hill, 1974; Parker & Smith, 1979; Smith & Parker, 1980).

In addition to these demographic factors, in order to appropriately assess the impact of minimum legal drinking age policy changes, we must also consider the impact of other social policies, particularly policies which are deliberately directed toward homicide prevention, such as criminal justice sanctioning policies and activities, as indicated by sentencing and arrest rates. Although it is the case that these factors have been found to have no discernible empirical effect on homicide rates (Smith & Parker, 1980; Bowers, 1984; Bailey & Peterson, 1989; Bailey, 1990), including them in the model is important for a number of reasons. The proposed research is designed to evaluate the impact of a policy change, that is, increasing the minimum age of alcohol purchase, and therefore other policy-related attempts to control homicide should be included in the model in order to prevent the changes in the minimum age of purchase from assuming covariance in the homicide equation which is actually due to variance from some other policy/sanctioning practice.

Also included in our models are a variety of indicators of the level of alcohol consumption. Any impact of changes in the minimum age of legal availability of alcohol must be considered in the context of controlling for variability in baseline rates of consumption, as well as variables that may directly or indirectly affect both availability and consumption rates, such as state regulation strategies and differences in taxation rates.

HYPOTHESIS: MINIMUM DRINKING AGE CHANGES AND YOUTH HOMICIDE RATES

Overall, we expect that increases in the minimum drinking age will have a statistically significant and negative impact on youth homicide rates. In light of evidence that predictive factors operate differentially to produce variation in race- and gender-specific rates of homicide (e.g. Messner & Sampson, 1991; Huff-Corzine et al., 1991; Sampson, 1987; Browne & Williams; Gartner, 1990; Parker, 1992b), we propose that increases in the minimum drinking age would similarly exert differential effects on the risk of homicide victimization in subpopulations divided by gender and race. Given the nature of the proposed relationship between alcohol and homicide, our predictions are based primarily on the empirical literature regarding alcohol consumption rates in different segments of the youth population.

Race

There is some evidence that the average rate of alcohol consumption is lower among African Americans than among whites at all ages (Barr et al., 1993; Johnson et al., 1995). This holds true for African American adolescents as well, who have some of the lowest rates of drinking and binge drinking (National Institute on Alcohol Abuse and Alcoholism, 2002). And, as mentioned above, research has shown that poverty has a much stronger impact on African American rates of violence than on rates of violence for other ethnic groups (Sampson, 1987), an effect which might overwhelm any potential impacts of an policy intervention such as raising the minimum legal age for alcohol purchase. For these reasons, we predict no significant impact of minimum drinking age changes on rates of African American youth homicide. This is mainly due to the structure of the data. The category of "non-African American" encapsulates many diverse ethnic groupings (at the very least, Hispanics and non-Hispanics) for whom different etiological models of youth homicide may apply; for this reason, the analytical utility of making a prediction about a specific policy intervention as if non-African Americans comprised a homogenous group is questionable.[1]

Gender

Males are overwhelmingly more likely to be both victims and offenders of homicide than females (Maguire & Pastore, 1997; National Institute on Alcohol Abuse and Alcoholism, 2002; Wilsnack et al., 2009). Additionally, males have higher rates of alcohol consumption than females (Johnson, 1982; Wilsnack et al., 2009). For these reasons, we predict a significant negative effect of minimum drinking age on rates of both male and female youth homicide. In the context of the selective disinhibition explanation of the link between alcohol consumption and homicide, we expect the negative impact of minimum drinking age changes to be strongest for female youth homicide, given the evidence that female homicides are most often characterized by primary victim-offender relationships (Riedel et al., 1985; Gartner, 1990; Browne & Williams, 1989) which are frequently characterized by normative ambiguities (see Parker & Rebhun, 1995).

DATA ANALYSIS

Pooled cross-section time series analysis was used to determine whether changes in the rate of various types of youth homicide were linked to changes in the minimum drinking age. The models were estimated using cross-sectional data for the fifty US states, for the time period 1973 to 1992.[2] States are the appropriate unit of analysis for this question because that is the level at which the intervention of interest (increases in the minimum drinking age) were implemented. These changes were implemented across the nation in the time period 1976 to 1987; the time frame of 1973 to 1992 thus affords us the opportunity to examine the relationships between the variables in "baseline" conditions, both before and after the intervention period. The pooling of these data resulted in 1000 observations (*NxT*, 50x20), for which Least Squares Dummy Variables (LSDV) models were estimated.

Using LIMDEP software, a three-stage panel model procedure was employed. The first stage of analysis consisted of running the model as an uncorrected OLS regression; the second stage included running the OLS with dummy variables added to correct for cross-sectional variation, also called a "fixed effects" model. The third stage was an error components model (random effects) estimated by GLS. Hausman tests indicated that the LSDV model was the most appropriate model for all types of homicide examined.

One advantage of the pooled cross-sectional time series approach is that it allows us to robustly estimate the regression equations utilizing all 1,000 observations. The time period covered in our data set, the twenty years over which minimum purchase age changes took place, is of too short a duration to produce reliable estimates in a standard multivariate time series or intervention analysis (McCleary & Hay, 1980). One dummy variable for each cross-sectional unit is present in the equation, which corrects for systematic differences due to cross-sectional variation on unmeasured characteristics (England et al., 1988).

Fixed-effects models have been criticized generally on the grounds that the generalizability of the results is limited to only the sample data (Greene, 1990). This is not at issue for the present study. We have data for all fifty US states, which is the population about which we wish to draw conclusions. Additionally, we are interested only in drawing conclusions applicable to a specific point in time, namely the time period surrounding and including the intervention of legal minimum purchase age changes for alcohol. In fact, given the limited viability of cross-national research in the area of violence and homicide prevention due to the uniquely high rates of violence in the United States, a pooled cross sectional time series analysis would seem to be an excellent method for the development and testing of general theories about crime and violence in the United States.

VARIABLE MEASUREMENT

Homicide Rates

Youth homicide rates are here measured by the rates of youth homicide victimization in four different subcategories: males aged fifteen to twenty-four, females aged fifteen to twenty-four, African American and non-African American victims (aged fifteen to twenty-four). These specific rates were compared to the overall rate of homicide victimization per 100,000 population aged fifteen to twenty-four. The rate of victimization is used because it is the most accurate measure of the actual rate of occurrence of homicide. Arrest rates for homicide tend to be artificially inflated due to the involvement of multiple offenders; this may be especially problematic for youth homicide, given the tendency for youths to be arrested in groups, thereby inflating crime rate statistics (National Criminal Justice Commission, 1996: 4). It is a well-established fact in homicide research, however, that homicide offenders tend to be remarkably similar to their victims on demographic characteristics (Maguire & Pastore, 1997; Sampson & Lauritsen, 1990; see also Broidy et al., 2006). For example, in 1995, for all homicide victims about which information on the offender was known, 93 percent of African Americans were killed by other African Americans, and 85 percent of whites were killed by other whites.

An exception to this "principle of homogamy" (Lauritsen, Sampson, & Laub, 1991) is the sex difference observed in rates of homicide offending: males are responsible for perpetrating approximately 90 percent of all homicides; 89 percent of male victims were killed by other males, as were 91 percent of female victims (Maguire & Pastore, 1997). In fact, this wide disparity in homicide offending by gender has held firm over the last thirty years, with females committing only 11.2 percent of all homicides from 1976 to 2005 (Bureau of Justice Statistics).

Minimum Drinking Age Changes

Many states increased their minimum age of purchase laws for alcohol between 1976 and 1987. Before these increases, however, some states had different minimum age of purchase requirements for beer and for spirits, and for this reason these are measured separately in our data. In order to take into account this variability in original conditions, we constructed an interaction-type indicator for changes in the minimum drinking age, whereby *only* states that increased the minimum age of purchase for *both* beer and spirits register as having increased the minimum drinking age. This is important for both symbolic and practical reasons; the symbolic aspect is that increasing minimum purchase ages for all types of alcohol beverages can be seen as a more dramatic policy shift than only increasing one.

On the practical side, if, for example, a state only increased the minimum purchase age for one type of beverage (for example, spirits but not beer), several things could happen. There could be substitution effects, resulting in no decrease in availability but simply a substitution to the more readily available beverage. Another possible scenario is that a state might have initially had a minimum age of purchase for spirits of twenty-one, but a lower minimum age (such as eighteen or nineteen) for the purchase of beer. While an increase in the beer purchase age might well reduce availability, it is also possible that such a state simply had a lower *baseline* alcohol availability to youth populations to begin with. For this reason, the measure included here may be considered by some to be overly restrictive; however, constructing the measure in this way reduces the likelihood of Type I error.

Alcohol Consumption

Parker and Rebhun (1995) found evidence for an association between alcohol consumption and homicide rates at the aggregate level. This hypothesis is tested for various types of youth homicide. Available evidence suggests that spirits account for a small fraction of the alcohol consumed by the youth population; a recent national survey indicated that more than 6 million high school students drink beer on a weekly basis; approximately half that number consumes spirits on a weekly basis (Bellenir, 1996). Indeed, youth who specifically seek out and over-consume hard liquor, though this is less common, may represent an especially at-risk population (Maldonado-Molina, 2010). Nevertheless, we would expect the relationship between beer consumption and youth homicide to be the most substantial.

Both consumption indicators are standardized for population size. Beer consumption is measured in barrels per capita; spirits consumption is measured in wine-gallons per capita. We have also included variables to account for the "demand" side of the consumption equation, in the form of an adjusted index of liquor prices and the taxation rate on beer, in order to control for other potential sources of variability in alcohol consumption. An additional factor that may influence consumption levels is the type of regulatory scheme for the distribution of alcohol imposed by the state. Some states have very strict controls on alcohol sales, requiring that all sales of alcohol be conducted through state-operated outlets; others impose partial restrictions, for example requiring spirits sales to be more strictly monitored than beer or wine, while others simply have a licensing process for independent retail agents. Included in all models is a dummy variable for the strictest type of regulation, state retail monopoly, expecting that consumption (and, concurrently, homicide) may be lower in states with more restricted alcohol availability.

Poverty and Inequality

The infant mortality rate is used here as an indicator of poverty (Loftin & Hill, 1974; Loftin & Parker, 1985; see also Messner et al., 2010). The models also include a measure of economic inequality between whites and African Americans, calculated by summing the differences between the proportion white and proportion African American in each of the six income categories defined by the US Census. In this way, we are able to reflect race-specific inequality at all points of the income distribution.

Formal Social Control/Deterrence Effects

It has been argued that the threat of sanctions will deter some offenders from committing criminal acts—two dimensions of the deterrence-sanctions relationship are the certainty and severity of sanctions (Van den Haag, 1975). These two dimensions of deterrence theory are explored here. The severity of sanctions is measured by the ratio of executions per homicide; the certainty of sanctions is measured by the ratio of homicides known to the police that are "cleared" by arrest.

Population Composition

Research that attempts to explain variations in patterns of homicide must take into account the demographic/compositional variables that are known to be associated with rates of homicide. Toward this end, we have included the effects of the relative size of the male population aged fifteen to twenty-four, and the percent of the population living in metropolitan areas as defined by the US Bureau of Census.

1984 as a Watershed Year

Rates of lethal violence committed by persons aged fifteen to twenty-four began to increase dramatically in the mid-1980s. Various explanations have been advanced for this increase. Blumstein (1995) argues that the increases in lethal youth violence are largely attributable to expanding drug markets and increasing availability of guns to youth, as reflected in the huge increases in youth homicides involving guns, relative to non-gun youth homicides, which have *not* increased substantially. Others cite the increased volatility of drug markets during this period due to the introduction of crack into American cities during this period (Blumstein, 1995; Reuter, 2009; Browne et al., 2010). These explanations have been rapidly gaining popularity in the research community despite the fact that they remain largely untested (for an exception see Parker et al., 2011).

As the reasons for this mid-1980s increase are far from resolved, we include a dummy variable for the time period 1984 and after. Our data indicate that 1984 is the point at which youth homicide rates clearly begun their upward trend. This variable acts as an additional "fixed effect," in the sense that it is not included for its explanatory value per se, but rather to exclude bias from the equation due to unmeasured variables. Tests of the various explanations for the post-1984 increase in youth homicide rates are beyond the scope of the present study, but the inclusion of this dummy variable provides a crude test of the potential explanatory value of these alternative explanations, controlling for other predictors.

Urban Minority Concentration

Wilson (1987) has asserted that deindustrialization and "white flight" (a phenomenon where whites flee residential communities when non-white peoples begin to move in) have resulted in the concentration of poor minorities in America's inner cities, one effect of which is the creation of an "underclass" that becomes stranded in increasingly deteriorating urban areas, resulting in the social isolation of poor, overwhelmingly African American inner city residents. Wilson argues that the combined effects of concentration and social isolation exacerbate the "tangle of pathology" in the inner city, a constellation of factors that includes high rates of violent crime. The present data provide a unique opportunity to empirically investigate Wilson's theory. It is possible that the increases (largely realized in African American populations) of youth homicide in the past decade are a consequence of minority concentration. An interaction term was constructed in order to assess the impact of urban minority concentration on rates of youth homicide. This interaction measures the unique effect of the combination of racial economic inequality, the proportional contribution of African American female-headed families to the population[3] and the proportion of the population living in urban areas.

MODELS

Three nested models were estimated for each dependent variable using the three stage panel procedure in LIMDEP. Preliminary analysis indicated that the relationship between minimum purchase age changes and youth homicide is curvilinear over time. The dramatic increase in youth homicide that begins in 1984 seems to change the relationship between the legal intervention of minimum purchase age increases and homicide rates. For this reason, we introduce, in the second model, an interaction term which specifies the impact of minimum purchase age changes before 1984 only; once this term is introduced, the minimum drinking age variable specifies only the effect of changes taking place 1984 and after. Also added to the model is the dummy variable representing a period effect for cases 1984 and after. The final model also incorporates the concentration interaction term.[4]

In the third and final model, we also perform a test for floor effects. Sparseness in the data can sometimes bias the coefficient estimates; a correction for this type of specification bias consists of the introduction of a dummy variable accounting for the effect on the model of cases with zero values on the dependent variable.

RESULTS

Overall Youth Homicide

Minimum purchase age increases *do* appear to have a negative influence on the overall youth homicide rate for the period before 1984 only; when race- and gender- specific effects are considered, these effects are present only in the model of male youth homicide, which accounts for nearly all of the covariance explained by minimum purchase age changes in the overall model. The relationship between minimum age changes and homicide rates over time is indeed curvilinear, and a close examination of the standardized coefficients reveals that the increases in youth homicide in the period after 1984 appear to dominate the series, resulting in larger, positive effects of minimum purchase age changes on overall rates of youth homicide (see table 7.1).

Modest positive effects for beer consumption and modest negative beer taxation effects were observed, consistent with expectations. In addition to this, significant effects are present for the spirits-related consumption variables, in directions contrary to what our theory of the relationship between alcohol and homicide would predict.

Table 7.1.   Overall Youth Homicide: Standardized Coefficients

	Model 1	Model 2	Model 3
Males Fifteen to Twenty-Four	.178*	.181*	.168*
Infant Mortality Rate	.244*	.227*	.210*
Executions per Homicide	−.012	−.011	−.012
Homicide Clearance Rate	−.078*	−.079*	−.084*
Racial Inequality	.325*	.312*	.157*
Urbanization	1.075*	1.202*	.952
Spirits Consumption	−.840*	−.848*	−.775*
Beer Consumption	.180*	.186*	.246*
Liquor Prices	.237*	.255*	.317*
Beer Taxes	−.192*	−.208*	−.283*
Strong Regulation	.303*	.361*	.172
Minimum Age Increases	.096*	.141*	.157*
Minimum Age Increases Before 1984		−.072*	−.065*
1984 and After		−.063	.009
AA Female Headed hh			−.954*
Concentration			.682*
Floor Effects			−.020
R2	.666	.668	.690

* p < .05

This seemingly paradoxical finding, which is common to all the models of youth homicide, will be discussed below.

As far as control variables, most of the coefficients are in the expected direction, with poverty and racial inequality exerting significant positive effects on the overall rate of youth homicide victimization; urbanization, as well, exerts a relatively large positive effect. Urban minority concentration, net of other predictors, exerts a large positive effect on the overall rate of youth homicide.

There is also evidence for a modest deterrent effect, as measured by the homicide clearance rate. In the first two models of the overall youth homicide victimization rate, there is a moderately sized positive effect associated with strong alcohol regulation, which drops out of the model when the concentration term is introduced. No support was found for the hypothesis that the introduction of crack into drug markets in the mid-1980s somehow changed the dynamic processes that generate youth homicide; this is indicated by the lack of a significant explanatory finding for the fixed effect term representing the post–1984 period.

African American Youth Homicide

Contrary to our prediction, minimum drinking age increases in the period prior to 1984 had a negative and significant effect on the rate of African American youth homicide victimization. No significant effect of minimum drinking age changes was observed in the subsequent period. Once again, we fail to find support for period effects after 1984 (see table 7.2).

Beer taxation rates were found to be inversely related to rates of African American youth homicide, while the effect of liquor prices was positive and significant, and spirits consumption effects were negative and significant.

Consistent with Wilson's (1987) assertion that the consequences of historic discrimination are more relevant to the various social problems that plague African Americans today than are the effects of contemporary discrimination, racial inequality persists in the first two models as a significant predictor of African American victimization rates, but when urban minority concentration is introduced into the model, the unique effect of contemporaneous racial inequality disappears from the model, and concentration emerges as the strongest predictor of African American homicide rates as can be seen in table 7.2. The independent effect of poverty maintains the same magnitude of strength, even after the introduction of the concentration term. An additional change that results from the introduction of the urban minority concentration term is a moderate positive association between beer consumption rates and African American victimization that emerges in the presence of the concentration interaction. As in the overall model, there are moderate positive effects of strong alcohol control policies, but these effects disappear when minority concentration effects are introduced. It's important to note that the large negative

Table 7.2. African American Youth Homicide: Standardized Coefficients

	Model 1	Model 2	Model 3
Males Fifteen to Twenty-Four	−.122*	−.158*	−.077
Infant Mortality Rate	.313*	.286*	.272*
Executions per Homicide	−.023	−.023	.013
Homicide Clearance Rate	−.105*	−.107*	−.070*
Racial Inequality	.289*	.267*	.048
Urbanization	.419	.515	.308
Spirits Consumption	−.471*	−.488*	−.392*
Beer Consumption	.129	.130	.124
Liquor Prices	.226*	.238*	.387*
Beer Taxes	−.235*	−.236*	−.293*
Strong Regulation	.400*	.427*	.131
Minimum Age Increases	.012	.046	.046
Minimum Age Increases Before 1984		−.048	−.064*
1984 and After		−.099	−.057
AA Female Headed hh			−.848*
Concentration			.883*
Floor Effects			−.849*
R2	.467	.469	.621

* p < .05

main effect observed for the proportion of African American female-headed house-holds relative to all households is due to multi-collinearity between this measure and the concentration measure, of which it is a component.

Non-African American Youth Homicide

Overwhelmingly, the strongest predictor of non-African American victimization is the degree to which a states' population resides in urban areas. There are no significant effects for poverty, racial inequality, or minimum purchase age increases in either time period (see table 7.3).

Once again, the effect of spirits consumption is negative and significant, and liquor prices are found to be positively associated with homicide. No significant effects associated with beer consumption are found in the model for non-African American youth homicide. A negative period effect for 1984 and after appears in the first model in which it is introduced; however, this disappears when the urban minority concentration effect is added to the subsequent model.

Male Youth Homicide

The explanatory model for male victim youth homicide looks remarkably similar to the overall model (see table 7.4).

Table 7.3. Non-African American Youth Homicide: Standardized Coefficients

	Model 1	Model 2	Model 3
Males Fifteen to Twenty-Four	.141*	.113*	.110*
Infant Mortality Rate	.059	.036	.018
Executions per Homicide	−.018	−.019	−.021
Homicide Clearance Rate	−.053*	−.055*	−.051*
Racial Inequality	.016	−.003	.098
Urbanization	.704*	.794*	.100*
Spirits Consumption	−.226*	−.240*	−.235*
Beer Consumption	.011	.013	.021
Liquor Prices	.186*	.197*	.213*
Beer Taxes	−.003	−.006	−.029
Strong Regulation	.228	.254*	.249
Minimum Age Increases	−.125	.020	.020
Minimum Age Increases Before 1984		−.046	−.044
1984 and After		−.086*	−.074
AA Female Headed hh			−.042
Concentration			−.159
Floor Effects			−.081*
R2	.706	.708	.715

* p < .05

Table 7.4. Male Youth Homicide: Standardized Coefficients

	Model 1	Model 2	Model 3
Males Fifteen to Twenty-Four	.184*	.190*	.171*
Infant Mortality Rate	.253*	.236*	.216*
Executions per Homicide	−.011	−.010	−.013
Homicide Clearance Rate	−.074*	−.075*	−.082*
Racial Inequality	.344*	.333*	.167*
Urbanization	.001	.13*	.833
Spirits Consumption	−.885*	−.892*	−.815*
Beer Consumption	.192*	.198*	.258*
Liquor Prices	.225*	.244*	.306*
Beer Taxes	−.178*	−.195*	−.275*
Strong Regulation	.303*	.353*	.153
Minimum Age Increases	.108*	.154*	.171*
Minimum Age Increases Before 1984		−.074*	−.067*
1984 and After		−.060	.014
AA Female Headed hh			−1.00*
Concentration			.717*
Floor Effects			-.030
R2	.641	.644	.668

* p < .05

This is not surprising, given the relative size of the contribution of male victim homicides to the overall youth homicide rate. The size of the male youth population and poverty exert significant positive effects yet urbanization exerts no significant effect in any of the models of male victimization. Additionally, there are no significant period effects for the post–1984 era. When the urban minority concentration term is added to the model, it emerges as a very strong predictor of male victim homicide. Even when urban minority concentration effects are controlled for, racial inequality continues to exert a positive and significant effect on rates of male victimization, although the strength of the effect is reduced to nearly half of its prior value. As in all models, a modest negative effect is present for deterrence via the homicide clearance rate. A positive effect of moderate strength is observed for strong alcohol control, but as in the model for African American victimization, it drops out when the concentration measure is introduced.

Minimum age of purchase changes before 1984 exert significant negative effects on the rate of male youth homicide victimization; however, the positive effects observed in the subsequent period dominate the series, with standardized coefficients more than twice as large as the negative pre-1984 effects.

In all three models of male youth homicide victimization, there are moderately sized beer consumption and taxation effects, in the expected directions; it should be noted that both the coefficients for beer consumption effects and the effect of the rate of beer taxation increase noticeably in strength when the urban minority concentration term is introduced into the models. As in previous models, significant effects for spirits-consumption-related variables are present, and for some reason, in the direction opposite that predicted by our theory.

Female Youth Homicide

The best and most consistent predictor of female youth homicide victimization is the proportion of the population living in urban areas. As in all other models, there is a modest negative effect for deterrence as measured by the homicide clearance rate. There are no significant effects of minimum age of purchase changes in either period on female youth victimization rates.

Adding explanatory variables to the original model does not change the picture for female victimization very much; in the initial model there are modest positive effects for the size of the male youth population and poverty, but these effects are rendered nonsignificant by the introduction of the term measuring minimum purchase ages before 1984 and the 1984 and after dummy variable. There is no significant effect for the period after 1984. A modest negative effect is present for the homicide clearance rate. Urban minority concentration has no apparent effect on female youth homicide victimization (see table 7.5).

Beer consumption and beer taxes exert, respectively, significant positive and negative effects on female youth homicide, as predicted by the theoretical model of the

Table 7.5.   Female Youth Homicide

	Model 1	Model 2	Model 3
Males Fifteen to Twenty-Four	.099*	.083	.068
Infant Mortality Rate	.112*	.097	.122*
Executions per Homicide	−.008	−.008	−.017
Homicide Clearance Rate	−.069*	−.071*	−.067*
Racial Inequality	.075	.063	.068
Urbanization	.207*	.269*	.206*
Spirits Consumption	−.250*	−.258*	−.189*
Beer Consumption	.593	.608	.12*
Liquor Prices	.200*	.208*	.218*
Beer Taxes	−.221*	−.223*	−.251*
Strong Regulation	.221	.241	.209
Minimum Age Increases	−.004	.018	.045
Minimum Age Increases Before 1984		−.032	−.042
1984 and After		−.054	.025
AA Female Headed hh			−.227
Concentration			.133
Floor Effects			−.263*
R2	.586	.587	.632

* p < .05

relationship between consumption and violence. Spirits consumption appears to be inversely related to female homicide, while the effect of spirits prices is positive and significant.

DISCUSSION

The analysis presented in this chapter yielded qualified support for some of our predictions concerning the relationship between minimum drinking age changes and different types of youth homicide. It appears that prior to 1984, minimum drinking age increases had negative and significant effects on youth homicide rates overall, and for male and African American victims. This is entirely plausible given the history of the period. Nearly all changes to minimum purchase age laws had been implemented by 1984, and grassroots support for such increases (and, it can be argued, the heightened enforcement that likely accompanied this public pressure) had largely diminished by 1984. For these reasons, it is logical that it is in the period prior to 1984 that we would see the greatest impact of minimum drinking age increases. In addition, data from a number of natural experiments and evaluations of legal interventions show a similar pattern to that reported here (Ross, 1982). The curvilinearity of the relationship between minimum purchase age increases and youth homicide was evident for all dependent variables, yet was only statistically significant in the model for the overall youth homicide rate and in the model for male youth homicide victimization.

Impacts of minimum drinking age changes after 1984 are found to be positive and significant in the models of overall and male victim youth homicide. To investigate whether this was due to collinearity with the 1984 and after dummy variable, we estimated the final model for each type of homicide without the dummy variable representing minimum drinking age changes after 1984. However, the results were virtually unchanged with the exclusion of this variable.

In addition, we investigated the possibility that this positive effect of the minimum drinking age after 1984 was due to collinearity with the pre 1984 minimum drinking age indicator. If there really was no watershed for youth homicide in the mid-1980s, then entering two versions of the same minimum drinking age variable divided by an arbitrary date could result in this kind of anomalous finding. However, the positive and significant effects remain even when we remove sources of collinearity in these indicators. The most likely explanation, especially given that there were not as many changes in minimum drinking age laws after 1984, is that an additional untapped process driving youth homicide higher occurs after 1984, and it is a process that occurs in the states that made changes after 1984 in their minimum drinking age laws, as well as others.

Although the positive effects of alcohol regulation found in Models 1 and 2, regarding male youth homicide, for example, are also anomalous, these effects disappear when the urban concentration measures are entered in the equation in Model

3. Even in a state with strong alcohol regulation, that is, reduced availability due to the lack of private retail outlets and restricted hours of sale, urban areas will still have greater alcohol availability than non-urban areas. This contention is supported by the fact that poor urban neighborhoods have higher concentrations of alcohol outlets than other types of locations (Alaniz et al., 1997; Watts & Rabow, 1983). Therefore, once urban concentration is adequately controlled for, this effect disappears.

One of the most important findings of this research is the support given to Wilson's theory of urban minority underclass concentration resulting from deindustrialization and its relationship to rates of criminal violence. The results of our analysis of African American youth homicide supports Wilson's assertion that the compounded effects of historic discrimination, realized as a concentration of extremely impoverished, primarily African American, inner city residents. In the first two models, contemporaneous racial economic inequality exerts a strong and positive effect on rates of African American youth homicide; however, when the urban minority concentration interaction term is introduced into the model, it eclipses this effect and renders it non-significant.

In the models for male and overall youth homicide, a significant effect of contemporaneous racial inequality on homicide rates persists even in the presence of minority concentration effects. Our data do not allow us to estimate the proportion of youth homicides that are inter-racial, but for all homicides, 7 percent of African American victims are killed by non-African American perpetrators, and 15 percent of white victims are killed by nonwhites (Maguire & Pastore, 1997). It is possible that this effect is reflecting the small proportion of homicides in which the victims and perpetrators are of different races.

Poverty has consistently positive and significant effects in every model (except for non-African American victimization) thus replicating the common finding that homicide is persistently associated with a lack of resources and access to basic necessities like housing, health care, and consumer goods. In inner city areas where Wilson's process of increased isolation and concentration of a lack of opportunity occurs, higher rates of poverty occur as well. Our results indicate, however, that persistent poverty has broader effects than in those areas alone.

It is likely that the negative significant effect of the clearance rate is due to the fact that as homicide rates rise, law enforcement will be unable to effectively respond to the sharp increases evident in these data. As more and more homicide investigations overwhelm the more or less constant resources available to deal with these events, arrests will decline or at best remain constant, resulting in a drop in the rate of arrests per homicide. Thus it is likely that rising homicide rates result in a decline in clearance rates, rather than the latter indicating some success in deterring youth homicide in the face of increasing rates.

The previous discussion applies primarily to results for overall, male, and African American youth homicide, but not necessarily to female and non-African American victimization. Although the pattern of predictors for female youth victimization shares some characteristics in common with results for other types of victimization, that is, beer consumption, beer taxes, and poverty, no significant effects of the minimum drinking age nor for urban concentration were found. This suggests, at the very least, that the dynamic of female youth homicide is different than that of male youth victimization, and that the models developed here are less successful in explaining variation and change in female rates in this period. Additional indicators of this are the large and significant effects of the metropolitan indicator, a proxy for a number of potential unmeasured effects, and the presence of substantial floor effects. Even some approaches suggested in the domestic violence/homicide research (Browne & Williams, 1989; Silverman & Kennedy, 1987), which emphasize the role of males as potential offenders in female victimization, are less than successful in this case: the proportion of young males in the population is not a significant predictor of female victimization in this model. Perhaps additional concepts drawn from other perspectives that seek to explain the impact of economic power and labor market competition might be useful in explaining female victimization more fully (e.g., see Hagan et al., 1989; Gartner, 1990; Parker, 1998).

Results for non-African Americans are even more problematic, but for an obvious reason: given the limitations of these data, we cannot disentangle the various ethnic/racial groups contained in the omnibus classification. This limitation is severe, and the implications of it have been discussed elsewhere (Martinez, 1996). Similar to the results for female victimization, the model of non-African American victimization shows significant effects for metropolitan population and floor effects, indicating that a number of unmeasured but important determinants of homicide have been excluded; the inability to distinguish Latino from Anglo victimization in these data is a likely source of this difficulty, among others.

One result that requires some additional explanation is that in every model, spirits consumption has a significant and negative effect on youth homicide. However, it would be foolish to conclude that increases in spirits consumption lead to decreases in youth homicide; evidence from the study of beverage preferences and consumption of alcohol indicates clearly that spirits consumption is the provenance of older drinkers in the United States (Treno & Parker, 1994; Kerr et al., 2004), and indeed has declined in parallel with an increasing proportion of the population in younger age categories. This effect is not caused by collinearity with other measures of consumption or alcohol policy, as the negative effects persists when these variables are removed from the model. Rather we would argue that the negative and significant effect of spirits consumption on youth homicide is simply a reflection of the fact that spirits are so closely tied to older age groups, while our dependent variables, youth homicide victimization, are closely tied to the proportion of young people. Indeed, our indicator of this compositional effect, the proportion of young males, is significant in three of the five models we consider.

CONCLUSION

Our findings indicate that alcohol policy, primarily in the form of the minimum drinking age, but also in terms of consumption taxes on beer, can be an effective mechanism for the control and prevention of youth homicide. Although we did not find this to be the case in every model or every type of victimization we examined, it was the case consistently enough to recommend the reexamination of alcohol policy as a means of reducing youth violence, particularly in terms of enforcement of existing policies. This is further underscored by a number of significant positive effects of beer consumption on offending reported here. Not only will control measures have a direct effect on youth violence, but the possibility of indirect effects via reduced consumption by young people is also indicated. In addition, our indirect tests of Wilson's notions of the impact of the increasingly marginalized and deprived inner city also indicate directions for policy research and intervention. Finally, it is clear that we need to further theorize female and other types of homicide, as the models used here do not provide satisfactory explanations. New developments in feminist approaches to violence and in the increasing interest in ethnic and racial differences in violence have begun to provide some direction for this effort (Martinez, 1996; Crutchfield, 1995; Radford, 1994; Bart, 1993; Pizarro et al., 2010; Vieraitis et al., 2011).

Also significant is the failure to find a significant period effect for the time period after 1984. It is a widely held belief in the field of homicide research that the increases in youth homicide during this period can be attributed to the increasing availability of guns to youth, as well as increased volatility in illicit drug markets, fueled by the introduction of crack into inner-city communities (Blumstein, 1995). It should be pointed out that were we to find a significant effect for the 1984 and after period variable, this could *not* be taken as support for any particular explanation. However, the *lack* of any significant effect on homicide rates for this variable indicates that the increases in youth homicide are not due to a change in the dynamic processes that generate youth homicide associated with this period. This is consistent with more recent data which show that youth homicide trends decreased after the period analyzed in this chapter. In fact, according to the US Department of Justice, youth homicide offending fell 65 percent from 1994 to 2003. As a result, juvenile homicide offending rates today resemble those prior to the 1984 increase (US Department of Justice).

Although alcohol policy is no panacea for youth violence, this study demonstrates that alcohol policy can be a useful tool among others for communities concerned about recent increases in youth violence. It is especially appealing to consider the minimum drinking age, as this policy already exists on the books in every state in the United States. In this case the hard work of creating policy has already taken place; what remains is the effort to enforce the policy and evaluate its outcome, an outcome that may result in fewer youth homicides.

NOTES

1. We acknowledge the limitations of any structural-categorical analysis in terms of obscuring variability within the categories. This limitation is a feature of any macro-level study. In

addition, data limitations restrict our analyses to the "non African American" category; we include this category for the sake of comparison while acknowledging that the results are not likely to be very informative.

2. Due to large amounts of missing data for Hawaii, this state was not included in the analysis; but data from the District of Columbia was included.

3. The proportional contribution of African American female-headed families to the population is a multidimensional indicator, and for this reason was not included in the original specification of the model as a general indicator of poverty. It measures not only the *extent* of poverty in the African American population, but also its impacts: that is, the feminization of poverty. This impact is a central component of Wilson's thesis concerning the specific effects of inner-city urban poverty. The demographic specificity of this indicator can been seen in the trends across time for the two variables. The infant mortality rate, chosen as the overall indicator of poverty for purposes of comparison across states over the time period, is declining over this period. However, the proportion of African American female–headed households has been steadily increasing.

4. All models were estimated including all two-way interactions subsumed by the three-way interaction term representing urban minority concentration. The presence of these terms did not alter any of the main or interaction effects, so, in the interest of parsimony, they were eliminated from the models presented here.

8

The Impact of Banning Alcohol on Criminal Assault in Barrow, Alaska

Robert Nash Parker and Kevin J. McCaffree

INTRODUCTION

Researchers have consistently found that there is a relationship linking alcohol availability in a community, alcohol consumption by individuals, and the level of associated alcohol and other health problems (Gruenewald, 1996; Holder, 1998; Parker & Rebhun, 1995; Albrecht, 1984; Bondy, 1995). One of the best historical examples is that of the twenty-one-year-old minimum drinking age in the United States and youth drunk driving: during the 1960s and early 1970s, when drinking ages were being lowered in many states to eighteen or nineteen, youth drunk driving accidents and fatalities increased (Vingilis & DeGenova, 1979). When states began to raise the drinking age in the late 1970s and 1980s, until the uniform twenty-one-year-old minimum age was reached in 1985, youth drunk driving accidents and fatalities declined (O'Malley & Wagenaar, 1991). Increases in the minimum age also reduced some kinds of homicide among youth (Parker & Rebhun, 1995) and resulted in decreases in alcohol consumption and binge drinking among cohorts who came of age under the twenty-one-year-old minimum age compared with those who came of age under the eighteen-year-old minimum age (Vingilis & DeGenova, 1979). Although several studies have taken advantage of large scale "natural" experiments, in which policy changes driven by other dynamics have occurred and thus allowed researchers to assess the impact of the change in alcohol availability on consumption and problems (e.g., Parker & Rebhun, 1995; Vingilis & DeGenova, 1979; Wagenaar & Holder, 1991), what has been lacking is a policy experiment in a limited and isolated geographic area in which alternative policies were implemented over a relatively short period of time. A remote and isolated case study would limit substantially the possibility that various threats to validity applicable to natural experiments, and nonexperimental research in general, would be responsible for any relationship found between availability and alcohol and problems. During the 1990s, Barrow, Alaska, the northernmost city in the United States, with a population of about four thousand residents, provides an opportunity to better assess the impact of a severe restriction on alcohol availability on the number of criminal assaults in this isolated community. This curious natural experiment that occurred in Barrow must be analyzed at numerous intersections, and perhaps most prominently, the intersections of indigenous life and alcohol use (as Barrow's population includes a majority of indigenous Eskimos), and alcohol use/control/policy and violence.

INDIGENOUS ALCOHOL USE

In 1867, the fates of Alaskan Natives and those of American Natives became inextricably intertwined. The Treaty of Cession, signed in that year, transferred the jurisdiction of Alaska from Russia to the United States and, not long after, traders brought large quantities of alcohol with them as a way of establishing business avenues and political alliances, a practice common at the time (Kelso & DuBay, 1985). This method of lubricating trade with large quantities of alcohol (and, no doubt, with a "frontier-style" of drinking) was also a strategy that Russia's vodka had served before the Treaty of Cession, and there is historical evidence that natives often decried the infusion of problem drinking and made efforts to control it, often to no avail and with little assistance from the broader European population (Abbott, 1996; Price, 1975; see also MacAndrew & Edgerton, 1969).

Anthropologists and others began to take the drinking practices of natives as a subject matter in and of itself around and after the 1950s. In 1956, for example, Berreman studied the Aleuts of Nikoiski, a people with a long history of contact with Europeans (again, mostly Russian influence). Berreman offered that stress, uncertainty, anxiety, and a general lack of self-determination may be driving the problem drinking he observed (Berreman, 1956). The exogenous and imposed influence of colonialism had debased village stability and it was for sorrowful and not celebratory reasons that the Aleuts drank. Others would support this general interpretation of the causes of problem drinking, isolating the cultural and structural disjuncture between the dominant interests of the US government and the desires for autonomy and self-determination not uncommon to native villages (c.f., Kelso & DuBay, 1985).

A caveat should here be mentioned before going further. The consumption of alcohol for purposes of intoxication was not, of course, unknown entirely to American Natives before European contact. As Abbott (1996) points out, the use of alcohol among natives originated in Middle America, and was tied to the requirement of an agricultural base, as alcohol during this time was made primarily from domesticated plants. From Middle America, however, the use of alcohol rapidly diffused to Northern Mexico and to the Southwestern United States (Abbot, 1996). Alcohol was used by indigenous Americans primarily in ritual ceremonies, and European accounts of early Native alcohol use do not describe frequent periods of impulsive binge drinking. As MacAndrew and Edgerton (1969) argue, the Natives in essence learned the reckless frontier-drinking mentality from white colonists. As for why American Indians fell victim to this socialized mentality, Abbott (1996) writes:

> Several hypotheses are likely: alcohol became increasingly more available through the active commercial and fur trade; tribes did not have to divert valuable food supplies into producing alcoholic beverages; the content of alcohol in beverages increased dramatically with the introduction of distilled spirits, which was largely unknown to American Indians except by the Aztec who had some familiarity with rudimentary distillation processes; and lastly, and perhaps most likely, massive social and cultural changes came about as the result of outside [European] contact. Social rules governing drinking behavior shifted as a result of these changes. Alcohol became a menace, not necessarily because it was novel in use, but as an expression of a dramatic socio-cultural shift. (Abbott, 1996)

Indigenous alcohol use has certainly been studied outside of the United States, as well. Anderson (2007), for example, recently found that Aboriginal drinkers in Canada are less than half as likely to drink on a regular basis but *more than twice as likely* to binge drink than the general Canadian drinking population. Consequently, aboriginals in Canada experience a rate of alcohol-related hospitalization and death much higher than the general population (Anderson, 2007). This disparity is a very real reminder of the history of colonization, frontier-minded recklessness, and disregard, and the very real structural strain felt by indigenous peoples. Or, take the case of Australian Aboriginals. Indigenous imprisonment rates are a continued focus of social policy and recent research in Australia and, though a variety of explanations exist for the high imprisonment rate, especially viable explanations point to alcohol abuse. Weatherburn (2008), for example, points to data showing that, controlling for sex and age, the amount of alcohol consumed predicts indigenous contact with the law. Weatherburn also uses data that show that the effect of alcohol use on risk of arrest is as powerful as the effect of unemployment to argue for a causal role of alcohol assumption in aboriginal arrest rates. Though he acknowledges the impact of financial stress and general structural instability on Aboriginals' propensity to abuse alcohol, Weatherburn suggests that parental/peer modeling and alcohol availability play very important roles as well.

We might also look to Venezuela for further research into aboriginal alcohol use. A recent study of two small indigenous villages of about forty to fifty families each reveals a great deal. Aboriginal focus-group participants report that, prior to the mid-twentieth century, alcohol was brewed in limited quantities and reckless drinking was reserved largely for festivals which occurred only a few times a year (Seale et al., 2002a). Injuries were, on balance, few, and domestic violence wasn't considered a serious problem. Exposure to Westerners and to Western economies opened up not only access to larger quantities of commercial alcohol but also to a normative style of drinking behavior at variance with the traditional aboriginal subculture. Though sales of alcoholic beverages are increasingly becoming regulated, the impact of problem drinking on these villages has already been felt, including dismally predictable spikes in injuries and domestic violence. A subsequent focus group interview revealed that these natives had gradually reduced their festival-related consumption of culturally traditional corn liquor in favor of commercial beer and rum, which they subsequently drank more frequently (Seale et al., 2002b). Seale et al. (2002a) explains the perspective of the natives they studied:

> Many of the reasons for drinking mentioned were external. Some described how others pressured them to drink. Others blamed the alcohol itself, describing it as "deceptive" or a betrayer. Some felt that the Black Spirit enticed them to drink. Focus group participants stated that they had learned their current drinking patterns from the White man. According to one man from Village A: "Little by little, people began to get closer to the city. . . . Little by little, they sought out more contact with the White man. Let's say, they start working at the cattle ranch for two weeks or a month. There they earn some money. Then you know that the White man has a different kind of drink, different from ours. After [our people] are mixed with the White man, they see the White man drink. It is just like the way children learn in school."
>
> Focus group participants frequently commented on how dramatically their culture had changed, and how many of the changes they were seeing were not good. There was a general sadness over the loss of the old ways and of good aspects of their culture that were disappearing. Nonetheless, no focus group participant described drinking due to sadness, depression or despair. (Seale et al., 2002a: 606)

NATURAL EXPERIMENTS AND
THE CITY OF BARROW, ALASKA

What follows in this chapter is a sociological analysis of what occurred during a natural experiment in Barrow, Alaska, over a thirty-three-month period. The cause of the natural experiment was a series of electoral decisions that served to ban the possession and importation of alcohol in Barrow. A ban on retail sales of alcohol was also extended. This ban, over thirty-three months, was sequentially repealed and reinstated allowing researchers to assess the effects of the alcohol ban on violence and other negative health-related outcomes.

Before moving forward, a few ideas on the notion of a natural experiment should be discussed. Natural experiments are broad, exogenous (i.e., "from the outside") or endogenous (i.e., "from within") changes to a social system. Generally speaking, large social interventions are "natural" to the degree that the researcher often has no control over the implementation or the diffusion of the change—the researcher is relegated to observing and analyzing an intervention largely or utterly outside of his or her control (Petticrew et al., 2005). Within criminology and sociology, a natural experiment is not always literally an intervention of the natural environment but, as with the study that constitutes this chapter, natural experiments can also be novel structural changes to a social system voted on or encouraged by the populace.

As Petticrew et al. (2005) note, natural experiments occur frequently but are rarely systematically and appropriately analyzed to glean useful data on public health. Undoubtedly, much data is gleaned from controlled, randomized experiments on a sample of people, but such data is often expensive to obtain and it can be difficult to persuade governments to initiate interventions in a way that would produce robust outcome measurements (Petticrew et al., 2005). Natural experiments, then, are an attractive, cost-effective (for the researcher, at least) alternative. So long as the researcher can reconcile himself with the experimental control he has relinquished, much useful analysis can follow from a "natural" change to a social system.

The electoral decision of Barrow residents to ban alcohol in October 1994 constituted an especially unique natural experiment, as Barrow is a very remote location—over 300 miles north of the Arctic Circle. The citizens of Barrow, in adopting the ban against alcohol, then rejecting it, then adopting it once more, effectively visited upon themselves a controlled, time-varying intervention. This intervention, because it occurred over a relatively short interval, served to hold other characteristics of Barrow which might affect crime constant (e.g., large scale-economic organization, and population demographics). A natural experiment of this sort, because it occurs in a remote location (safe from outside "influence" during the experimentation period), because it occurs over a relatively short amount of time, and because the ban was time varying (that is, the ban existed in full effect at time1, was repealed at time2, and resumed existence at time3) has a very high level of external scientific validity.

According to available census data,[1] Barrow, Alaska, has a population of just over 4,200 people with a median age of 28.7 years. Importantly, 61 percent of the population of Barrow is composed of Iñupiat Alaskan natives. In fact, the website for the City of Barrow remarks on the prominent presence of this indigenous population of Iñupiat Eskimos.[2] Indeed, only 17 percent of the population of Barrow is white. Because the natural experiment discussed in this chapter occurred in the mid-1990s, it would of course help to compare the more recent census demographics to the demographics of Alaska during this period[3]. As it turns out, though, little has changed in the overall population proportion of residents that are indigenous Alaskans—63.9 percent in 1990 compared to 61 percent in 2010.

Background

In October 1994, the citizens of Barrow, Alaska, voted to pass a referendum banning the sale and importation of alcoholic beverages. The referendum marked the beginning of a new strategy to reduce Barrow's history of heavy alcohol consumption, and came with the encouragement of local Eskimo leaders as well as the city's tribal government. The referendum (which passed narrowly) was meant as an assertion of political autonomy on the part of the Eskimo community in Barrow, which had been devastated by alcohol-related disease and violence.

The *Los Angeles Times*, for example, reported that, in the four years leading up to the ban, Barrow had had 87 arrests for rape, 2,057 arrests for drunken and disorderly conduct, 675 drunken assaults, 230 children arrested for drinking, and some of the highest fetal alcohol syndrome rates in the world—all in a city of only 4,000 people (*LA Times*, 1995a). Dorcas Stein, executive director of the Native Village of Barrow tribal council at the time, argued that this referendum against alcohol was truly an effort on the part of Eskimos to defend the health and future of their people (*LA Times*, 1995b).

Backlash against the ban appeared to be immediate and was concentrated in the comparatively small non-Eskimo (i.e., white) population of Barrow. The majority white so-called Barrow Freedom Committee led the charge against the referendum, calling for its immediate repeal. The tribal leaders of the Iñupiat Eskimos (representing, again, over 60 percent of the population), by contrast, stressed the continuing importance of the ban for their health and culture. In fact, the Sober Life Movement, composed of Iñupiats in favor of the ban, campaigned against the Barrow Freedom Committee's desire to repeal it with one tribal leader pointing out that, "The graveyard is full of young men who died as a result of alcohol. Where is the Barrow Freedom Committee when we hold the funerals?"[4]

Nevertheless, the backlash from the Barrow Freedom Committee was palpable as committee members sought out signatures for a petition to overturn the ban. They were successful, and a year later, on October 3rd, 1995, with a city council vote of 4 to 2, the ban on alcohol was lifted. Once again, the sale and importation of alcohol was legal, despite the concerns and activism of Iñupiat leaders. This lifting of the ban caused an eruption of ethnic tension between Native Eskimos and the white immigrants, who insisted on their right to have a drink whenever and however damaging and profound the consequences. The Iñupiats, undeterred, were once again galvanized, and on March 1st, 1996, the ban on alcohol was once again reinstated.

Methods

Barrow's law enforcement is the responsibility of the North Slope Borough Police Department. The department headquarters is in Barrow, where the jail run by the department is located as well as the central dispatch and the office of the chief of police. About one-third of the approximately thirty sworn officers work out of the Barrow headquarters, with about one-third involved in the operation of the jail and the remainder of the sworn officers working in seven outlying villages that exist in the North Slope Borough. Data on assaults and alcohol-related assaults were obtained directly from the North Slope Borough Police Department, with the contact at the time being Lieutenant James Wood. Monthly counts of these criminal reports were provided to the researchers.

Figure 8.1 shows these data summed into an overall time series of total assaults and alcohol-related assaults; table 8.1 gives descriptive statistics on the overall series and the subseries. In order to assess the impact of the alcohol bans on assault and alcohol-related assaults, we need to specify the hypothesis that the bans indeed resulted in the drops evident in figure 8.1; when the first ban takes effect in November

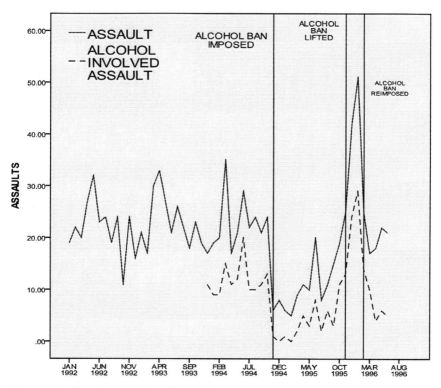

Figure 8.1.   Courtesy of Robert Nash Parker.

1994, the monthly number of assaults drops precipitously, and remains low until November 1995, when the ban is lifted.

At this point, the number of assaults increases to a level significantly higher than the pre-ban average of 1992–1994. When the second ban is enacted, in February 1996, the number of assaults drops again, to levels similar to the 1994–1995 period of the first ban. However, it is well known that a time series of the sort depicted in figure 8.1 can be driven by a number of processes that can appear to be related to some external impact or shock to the system underlying the observed series, but are in fact due to these internal processes or components and are independent of, in this case, the intervention represented by the alcohol bans and their reversal. This is analogous to the waves observed on an ocean beach—the exact height and pattern observed is due to a number of factors: the tidal cycle, the shape of the shore underneath the waves, storm patterns at sea, seasonal variations in gravity, and so on. In order to understand why the waves hit the beach as they do, it is necessary to decompose the wave into its constituent components, and, therefore, this analysis must also be decomposed first in order to rule out the fact that the observed pattern

Table 8.1. Descriptive Statistics for Total and Alcohol-Related Assaults

Variable	Mean	Standard Deviation	Range and N
Total Assaults	20.67	8.58	5 to 51; 54
Alcohol-Related Assaults	8.67	6.84	0 to 29; 31

is due to some internal dynamic before we can determine if any relationship exists between the interventions and the assault series (see table 8.1).

Drawing on the work of Box and Jenkins (1976), McCleary et al. (1988) demonstrated the utility of Auto Regressive Integrated Moving Average, or ARIMA modeling as a practical and effective method for decomposing the types of series often observed in the social and behavior sciences. In addition, they show how the interrupted time series model, so named because the intervention is seen as an "interruption" to the prior path of the series, so that the series following the interruption takes a different path over time, is an effective way of ascertaining the impact of an intervention on such series. Interrupted time series methods have had a long history of use in alcohol policy research, and have been used in a number of studies to show the impact, if any, of a variety of interventions (Holder & Wagenaar, 1990; Wagenaar, 1983; Skog, 1986; Loftin & McDowell, 1982). The reader is referred to McCleary et al. (1988) for further information on this approach.

We first summarize the results of the identification phase of the modeling for the total assault series, and then the results of the interrupted time series model relating the alcohol bans to the assault series. We will also summarize the results of the same analysis on the shorter alcohol involved assault series as a replication and reliability check on the total assault series.

Identification Phase

Examining the total assault series as observed via the autocorrelation and partial autocorrelation functions suggested that an AR model at lag 1 time period would be an adequate representation of the internal processes driving this series. This model was estimated, and the coefficient for the AR1 parameter was significant; table 8.2 presents a summary of the models estimated. Examination of the residuals from this model suggested that this model was an adequate representation of the internal components of the total assault series. The Box-Leung Q statistic, used to test whether or not a residual series from a fitted ARIMA model is "white noise" (i.e., that no significant internal components of variation exist), was equal to 9.49 at 16 lags, with a probability of .8919. The Q statistic for the original series was 39.029, with a probability of .001. Table 8.2 also shows the estimation results from the AR1 model, indicating that the AR1 coefficient and the constant term were both significant for the total assault series.

Table 8.2. ARIMA Model Results from Identification Phase, Total Assaults, and Alcohol-Related Assaults

Model	Box-Leung Q, Original Series or Residuals	Constant (Significance)	Time Process Coefficient (Significance)	Intervention Coefficient (Significance)
Total Assaults Original Series	39.03, P = .001, 16 lags	—	—	—
Alcohol-Related Assaults	32.72, P = .003, 10 lags	—	—	—
Total Assaults, AR1	9.49, P = .892, 16	20.64 (8.77*)	.539 (6.01*)	—
Alcohol-Related Assaults, AR1	3.54, P = .966, 10 lags	8.87 (2.89*)	.636 (5.16*)	—

Considering the identification analysis for the shorter alcohol-related violence series, similar results were found for the original series. The Q statistic was equal to 32.72, with a probability of .0003. The ACF and PACF were similar to those found for the total assault series, indicating an AR1 model was appropriate; these graphs are shown in figures 8.2 and 8.3. An ARIMA model with an AR1 component was estimated, and the results indicated that this model was an adequate representation for the alcohol-related assault series. The Q statistic was equal to 3.54 at 10 lags with a probability of .9656.

The ACF and PACF graphs for the original and residual alcohol-related assault series are shown in figures 8.4 and 8.5; table 8.2 also shows the results from this estimation, again demonstrating that the AR1 and constant terms were statistically significant.

Conceptualizing the Alcohol Ban

The next issue in this analysis was the way in which the ban or series of bans, reversal, and reinstatement would be conceptualized and measured. Although there are a number of alternatives, the approach we report on here is the most straightforward one, in which the imposition of the ban is treated like an electrical switch: the ban is initially "off" or 0 at the beginning of the series, November 1993. In November 1994, when the ban is first imposed, the switch is "on" or 1; when the ban is lifted in November 1995, the ban series is set back to 0, and when the ban is fully reinstated, on April 1, 1996, the ban series is reset to 1, where it remains through the last data point, July 1996. We have examined a number of alternative specifications of the ban indicator, and the results from those models do not differ in any substantial way from those presented here.

As table 8.3 reports, we estimated a model in which the AR1 parameter was specified along with the ban indicator as described, and the ban indicator was significant

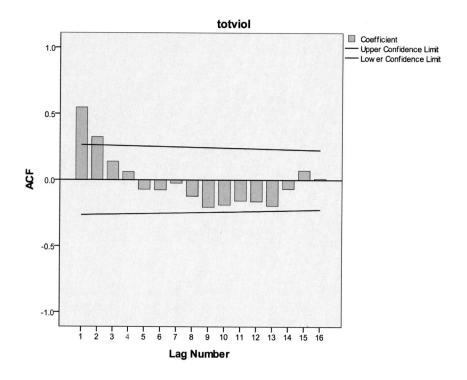

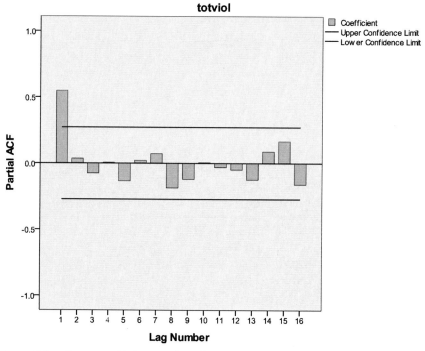

Figure 8.2. Courtesy of Robert Nash Parker.

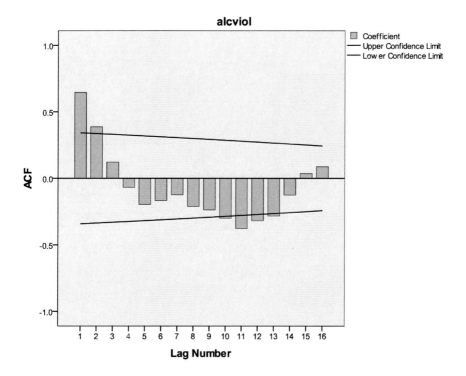

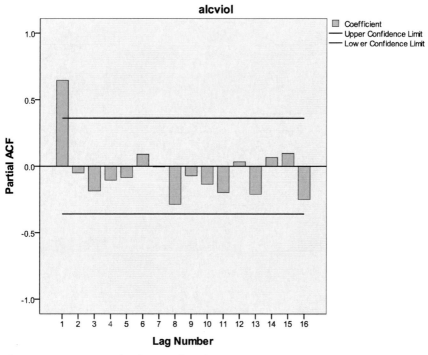

Figure 8.3.   Courtesy of Robert Nash Parker.

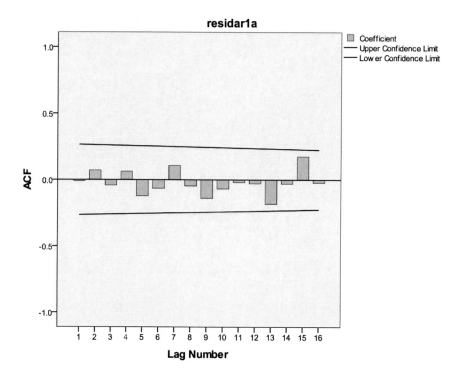

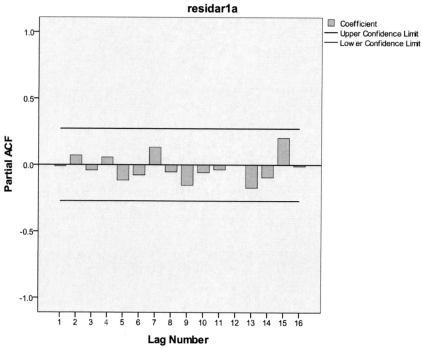

Figure 8.4. Courtesy of Robert Nash Parker.

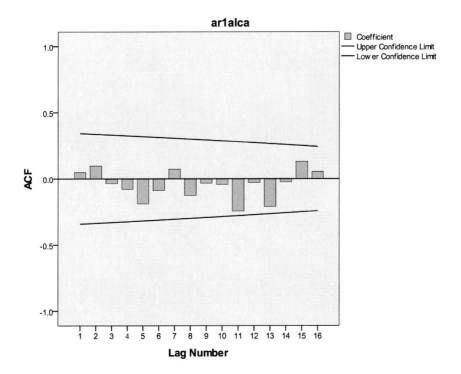

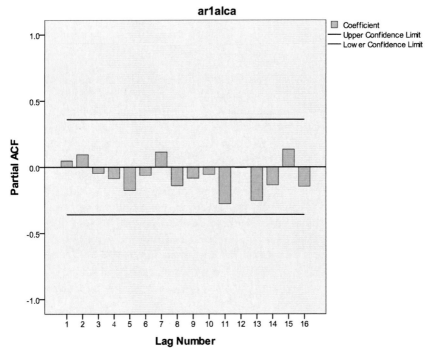

Figure 8.5.   Courtesy of Robert Nash Parker.

Table 8.3. Final ARIMA Models and the Impact of the Alcohol Bans of Assault and Alcohol-Related Assaults

Model	Box-Leung Q, Residuals	Constant (Significance)	Time Process Coefficient (Significance)	Intervention Coefficient (Significance)
Total Assaults, AR1 and Alcohol Ban	7.31, P=.967, 16 lags	24.46 (12.41*)	.477 (4.33*)	-11.89 (3.13*)
Alcohol-Related Assaults, AR1 and Alcohol Ban	3.38, P=.971, 10 lags	14.00 (5.93*)	.515 (3.28*)	-9.38 (3.29*)

* = Coefficient Significant at .05 or greater

and negative in direction, indicating that the ban resulted in a reduction in both the total assault series and the shorter alcohol-related assault series. The AR1 parameter and the constant were also significant, and the ACF and PACF, shown in figures 8.6 and 8.7, show that the residual series from these models are equivalent to "white noise." The ARIMA analysis presented here substantiate the conclusion that the alcohol ban in Barrow was responsible for the reductions in assaults and alcohol-related assaults during this period.

Threats to Study Validity

Although the statistical analysis we have presented is conclusive, any statistical model is subject to threats to the validity of the design, especially those based on nonexperimental data such as that used here. In this section we examine some of the more likely threats, and present arguments concerning the possible impact or lack thereof on our analysis and conclusions.

One possibility is that although the North Slope Police were generally in favor of banning alcohol, and were interested enough in the issue to have developed an alcohol-related assault data series, something not required by state or federal reporting systems, some officers might have underreported assaults during the bans. Perhaps they transported potential offenders to the local detoxification center and failed to fill out a crime report on these assaults. If this were the case, we would expect to see an increase or at least not much of a decrease in admissions to the detoxification center, but in fact available data show that the detoxification center had a dramatic decrease in admissions after the ban went into effect as well. Admissions for alcohol detoxification ranged from thirty in March 1994 to sixty-two in September 1994; after the ban went into effect in November 1994, admissions ranged from a low of twelve in January 1995 to a high of twenty-nine in November 1994, the month the ban was imposed. Another similar possibility is that assaults declined overall after the ban was imposed because of some other factors operating in the community, so

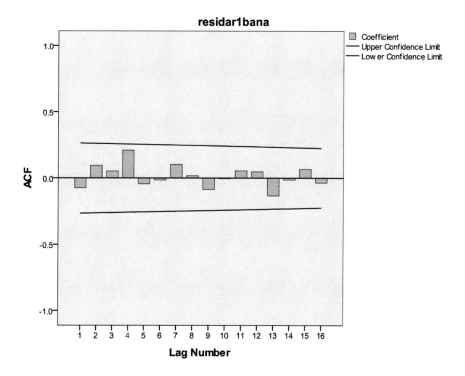

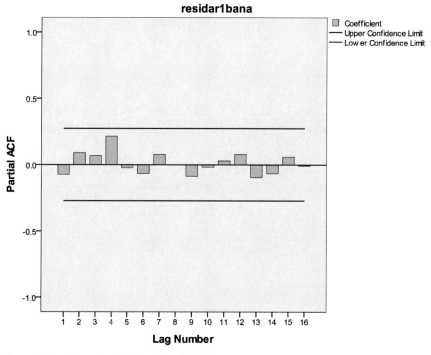

Figure 8.6.   Courtesy of Robert Nash Parker.

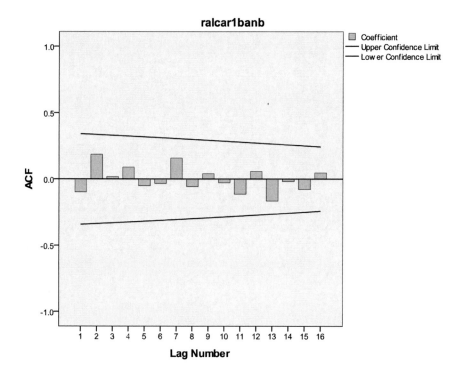

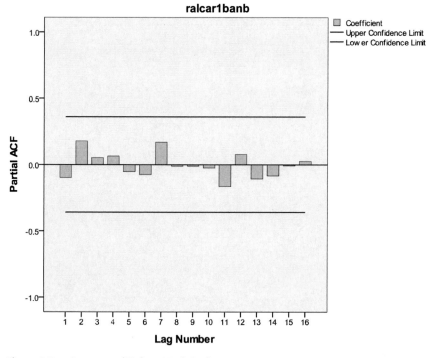

Figure 8.7. Courtesy of Robert Nash Parker.

that the decline in alcohol-related assaults simply reflects an overall decline in crime. Once again, however, available data do not support this argument: in fact, other than assaults and some other alcohol-related offenses like drunk driving, crime rates in other categories like property crime were similar during and after the bans were imposed compared to before.

Given the isolation of this community, are there any other contaminating factors? One possibility is that those seeking alcohol-related activities during the times the bans were in effect might have traveled to Fairbanks, which is reasonably accessible twelve months of the year by scheduled and charter air service. However, there is no indication that assaults and alcohol-related assaults increased in a corresponding pattern to the bans in Barrow, and certainly no crime data available that could account for the dramatic changes observed in the Barrow assault series examined here.

Or, another possibility exists. Perhaps there has been a substitution of other substances for alcohol, after it became illegal and difficult to obtain. However, discussions with the North Slope PD provide little evidence that there have been any major increases in other drug trafficking as a result of the alcohol bans.

Another possibility is that alcohol-related problems are being handled privately by individuals, at home, either successfully or not. For example, perhaps domestic violence calls that involved alcohol decreased after the ban because of enhanced reluctance to be involved in the additional legal trouble violating the bans would add to the situation. Police data show that domestic violence calls in fact decreased significantly after the ban was imposed, but data from the Barrow Women's Shelter, Arctic Women in Crisis, do not show much of an increase or a decrease after the ban was imposed. Discussions between the senior author of this chapter and the director of the shelter suggested that the severity of domestic violence in Barrow decreased after the ban was imposed. If this threat to validity were important, domestic violence severity would most likely have increased after the ban's imposition. In any case, domestic assaults are not included in the series analyzed here, as they were recorded in a separate series; not enough data were available during this period for an additional analysis.

Finally, although alcohol-related assaults in total declined, perhaps mortality due to alcohol nevertheless increased. We examined death certificate data from 1990 to mid-1996, and could find no pattern which would suggest an increase in mortality due to alcohol-related causes after the imposition of the ban in Barrow. Although there may be other potential threats to the validity of the analysis presented here, we believe that the most important ones have been dealt with and that available evidence suggests that they do not undermine the results reported here.

CONCLUSION

The results of this study clearly demonstrate that in Barrow, Alaska, banning the sale, consumption, and possession of alcohol has had a significant impact on the reduction of total assaults and alcohol-related assaults known to police. In a geographically isolated community where concern about alcohol problems and their prevention have become important community values, banning alcohol can be a very effective violence prevention technique. Other similarly isolated communities may benefit from the experience of Barrow, and more geographically mainstream communities may also be able to benefit from conclusive evidence that reducing the availability of alcohol will result in a reduction in violence overall and alcohol-related violence in particular.

NOTES

1. Census.gov, Census 2010:
http://factfinder2.census.gov/faces/tableservices/jsf/pages/productview.xhtml?src=bkmk.
2. http://www.cityofbarrow.org/content/view/5/46/.
3. www.census.gov/prod/cen1990/cp1/cp-1-3.pdf.
4. http://ndsn.org/jan96/alaska.html.

9

What Happens When Alcohol Outlet Density Decreases?

A Natural Experiment in Union City

Robert Nash Parker, Kevin J. McCaffree, Maria Luisa Alaniz, and Deborah Marie Plechner

INTRODUCTION

In chapter 4, we reported on the overall results of a study which examined the links between youth violence and outlet density in three cities with significant Mexican American populations. One of the three cities included in the study was Union City, California; Union City is part of a "tri-city" area in the San Francisco East Bay which includes Hayward to the north and Fremont to the south. This city was selected because of its largely suburban population, which served to balance findings across urban Redwood City and rural Gilroy, the two other sites of the project. Though Union City does have a commercial strip, the surrounding environment is largely residential. At the time of data collection, Union City had a population of 53,762 and a Mexican population of around 24 percent.

In chapter 8, we reported on the results of a "natural experiment" in the banning of alcohol in an isolated community. Events in Union City presented us a similar opportunity for evaluating the impact of a similar intervention which occurred without input or advanced knowledge of the investigators of the Youth Violence and Outlet density, or Three City project. In this case, the "experiment" was to change the way zoning rules were used in Union City in such a manner as to cause a drop in the outlet density in five of the thirty-two block groups that constituted the city in the 1990 census definitions. As we were in the midst of a three year data collection, and the policy change enacted by the Union City Council was effective as of January 1, 1994, the final year of our data collection, we were provided with a relatively strong before-and-after design. Data from the years 1992 and 1993 gave us a baseline, and the 1994 data, subsequent to the implementation of the zoning change, provided the experimental stimulus and the post stimulus data on youth violence.

A ZONING INTERVENTION IN UNION CITY

About every ten years or so, many cities in the United States undertake what is generally referred to as a General Plan Review. The General Plan is a term used in many cities in the United States for the collection of reports and documents that describe the current land use patterns within the city boundaries and the rules that will generally govern the development of new and modified land use patterns over the coming decade. As with any such general planning document, there are often exceptions to the general plan stipulations about which areas are supposed to be strictly residential, strictly commercial, and so on. Sometimes, traditional and historical land uses are "grandfathered" into the general plan, in recognition that certain city business and institutions may be important to continue in their current form and location, even if more recent development has changed the nature of the location overall. So, a once rural roadhouse restaurant and bar, well known in the area as a traditional watering hole, can be maintained even in a neighborhood that sees significant increases in new single and multi-family housing. Such housing is often constructed as cities grow and co-opt some of the formerly rural areas away from the central core. A city planning commission, or some similarly constituted body, is charged with reviewing the current general plan in light of new development, so that the overall character of the land use patterns, consistent with the general plan, is maintained.

During 1993, the Union City Council became concerned with variances that had been granted in the past, and which had accumulated in various neighborhoods around the city. As part of their efforts to maintain the intent of the General Land Use plan, they decided to revoke variances for commercial establishments that had been allowed to infiltrate areas classified as residential only in the previous general plan. The result was that in five locations around the city, businesses, including alcohol outlets, were forced to close their doors and cease their commercial activities. This decision had nothing to do with our project; we had made a presentation to the council early in 1993 to inform them about our project and activities in Union City. There was no indication, however, that our focus on alcohol and youth violence was related to the revocation of the zoning variances. The fact that all such variances given to commercial establishments were revoked meant that the Alcohol Industry could not claim that they were being targeted by this zoning review, and there were no court challenges, that we are aware of, to this action by the city council.

In short, the actions of the Union City Council provided the "stimulus" for our natural experiment; as of January 1, 1994, the final year of our data collection for this project, five US Census block groups in Union City showed a decline in outlet density. Figure 9.1 shows a map of Union City based on 1990 census data, and dots in five of the block groups where the zoning changes occurred.

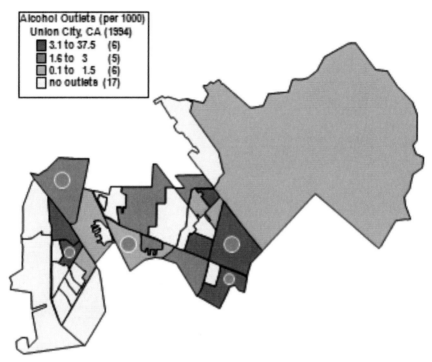

Figure 9.1. Courtesy of Robert Nash Parker.

Data, Measures, and Analytic Strategy

We refer the reader to chapter 2 for a full discussion of the motivating literature for a general analysis of youth violence, especially in communities with significant Latino populations, and outlet density (See also Parker, 1993; Parker & Rebhun, 1995; Pratt & Cullen, 2005). These previous studies and others suggest that variables representing poverty, family structure, and racial/ethnic composition are important at a minimum to include in any analysis of violence. Similar to the analysis presented in chapter 2, we include as control variables the percent of those living in the block group with an occupation who worked at professional, technical, and managerial jobs; the percent of the adults over eighteen who reported their marital status as divorced; unemployment rate; percent of households that reported earning $10,000 or less as a poverty measure; percent Latino and percent African Americans living in each block group; and outlet density for off sale alcohol stores. All of these measures are taken from the 1990 US Census, with the exception of outlet density, which is from the California Department of Alcoholic Beverage Control. These measures are used as predictors of youth violence, including murder, rape, assault, sexual assault and robbery, in which the victim and/or the offender was aged fifteen to twenty-four. All of these data were provided by the Union City Police Department. Finally, in the intervention equation, we also used a variable that was equal to 1 for the block group if the zoning review resulted in a decrease in outlet density, and 0 otherwise; as previously noted with figure 9.1, the zoning review impacted five block groups in 1994.

The statistical approach utilized here is somewhat different from that reported in chapter 2. In the former case, we analyzed all three sites in the larger study individually, and then merged the data together in a spatially corrected model of pooled multiple cross sections; all data analyzed in that case come from 1993. The results of that analysis are presented in table 2.1 in chapter 2; and for site 2, Union City, the results show that off-premise outlet density and the percent of professionals have significant and predicted directional effects. The approach taken here is referred in the literature as a Panel Model approach (a general term of which the model we estimate here is one type) or, more specifically, a pooled cross sectional and time series model (see Marcus, 1988; Kmenta, 1985). Thus, instead of taking one of the three years of data we collected for this project, as was analyzed and presented in chapter 2, here we measure outlet density, youth violence, and the decline in outlets resulting from the zoning review dynamically, in each block group, for 1992, 1993, and 1994. There are thirty-two block groups in Union City as of the 1990 Census, so our analysis here has ninety-six block groups, one set from each year. The remaining measures, derived from the 1990 Census data, are the same in each yearly set of block group data, and are therefore considered to have "fixed effects" in this type of model (see Kmenta, 1985). In other words, these variables such as divorce, poverty, percent Latino population, and so on, have a fixed effect in this model, while we allow a dynamic relationship to exist between youth violence and the alcohol outlet density–related measures. Given the fact that we have one city analyzed over a relatively short period of three years, it is reasonable to assume that the variables derived from the large body of literature on youth violence causation would have fixed effects as a backdrop for the understanding of youth violence. The pooled cross sectional model allows us to address a vital question: do changes in youth violence respond, independent of the fixed effects of poverty, professional occupations, etc., to changes in outlet density, either overall, or specifically in the five areas indicated in figure 9.1?

As this model is based on data from a real geographic location, with units of analysis that share common boundaries and are in close proximity to one another, as well as pooled across three years, spatial autocorrelation is also an important statistical issue (see Parker & Ascencio, 2008). We utilize software designed to estimate pooled cross sectional and time series models with the possibility of spatial autocorrelation included in the model (see Ponicki & Gruenewald, 2005).

Figures 9.2 and 9.3 give a picture of the dynamic nature of the youth violence and outlet density data. In figure 9.2 we show the crime data for 1993, the second year of the study. In figure 9.3, we show the 1994 crime data, along with the locations where outlet density declined due to the zoning review.

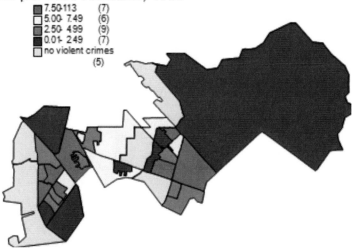

Density of violent crimes in Union City, CA
Crimes per 1000 residents, 1993

7.50-113	(7)
5.00- 7.49	(6)
2.50- 4.99	(9)
0.01- 2.49	(7)
no violent crimes	
	(5)

Figure 9.2. Courtesy of Robert Nash Parker.

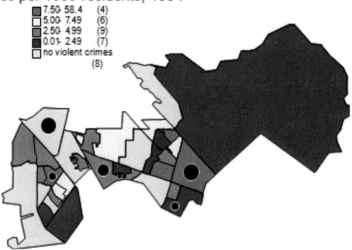

Density of violent crimes in Union City, CA
Crimes per 1000 residents, 1994

7.50- 58.4	(4)
5.00- 7.49	(6)
2.50- 4.99	(9)
0.01- 2.49	(7)
no violent crimes	
	(8)

Figure 9.3. Courtesy of Robert Nash Parker.

In comparing figures 9.2 and 9.3, the color scheme in both maps is identical, and this allows us to see less youth violence in three of the five block groups where the outlet density declined due to the zoning review. The other two block groups with declining outlet density remain in the highest violence category in both years, though a decline in violence may have occurred here as well, as our prediction suggests, within the upper range of the distribution across space in Union City.

We now present the results of two pooled cross sectional time series models with correction for spatial autocorrelation in table 9.1. These models are GLS estimators with a nuisance parameter estimated with a random effects approach; Hausman tests indicated that the random effects model was the appropriate estimator in both cases (for more detail about this issue and the Hausman Test, see Greene, 2011).

In the first column of table 9.1, we present the baseline model; the results indicate that the divorce rate, alcohol outlet density, and both population composition measures are significant positive predictors of youth violence across the three year pooled framework. These results are different than those presented in chapter 2 for site 2, Union City; in the latter case, the significant predictors were outlet density and percent professionals, with the percent of working professionals having the predicted negative effect on violence. Here, our variable measuring the percent of working professionals has the predicted negative sign, as the notion is that role models living in the neighborhood provide a protective factor for violence among youth. However, in the pooled cross section framework, this indicator is not significant. More importantly, the impact of outlet density is robust to the choice of data and statistical approach.

In the second column of table 9.1, we reestimate the pooled cross-section model with the addition of the closed outlets indicator. This indicator is significant and

Table 9.1.   Union City Zoning Intervention Results, 1992 to 1994 Overall Youth Violence Rate

Predictor Variable	Basic Model	Intervention Model	Interaction Model
Percent Professional Occupations	–0.915	–1.295	–6.233
Divorce Rate	19.070*	33.867*	31.447*
Percent African American	0.421*	0.664*	0.131
Percent Latino	0.049*	0.041	0.051
Unemployment Rate	4.536	27.128	–19.323
Alcohol Outlet Density	1.549*	1.154*	1.399*
Poverty	0.572	10.669	–38.142
Outlets Reduced (Five Block Groups)	—	–6.791*	–6.133*
African American/Poverty Interaction	—	—	5.391*
Constant	–4.868*	–7.960*	–1.628

* = Significant at p = < .05, Two-tailed test

Pooled cross section and time series analysis, three time points, N = 96 negative in direction, consistent with the prediction that reducing outlet density in these five areas resulted in a decline in violence among youth in these places. The divorce rate and overall outlet density remain significant predictors of youth violence, as does the proportion of African Americans who resided in the block group. This effect most likely represents unmeasured socioeconomic distress that urban African American communities often suffer from, and the possibility of an interaction effect between poverty and the African American population in Union City.

In column three of table 9.1, we examine this possibility by entering into the intervention model shown in column two a multiplicative interaction term measuring the combined effect of the proportion of the population that is African American and our economic poverty indicator (the percent of families with incomes equal to or less than $10,000.00). These results indicate that our speculation of an interaction effect is empirically supported by these results. The interaction term is significant and positive, and the previously significant positive effect (shown in column two) of African American population becomes non-significant once the interaction effect is controlled for. The effects of our variables measuring divorce, outlet density, and the decline of outlets in the five locations remain significant and in the predicted directions, as can be seen in column two of table 9.1.

DISCUSSION AND CONCLUSION

The results of this examination of the impact of a natural experiment in Union City show the impact of outlet density is indeed a causal factor for youth violence. Not only do we replicate the findings of countless studies in the literature that show a significant positive relationship between outlet density and youth violence, controlling for other important predictors of youth violence, but we also show explicitly what happens if outlet density is reduced within the context of a larger model of youth violence. It is of course unusual to find circumstances in which outlet density is actually reduced, although the recent recession in the US may have provided examples of such in a number of communities across the country; interested readers should seek out such circumstances and attempt to replicate the findings presented here.

The findings presented here should help to challenge the predominant market-oriented regime under which it has become so difficult to reduce outlet density as a protective measure in communities. The usual argument that prevents communities from taking action to reduce outlet density is the protection of private property elements that are an essential part of our legal system. An existing business generates income for its owners, provides employment for those who work there, and provides a service to the community. However, it is also enshrined within the legal and moral system of the United States that no business has the right to operate in a manner which harms the community in which it operates. It is this latter principle that allows local governments to regulate certain aspects of the way alcohol outlets operate, such as restrictions on hours of sale and the type of products that can be sold (see

Parker et al., 2011). Paying attention only to market factors (i.e., sales, taxation, and city income) to the detriment of legal and moral factors (i.e., the impact of alcohol sales on violence and underage and problem drinking) produces a disintegrative cultural climate where immediate monetary concerns take precedence over the health and well-being of the citizenry.

10

The Unintended Consequences of Alcohol-Based Environmental Interventions on Violence

Robert Nash Parker and Kevin J. McCaffree

INTRODUCTION

In this section of the book, we have examined a number of interventions that occurred independently of the goal of this research. Indeed, the researchers in these studies had no direct control over or influence on these community or environmental actions taken by state legislatures and national policy organizations, such as in chapter 7, with the minimum drinking age, in chapter 8, with the voters in Barrow going back and forth on the banning of alcohol in their isolated community, and in chapter 9, with the actions of a city council reviewing a land use plan for their community. In each of these cases, the actions taken were not in any way designed to impact violence in these communities or in the US states. By contrast, in the case discussed in this chapter, the community trials study, the interventions were designed by and either directly or indirectly implemented by the researchers. As you will see, the goal of these researchers was to reduce alcohol-related problem behaviors in each community they worked in: to reduce drunk driving, to reduce alcohol-related injuries in the local emergency room, to reduce underage access to and consumption of alcohol.

Our research question, different from the previous examples discussed in chapters 7, 8, and 9, is in this case to ask, were there unintended consequences of these deliberate interventions? Can we show that the implementation of these interventions in fact reduced violence, regardless of their impact on their intended targets? This is in its own way perhaps the most important test of the environmental approach presented in this book. It is one thing to come along after the fact and say that interventions that occurred due to the efforts of other actors for other reasons had the serendipitous effect of reducing violence, as we have shown in the previous three chapters. However, here we are directly testing an environmental prevention model; can deliberately organized and coordinated interventions designed to reduce consumption and related negative consequences other than violence, also be shown to reduce violence? Once again, we have upped the ante in our claim that alcohol consumption and availability have a *causal* effect on violence. We have shown in chapters 7, 8 and 9 that large scale legal changes in availability result in less violence; that dramatic changes in availability can have dramatic causal impacts on an isolated community; and that a direct reduction in availability can have a short term impact on violence in specific locations where that reduction has occurred, even in a general context where availability is still positively associated with violence. The consequences we predict here may be unintended, but they are not inadvertent; this is not an isolated community, and the interventions were not specifically designed to have the impact on violence we are looking for. This is a much stronger test of the environmental approach, and yet our results, as you will learn here, are strongly in support of this approach.

THE COMMUNITY TRIALS STUDY: BACKGROUND

The measure of any public health and safety intervention is the impact it has on improving the well-being of and opportunities for individuals. This may seem a banal point, but the positive benefits from smartly planned and targeted interventions cannot be overstated—especially as regards widely available, potentially dangerous, and largely misunderstood drugs such as alcohol. A well-executed community prevention strategy promises both an ecology conducive to the casual drinking demands of the majority while directing attention and efforts to stem misuse and abuse among vulnerable communities (such as youths and addicts). Within an ecological or community-prevention framework, the vulgarity and heavy-handedness of prohibitory efforts is set aside for more nuanced, attentive, and mobilized collaborative partnerships. The community is an ecology, subject to the limits and dangers and opportunities of any environment and the more one fortifies one's community against threats to its stability (whether these threats are related to crime, high rates of drug abuse, or infrastructure degradation), the better that community can grow and sustain itself for future members. An improvement of human life, and of the communities which sustain it, is a driving force not only of the science of prevention, but, as well, of sociology and of epidemiology more broadly.

Historically, alcohol policy was set at the national level and involved restricting commercial and economic access. This top-down approach imposes alcohol policy from the outside, with little or no attention to the specific dynamics operating in any given community. Alcohol policy imposed from above at the national, or even state, level is akin to a blanket policy that is assumed to work because of its own internal logic—little or no attempt is made to square the mandates of the policy with the local disposition and resources of the communities it will effect. Without question, many of these national or state-wide mandates on alcohol use have been effective in reducing crime and harm, for example, laws mandating a minimum legal drinking age (Voas et al., 2003) or those instituting alcohol beverage taxes (Chaloupka et al., 2002). Nevertheless, it is an argument of this chapter that the best possible prevention efforts are those that fully take the local community into account. Local communities may provide rich media and political resources that can help stabilize and institutionalize effective prevention efforts long after their initial implementation and funding has passed.

While educational interventions and alcohol recovery efforts have been used in the past to change individual attitudes toward drinking, community interventions that take a multi-pronged approach (including education and media) and which also engage local community leaders and policing agencies are far less common. Traditionally, interventions have focused on introducing new *programs*, be they educational or rehabilitative, as opposed to introducing new institutional *policy* buffered by a basic social and political infrastructure with which to sustain such policy. More modern and sophisticated approaches to community-policy intervention target the *environment* as the salient object of change or modification. An *environmental approach*, then, differs in its orientation to intervention only because of its greater emphasis on the total community. Treno and Lee (2002), for example, argue that environmental approaches to reducing alcohol use and misuse must target at least the following[1]:

- Vendors of alcohol, including both places where alcohol is consumed (e.g., bars and restaurants) and places where alcohol is sold (e.g., liquor stores and other shops)
- Social events where alcoholic beverages are sold and consumed
- Local laws, regulations, and enforcement agencies
- Local medical clinics and treatment facilities
- Social organizations that may support and promote public health campaigns, including schools and PTAs, churches, business organizations, and social clubs.

Focusing on the environment draws attention away from problem individuals or problem groups per se, and begins to take in a wider, more ecological, and more communal view of risk and prevention (see Holder, 2000 for a discussion). Indeed, community interventions targeted at reducing chronic illness such as heart disease and lung cancer have had some success, suggesting, in principal at least, the possibility of fertile opportunities to reduce rates of violence and addiction to alcohol using similar methods (Roussos & Fawcett, 2000). This may be doubly true in that threats of crime and addiction may be more proximate and visible concerns of a community compared with lung cancer or heart disease, as examples.

The community interventions described in this chapter begin to paint a picture of what thorough, and most importantly, effective, community prevention looks like. These community interventions were part of the most systematic and wide-ranging effort at the time to understand alcohol use and its consequences at local levels.[2] The Community Trials Project was initially designed in 1989 and included funding from the National Institute on Alcohol Abuse and Alcoholism and the Center for Substance Abuse Prevention for an intervention in one Southern California community. A follow-up proposal was submitted a year later for interventions in several other cities, as well, and the funding for these cities was also granted, thus officially beginning the Community Trials Project in 1991.

Over the next five years (1991–1996), interventions were launched in three diverse communities—in North Eastern South Carolina (Florence, South Carolina, the target site for this chapter, which will be discussed shortly) and Central and Southern California—and studied throughout this time by scientists at the Prevention Research Center in Berkeley, California. The communities chosen for intervention were not chosen at random but were, rather, carefully selected for their perceived conduciveness to policy change. In short, these communities had pre-existing coalitions in favor of the changes proposed by the Community Trials Project and, for this reason among others, were therefore assumed to be ideal locations to pilot the interventions.[3]

From the outset, the goal of the various interventions was to reduce alcohol-related accidental injuries and death through a unique combination of community outreach and policy change. Each community that received an intervention had a counterpart control community (matched for demographic similarity and existing in the same state or region) which received no intervention. This way, the specific effects of changed policy could be theoretically disentangled from simple random change or stochastic improvements which might have occurred regardless. Without the benefit of a control community, no meaningful conclusions could be drawn about the unique effects of the intervention. Without a control community for comparison, the internal validity of the entire project would be compromised.

THE FIVE COMPONENTS OF
THE COMMUNITY TRIALS PROJECT

Community Mobilization

The Community Trials Project consisted of five components, each addressing unique and uniquely important aspects of the intervention. The first component of the intervention addressed community mobilization and consisted of researchers and project members establishing and fostering local coalitions and task forces with common goals and aims related to the intervention. This coalition-building included local news media as well as public information campaigns led by community organizers. Such media advocacy provided legitimacy for both the Community Trials Project itself, as well as for the project organizers and researchers. Such efforts at community mobilization and outreach likely reduce the degree to which interventions seem like top-down impositions and foreign mandates, and increase the degree to which citizens and community leaders feel a sense of collective efficacy and ownership over the proposed social and policy changes.

Public information campaigns (including television and newspapers) can also bolster the positive effects of well-implemented social policy by faithfully reporting community improvements. This dissemination of information regarding the effects of community intervention is at least as important to educating the citizenry as the intervention itself. Local media advocacy also served to increase awareness of alcohol-related problems in the community, further reinforcing the legitimacy and importance of the intervention. Following Holder and Reynolds (1997), media can help demonstrate to community members that an intervention (a) has the potential to reduce alcohol-related problems, (b) is inexpensive to implement and maintain, and (c) has local citizen support (albeit along with opposition). Community Trials Project members also actively engaged in training community members to become local advocates, equipping them with both the information and network connections needed to bolster public information campaigns. In the case of the Community Trials Project, the sum total of these media and community outreach efforts resulted in both greater stability and greater awareness of the project goals and of local partnerships in the realization of these goals (for further discussion of the importance and dynamics of community mobilization, see Holder & Treno, 1997). This mobilization and media advocacy component was implemented toward the end of 1991 and was carried through 1995 (Holder et al., 1997)

Drinking and Driving

Cooperation with local law enforcement was critical to this second component of the Community Trials Project. All three experimental sites successfully implemented DUI checkpoints on at least two weekends per month. In addition, each police department received (on condition of their participation and their dedication to DUI enforcement units) technology that made detection of intoxication easier. Police in both California sites, for example, received pocket-sized alcohol sensors to aid enforcement (Holder & Reynolds, 1997).

Each site's task force members and project coordinator received training in media advocacy. In fact, an expert in media advocacy was made available to each site throughout the intervention period for this component (1993–1995). These media consultants worked closely not only with the project coordinators of each site (as part of the media component mentioned above) but also with the senior leadership in each police department to better coordinate and spread the news of impending DUI enforcement. DUI news and media coverage proved a crucial dimension to the success of this component of the intervention—numerous media events were planned around enforcement operations.

Also effective, was a strategy to continually shift media focus regarding enforcement every few months. Voas and colleagues (1997), all scientists involved in the intervention, described the effective media coverage: "News might focus on the novelty of the passive sensor flashlights [part of the new technology issued to officers to detect intoxication] at one time and on checkpoints at a later time, and on multi-jurisdictional 'sweeps' at a still later time even though the same basic enforcement techniques were being utilized throughout" (Voas et al., 1997, pp. 224). This roaming and attentive news coverage helped maintain the subjective perception of community members that, indeed, the local culture was changing regarding the seriousness of intoxicated driving. Thus the actions of researchers and community members to establish DUI enforcement checkpoints, along with ensuing media coverage, likely had direct and indirect effects on people's perceptions of risk of arrest (for a complete discussion, see Voas et al., 1997). This drinking and driving component was implemented in Florence, South Carolina, in January 1994 and carried through until the end of 1995 (Holder et al., 1997).

Alcohol Retail Access

In this third component to the Community Trials Project, each site was encouraged to construct a coalition of prominent community members, with each coming from, ideally, different social sectors (business, politics, education, lay citizenry). Local project staff also sought the participation of community advocacy groups such as Mothers Against Drunk Driving (MADD). The plan of the project staff was to have this newly constructed coalition, unique to each site, take novel steps toward addressing alcohol access issues and minimizing alcohol-related trauma.

The specifics of this component of the intervention were entirely dependent on the goals and concerns of each community-led coalition, but researchers emphasized the importance of identifying perceived problem areas, along with assessments of available community resources for combating alcohol-related problems. Among these suggested available resources were local city planning and zoning ordinances which often provide avenues for decreasing outlet density as well as implementing other preventive restrictions (Reynolds et al., 1997, and see chapter 9). Local media outlets were also, once again, used throughout this component to help increase local awareness of the dangers of high levels of outlet density as well as to inform the community of the ongoing implementation and prevention efforts.

This component, and the inter-community coalition building it encouraged, served, in part, to hand over autonomous prevention efforts to the community. Ideally, these coalitions at each site would establish themselves as viable forces for prevention and public safety *before* the Community Trials Project evaluation period ended. This way, community-led coalitions would be available to further institutionalize successful interventions and policies moving forward (for a complete discussion, see Reynolds et al., 1997). This underage access component was implemented in early 1994 and carried through until the end of 1996 (Holder et al., 1997).

Responsible Beverage Service

The fourth component of the Community Trials Project addressed the actions of those who directly disseminated alcohol in the community. The purpose of this component was to reduce the prevalence of intoxication at on-site and off-site alcohol establishments by educating vendors and their employees about the risks and consequences of serving intoxicated patrons (Holder, 2000; Holder et al., 1997). More specifically, alcohol beverage licensees and managers were expected to increase their monitoring of customer consumption, halt or avoid promoting "special deals" on alcoholic beverages (such as two-for-one), and increase promotions of food and non-alcoholic beverages. Beverage wholesalers and Alcohol Beverage Control (ABC) officials as well as local law enforcement were recruited to participate in and help enforce the policy changes of the intervention. Voluntary community associations such as Mothers Against Drunk Driving (MADD) and Alcoholics Anonymous (AA) were also recruited to participate.

In a variety of ways, researchers and project members established connections with local community members in order to implement new policies surrounding responsible beverage service (RBS). In the Northern California site, this networking consisted of public presentations by researchers regarding the experiences and past successes of such policies as well as visits to neighboring communities and meetings with local community leaders (Saltz & Stanghetta, 1997). In the Southern California community and South Carolina communities, similar strategies were adopted, along with successful attempts by researchers to tie their prevention efforts to preexisting activist committees and advisory groups.

After establishing training venues in each location and securing the endorsements of local Chambers of Commerce and ABC officials, researchers identified liquor stores and restaurants with high sales and customer volume to serve as targets for the intervention. The training curriculum used for managers and servers focused on three major aspects of RBS: knowledge requirements (participants must understand local and federal alcohol laws, signs of intoxication, and the physiological effects of elevated blood alcohol levels, etc.), skill requirements (participants must understand how to estimate BAC by number of drinks served, how to pace patron alcohol consumption, etc.), and various store policy recommendations (making visible "twenty-one and over" signs, etc.) that were provided to management only. It should be noted that training curricula was translated into Spanish for the California sites to ensure thorough implementation. This manager and server training was conducted routinely in all three sites during the implementation period (see Saltz & Stanghetta, 1997 for a full discussion). This component was implemented in Florence in early 1995 and carried through until the end of 1996 (Holder et al., 1997).

Underage Access

This component was the last to be implemented in the Community Trials Project. Holder and Reynolds (1997) point out that community members from each site were so incredibly eager to reduce consumption by minors that researchers worried other components might be overlooked. For this reason, the component targeting underage drinkers was slightly delayed to allow the full implementation of responsible beverage service instruction and other, perhaps less galvanizing, interventions.

This underage access component was made up of three basic interventions: enforcement, server and manager training, and media advocacy. Researchers mailed letters to vendors advising them of impending increased enforcement efforts regarding underage drinking laws. These letters were followed up by police "stings" or decoy operations whereby an underage confederate of the police attempts to purchase alcohol illegally. Across the three sites, 148 outlets were subject to decoy "stings" between July 1995 and May 1996 resulting in a total of twenty-two violations and subsequent citations (Grube, 1997). By rather stark contrast, in the year prior to this intervention, only four citations for illegal underage sales had been issued.

The second aspect of the underage drinking component included server and management training not unlike the training administered in the previous component mentioned above, but with a different focus. Server training in this component was meant to specifically address sales to minors and included improving off-site (i.e., liquor store as opposed to restaurant) server awareness of underage drinking laws, teaching servers to spot fake IDs, and teaching vendors conversational skills for refusing sales to underage customers (Grube, 1997). This server training took, on average, less than two hours and the manager training (which consisted largely of suggestions of effective store policies) took just slightly longer. Though participation in this training was voluntary, researchers solicited participation in various strategic ways within each community—in some cases where a simple letter from the project coordinator inviting participation was insufficient, supporting letters from the local police were used to further "motivate" participation (Grube, 1997).

As has been true throughout this discussion of the salient components of the Community Trials Project, media advocacy played a large role in this component as well. The project coordinator at each site arranged for news media coverage of enforcement activities where and when they occurred. Coverage wasn't restricted to local television news, but also included frequent newspaper articles updating readers as to the nature of the decoy operations as well as to the number of outlets targeted and the number of violators. In some cases, television news media was even able to set up hidden cameras during decoy operations to further immerse viewers and the larger community in prevention efforts (for a complete discussion, see Grube, 1997). This component was implemented in Florence in mid-1995 and carried through until the end of 1996 (Holder et al., 1997).

Florence, South Carolina

Florence, the biggest city in Florence County, South Carolina, serves as the backdrop for the findings presented in this chapter. The results of the Community Trials intervention in Florence were not only positive, but especially encouraging, given Florence's unique demographics. Indeed, each city involved in the intervention saw decreases in problematic alcohol use and each achieved some level of community mobilization for future alcohol regulation (see Holder et al., 2000 for a review of results from each city).

Florence County, as mentioned above, is located in Northeastern South Carolina, and is a primarily rural area. This rural countryside also contains a large amount of unincorporated territory—of all sites included in the Community Trials intervention, Florence best approximated an isolated community. This relative isolation serves as a kind of informal control variable, allowing researchers some modest certainty that outside influences and occurrences will have minimal impacts on the effects of the intervention.[4]

Demographically, as well, Florence is somewhat unique. Recall that the Community Trials study was initially funded in 1989 by the National Institute on Alcohol Abuse and Alcoholism and the Center for Substance Abuse Prevention, and that the interventions, from implementation to evaluation, lasted from 1991 to 1996. According to the 1990 decennial census, Florence City, South Carolina, had a population of 29,813 people, with just over 114,000 in the entire county.[5] Of this total population, about a quarter (7,472) of residents lived in a two-parent-headed household. Slightly under 30 percent (29.13 percent) of all households were occupied only by single mothers, with over half (51.4 percent) currently raising children under eighteen years of age. By comparison, nationally, female-headed households (with no husband present) in 1990 represented only 16 percent of all households. Additionally, only 69.1 percent of Florence residents had obtained a high school degree or higher, compared to a national average of 85.5 percent in 1990. The city of Florence was, however, nearly identical to the national average with regard to the proportion of its citizens with a bachelor's degree or higher (22.5 percent vs. 22.6 percent).

Racially, Florence is primarily split between Whites and African Americans who make up around 52 percent and 47 percent of the city's population. Hispanics and Asian/Pacific Islanders, according to the 1990 Census, collectively make up less than 1 percent of Florence's population. These population demographics (and, thus, the intervention) included a far greater proportion of African Americans compared to the United States population in general. In 1990, blacks made up only 12.05 percent of the nation's population, and whites, 80.28 percent. This "over-sampling" of minorities in the South Carolina intervention thus represents increased access to the African American community, indicating the results in Florence may be more generalizable to the African American community than other, more nationally representative cities with gross over-representation of Whites. Unfortunately, as mentioned above, Hispanics and Asians/Pacific Islanders represented only a small proportion of Florence's population, despite representing, collectively, around 12 percent of the population of the United States in 1990.

Again perhaps showing its rural character, the city of Florence in 1990 had only 60.6 percent of its population in the labor force, compared to the national overall labor force participation rate of 65.3 percent. Women, however, were only slightly under-represented in the workforce in Florence, with 54.6 percent of women in Florence working compared to 56.8 percent nationally. Economically, Florence, as well, lagged slightly behind the national average during the intervention period. Census data from 1990 shows the median household income in Florence to be $24,906 compared to $30,056 nationally. Poverty statistics tracked this disparity—10 percent of families nationally were below the poverty level in 1990 compared with 17.8 percent of families in Florence.

MEASUREMENT AND ANALYTICAL STRATEGY

The dependent variable we examine here is shown in figure 10.1: overall violent crime as reported to the Florence Police Department, measured in terms of the monthly count of all homicides, robberies, assaults, and domestic assaults.

Figures 10.2, 10.3, and 10.4 show the over time implementation of the interventions. In figure 10.2, we can see that the checkpoints for drunk drivers started in January of 1994, and reached a peak of forty per month in November 1995. The use of the breath sensors is shown as a cumulative percentage; the first one was introduced in February 1994, and the saturation point, at which all patrol cars were equipped with sensors, was reached in August 1995.

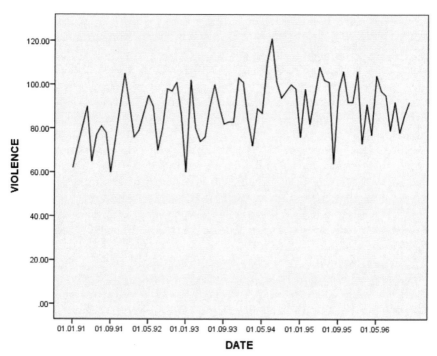

Figure 10.1.   Courtesy of Robert Nash Parker.

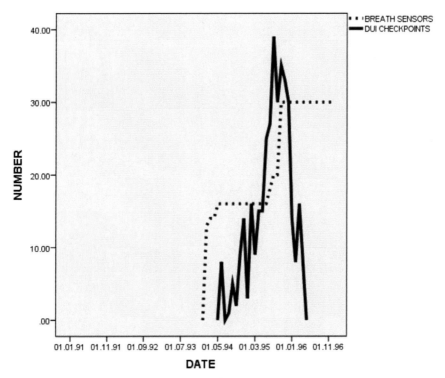

Figure 10.2.   Courtesy of Robert Nash Parker.

In figure 10.3, RBS training started in February 1995 for onsite establishments, and in February 1996 for offsite establishments; both types reached 100 percent of the establishments in both categories at the very end of the project, in December 1996.

Finally, in figure 10.4, we can see that the underage decoy operations began in August 1995, and finally reached saturation in December 1996.

These series as graphed are the interventions to be tested; they are measured for the analysis at 0 until the first occurrence, after which the series rise upward as penetration of the target is achieved, up to 100 percent; this is the case for the underage decoy series. For the RBS measures, we combined off and on site into one such cumulative measure. Finally, as the overlap of the checkpoints and usage of the sensors was considerable, we decided to use only the checkpoint series, measured as the number of checkpoints established per month.

Similar to the analysis in chapter 8, in which we analyzed monthly assault rates over a sixty-month period and looking for the effects of the interruption of the ban and lifting of the ban on alcohol in Barrow, this analysis uses Autoregressive Integrative Moving Average time series modeling to assess the impact of the interventions

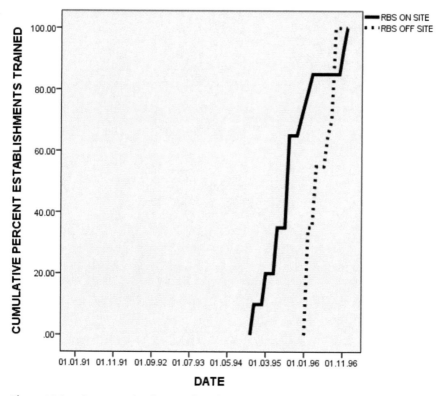

Figure 10.3.   Courtesy of Robert Nash Parker.

described above and graphed in figures 10.2, 10.3, and 10.4 on the series shown in figure 10.1, overall violence. Another term for this type of analysis is "interrupted" time series analysis (see McLeary & Hay, 1988). The logic of the analysis is that the dependent series, in this case, overall violence, is examined to see if the interventions "interrupt" the path of the time series over the period of the project. If the interventions have an impact, the series is interrupted from the path we could have expected it to take, and would show a statistically different path after the "interruptions" have begun and run their courses.

In addition, the dependent series has internal, time dependent processes that can be in effect so as to produce the path the series takes over time. These three components are the name of the model: Autoregressive; Integrated; and Moving Average. As in chapter 8, our first task is to identify which, if any, of these three components are operating in our violence series, and model their effects until what remains is the true underlying time series. Then and only then can we have confidence that any relationship we find in the model between violence and one of our interventions is due to the impact of the intervention on the violence series, and not due to some

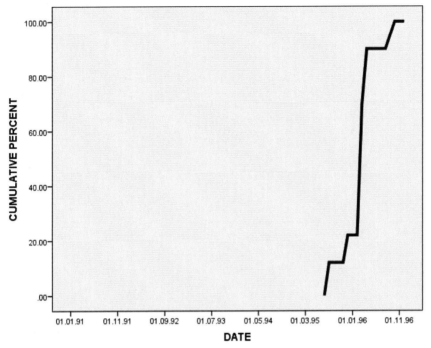

Figure 10.4.   Courtesy of Robert Nash Parker.

common component among the three basic components that is operating simultaneously in both the violence series and the intervention series.

Results

Although we will not go into the same level of detail as we did in chapter 8, the process started here as in chapter 8 with the identification phase, in which we look for evidence of the three components in our dependent series, model them, and examine the residuals for evidence that we have exhausted the internal components, and that the remaining "white noise" series is ready to compare to the interventions. As table 10.1 shows, we identified an autoregressive component in the DWI model, and the graphs of the residuals and the Q statistics both showed the adequacy of this model. For the RBS measure, we ended up modeling a seasonal autoregressive component; as these series are measured monthly over a six year period, the possibility of annual effects was present. Finally, for overall violence, we discovered and modeled a seasonal autoregressive component for the under-age decoy operations.

In the case of overall violence, we found that both RBS interventions and the underage decoys had significant and negative effects on overall violence. In other words, these interventions were sufficient to "interrupt" the expected path of the

Table 10.1.   ARIMA Results, Florence Site, Community Trials Project, Violent Outcomes

Independent Series	Overall Violence
DWI Measures	
Checkpoints	–.049
Movering Average	—
Autoregressive	–.481*
Seasonal Autoregressive`	—
RBS Measures	
On Site +Off Site	–.018*
Moving Average	—
Seasonal Autoregressive	–.698*
Constant	.033*
Off Site Decoy	
Decoy Measure	–.001*
Moving Average	—
Seasonal autoregressive	–.700*
Constant	.031*

*Indicates significance at p = < .05, two-tailed test

violence series in the post intervention section of the series. Although the DUI checkpoints effect is also negative, it did not reach significance. The findings then provide significant support for the idea that interventions designed to reduce alcohol consumption can be expected to have some impact, in the expected direction, on violence in the community.

CONCLUSION

In this chapter we made an assessment of the impact of a number of coordinated and researcher-initiated interventions in a community designed to reduce alcohol consumption overall in the community. The target of this effort was not to reduce violence, but we argue that given the substantial evidence of a relationship between alcohol, alcohol availability, and violence shown in the book in the previous nine chapters, and in the dozens and dozens of cited articles and books in the reference list, it is reasonable to hypothesize that interventions designed to reduce consumption would also have the benefit of reducing the amount of violence at the same time in the community. The results of this analysis show significant effects in one site of a three site national study. It is particularly interesting that the two interventions that show effects are those that both involve significant attention to the reduction of access and thus consumption among youth, responsible beverage service training, and underage decoy stings. Given that several of the chapters in this book, as well as many cited studies within these pages also focus on and find impacts of alcohol-related measures and alcohol-related interventions on youth violence specifically, it is perhaps not surprising that underage decoy operations, directed specifically at reducing access to and thus consumption of alcohol on the part of underage youth, and Responsible Beverage Service, especially in its off-site components, also directed significantly toward the reduction of sales to minors, would be the two conditions under which the reduction of violence would be found. Given all the evidence in this book and elsewhere that policies can indeed impact youth access, consumption, and related negative outcomes like violence but also drunk driving and accidents, the current study in this chapter provides yet another test, under different scope conditions, using a different methodology, that shows the same outcome. The Community Trials Project was a large-scale and relative expensive project, not by social science standards, but compared to the money spent on DARE and other aspects of the so-called war on drugs, declared recently by the Global Commission on Drug Policy to be a complete failure (Spokane, Washington, Spokesmen Review, June 2, 2011), the cost of reducing alcohol consumption among some members of the community, and the resulting decrease in youth violence, however modest, is truly an efficient way to spend public dollars.

NOTES

1. Adapted from Treno and Lee, 2002: 36.

2. For other contemporaneous community interventions which were also successful, see Perry et al., 1996, and Hingson et al., 1996. For examples of international community interventions outside of the United States, see Giesbrecht and Pederson, 1992.

3. Each city had an approximate population of around 100,000 people, with the California cities containing elevated populations of Mexican Americans (as compared to the national average) and the South Carolina location representing elevated levels of African Americans (see Holder, 2000).

4. For more on experimentations/interventions in isolated communities, see the chapter 8 discussion of Barrow, Alaska.

5. All statistics on the demographics for the United States and for Florence can be found in the 1990 decennial US Census: www.census.gov/prod/cen1990/cp1/cp-1.html.

11

Conclusion

Robert Nash Parker and Kevin J. McCaffree

Throughout this book, we have detailed a variety of ways in which researchers have studied alcohol consumption and criminal offending. Though scholars have been exploring a link between alcohol and violence for well over fifty years, much debate remains about how *causal* this link is. That is, does alcohol *accompany* violence or cause it? Note that implicit in this question is a concession that alcohol is often present during the commission of violence, as we have documented in this book. Statistically, one should be unsurprised if they are attacked by someone who has been drinking—though *causality* may be disputed, the presence of alcohol in an offender's system has become a disturbing regularity in American crime.

But what of the *causal* connection? As discussed in our chapter on violence and alcohol use in elementary school children (chapter 4), plenty of literature exists establishing the "myopic" effects of alcohol. Alcohol consumption narrows concentration, effectively over-focusing one on salient cues. Whatever cue is "salient" of course, depends on the situation. If this cue is another male at a bar who is picking a fight, intoxication can help escalate the situation by reducing behavioral inhibitions, increasing irritability, and focusing attention on the threat. Granted, *most* people who consume alcohol in any given setting, or on any given day, do not commit acts of violence or have acts of violence committed against them. Neither author of this book denies this. What matters, however, is that people understand the sources of their comfort with, and affection for, alcohol. As the first author of this book has detailed in a previous work (Parker & Rebhun, 1995), Americans have enjoyed a long history with alcohol. Starting with the colonial-style drinking of settlers, alcohol consumption became a daily activity, even among children, primarily because dirty water was hazardous and prevalent, but also because of a variety of folk myths about the nutritive and medical aspects of ethanol. Consequently, alcohol consumption was quickly woven into the fabric of American life; saloons and bars became both places to drink *and* hubs of social and cultural activity.

Thus, a major reason why *you* drink or enjoy the consumption of alcohol is cultural—this is what we do and how we enjoy ourselves. The very consumption of alcohol also has more proximate physiologically rewarding consequences, of course; alcohol is both an anxiolytic stress reducer and stimulating to reward centers in the brain that produce chemicals like serotonin. Nevertheless, a big reason why alcohol is the drug of choice for Americans—and not something else—is largely a consequence of the cultural preferences of those who settled here. As discussed in our chapter on the Barrow, Alaska, natural experiment (chapter 8), indigenous Native Americans indeed had and have customs where the consumption of alcohol is normative and traditionally appropriate. However, it was the rough-and-tumble binge-drinking *style* of European settlers that really placed alcohol in a central position in daily life.

Understanding the role of culture and history is critical. Alcohol is a part of who we are because we enjoy its use. This use, of course, can be responsible and fun or, conversely, excessive, irresponsible, dangerous, and under-regulated. Because of our cultural familiarity with alcohol, we forget how dangerous it really is. Alcohol is *consistently* found to be either the most dangerous or among the most physiologically damaging drugs one can consume. Alcohol's negative effects on organ function and interpersonal affairs are matched only by cocaine and heroin, and, most likely, not even by these (Nutt et al., 2010). We may tend to forget that alcohol is our cultural drug of choice because *we* have chosen this, and *we* have control over its influence, positive, negative, or otherwise.

Our chapters discussing environmental prevention and intervention (chapters 6 through 10) also highlight the important role of individual citizens in determining the impact of alcohol on their community's. A continuous theme with regard to alcohol policy and regulation has been the alcohol industry's insistence on unfettered, unregulated business practices. The controversy in Barrow, Alaska, is sadly not an unusual happening. The dynamic of natives trying to ban alcohol consumption to save their community, and alcohol industry–backed politicians fighting to keep stores open and selling, occurs commonly.

In fact, there is currently legislation in Nebraska that would curtail sales of highly concentrated single-serve malt beverages and circumscribe the operating hours of liquor stores. This legislation was introduced because of the devastating impact of alcohol abuse on the Oglala Sioux Native American reservation community located just over the state border in South Dakota (Williams, 2012). Small-town liquor stores near the Ogala Sioux reservation regularly sells over four million cans of high-alcohol content malt liquor annually to these natives and, consequently, the reservation has been nearly destroyed with alcoholism and dysfunction. Similar to the case in Barrow, Alaska, various Republican politicians in Nebraska have reportedly taken tens and hundreds of thousands of dollars from the alcohol industry (specifically, Anheuser-Busch) in order to keep liquor stores in the dilapidating community open and fully functioning (Williams, 2012).

As is typical, these industry-backed politicians appeal to "individual free choice." Everyone, they argue, can either choose to drink or not drink, choose to become an alcoholic or not. These, oftentimes Republican, politicians assert that it is immoral to regulate liquor store business because it is the fault of individual human drinkers if drinking becomes a problem, not the fault of the alcohol industry. This folksy over-emphasis on human "free will" is antiquated and all too easy to undermine with the literature of environmental crime prevention. Certainly, we all have the choice to buy this or that product, drink this or that drink. The rubber meets the road, however, with regard to the *structure of the environment within which people make purchase/ consumption choices*. Having "free will" to choose to drink responsibly means, almost literally, nothing if liquor stores dot each street corner and dominate the area as hangouts. People have to make choices within a structure of available options and if most of these available options are alcohol-related, addiction and abuse will be high regardless of the "willpower" of individual citizens.

Indeed, what does it even *mean* to say that individuals' "free choice" determines alcohol misuse and abuse? Does this mean, somehow, that the Oglala Sioux have *chosen* to be devastated by alcohol abuse? Does this mean that, as a collective, their life decisions have somehow *converged* on destruction-by-alcohol-consumption? Is not this hypothesis of self-destruction simply absurd on its face? Indeed, simply being born on a reservation that has been ravaged with alcoholism, poverty, and unemployment preferentially exposes new members of that community to the escapism of alcohol consumption and to the nihilism of addiction. Community members have the power to control the role of alcohol in their environment, if alcohol comes to take a massive toll on the social fabric of the collective. Alcohol outlets and in-dustry in a market economy exist to serve us, and to make our lives more enjoyable as consumers. If this business and this consumption gets out of hand, it is the moral responsibility of industry to bow to the wishes of a community and most certainly *not* the other way around. The shameless, thinly veiled bribery of alcohol-industry political lobbying demonstrates that the main concern of industry is not the citizens of a community, but the profit margins at the end of each fiscal quarter.

The issue of "harm" is very often treated as a simple subjective evaluation of a circumstance. One person's harmful situation is another person's excitement. Is harm purely subjective? Certainly, with regard to some contexts, yes, we might (and do) find it highly aversive to sky-dive, but this may be the life passion of another. On other matters, however, issues of harm converge dramatically. As members of a com-mon species, and members of a common society, all Americans must agree, almost by definition, that wanton and callous damage done to people and to communities is a harmful thing. Anyone who disagrees with this statement simply needn't be listened to, as a disavowal of the statement is nothing more than an open invitation to anti-social nihilism and indifference.

Clearly, of course, the crux of the above statement hinges on defining "wanton" and "callous" damage. Nevertheless, science advances by operationalizing constructs and testing them. There is nothing intrinsically metaphysical or fuzzy about the term "wanton" or "callous." By using the words "callous" and "wanton" we denote that the harm/damage is excessive, with no obvious benefit. In the case of Barrow, or of the Oglala Sioux in South Dakota, it is an *empirical fact* of the community, that the availability of alcohol now constitutes an eroding and undermining material force. This can be established by showing, as we have throughout this book, the role of alcohol in incidents of assault, homicide and sexual violence. When rates of these violent crimes are high, and alcohol can be statistically demonstrated to play a role in their occurrence, wanton and callous *harm* have been demonstrated empirically. One might make this more complicated, but we needn't. Harm is an empirical term, which cashes out in terms of violent and sexually violent acts. When these rates are excessively high, and linked to the arbitrary consumption of some drug, moral responsibility shifts to the drug-seller.

The Community Trials interventions in three cities, discussed in Chapter 10, are notable for reasons other than their beneficial impact on crime reduction. Recall, of course, that these Community Trials were highly effective in reducing alcohol-related crime. Community members were less likely to drink to intoxication and less likely to drive drunk; unsurprisingly, nighttime injury crashes declined 10 percent and assault injuries that required emergency medical attention declined by 43 percent (Holder et al., 2000). Additionally, relative to comparison communities, media attention to alcohol issues was significantly increased and over 400 managers and servers, working in restaurants with high-volume alcohol sales, received training in identifying and dealing effectively with intoxicated patrons (Holder, 2000). Perhaps as a consequence, underage drinking was reduced by nearly 30 percent (Holder, 2000). These, indeed, are encouraging results, but there is a great deal more to community intervention than crime reduction.

Oscar Newman, discussed in chapter 7 on environmental crime prevention, argued in his 1972 *Defensible Space* that a safe community is one in which a sense of territoriality has been established. By using the phrase "territoriality," Newman did not mean to reference a gang-laden, turf-defense kind of tribalism but, rather, that community members ought to embrace a sense of ownership of their entire community and not just of *their* house or *their* block. It may be a truism that humans by default think in terms smaller than the community level; indeed many undergraduates entering sociology find it much easier—more *intuitive*, even—to think about individual, micro-sociological dynamics than to conceptualize human life in terms of more abstract meso- and macro-level dynamics. Nevertheless, citizens live an embedded existence. One's house is embedded on a street, which is embedded in a neighborhood, sequestered in a single area of a city, which itself occupies a small niche within a county, and then the state. Thus, the more citizens can broaden the scope of their concerns, and take ownership of this territory, the more a sense of agency can be employed to stop or curb high crime rates, illegal or harmful advertising, underage drinking, and the like.

In many ways, researchers light the fire of this territoriality by simply reminding citizens that liquor companies and corporate alcohol interests have no more of a claim (indeed, far less of a claim) to the character of a city than the residents themselves. Researchers may, nevertheless, often be hesitant to even engage in community-prevention research (Holder et al., 1997). For one thing, researchers are often used to controlled conditions and a living, breathing, community is anything but controlled. Whether working in a laboratory, or within the confines of a specific statistical test, scholars are taught to control extraneous intervening variables so that *only* the target variables of theoretical interest are tested. Thus, in a researcher's perfect world, *all* community activity would remain identical throughout the intervention, with the *only change* being the intervention itself. Certainly if this were possible, and if crime declined, we would be able to attribute this to the intervention itself and nothing else. In reality, however, communities, and the individuals in them will do what they will do, regardless of what the researcher would prefer. This in itself likely turns numerous researchers off to the notion of community prevention research, but it needn't. Scholars, once getting over this limited point of view, have much to teach and, equally important, much to learn from such community research.

Researchers look at rates of behavior (e.g., crime) and use theoretical tools, gleaned from mountains of past research, to try and tailor beneficial changes, in the form of interventions, to a specific community. Community residents may unduly exalt the talents of researchers, for example assuming that researchers have some inaccessible privileged wisdom that cannot possibly be transmuted to the everyday person. As a point of fact, however, community members bring as much to the table as researchers. During the Community Trials Project, residents frequently assisted in pointing out neighborhood crime hotspots and gang hangouts and, perhaps more importantly, educated researchers on the "community culture" of the area which helps profoundly in determining which interventions are likely to work and how they might best be tailored to fit within the community with minimal disruptions (Holder et al., 1997).

Community members also need not only passively educate researchers about community dynamics. Nothing in the strategy book of community prevention research precludes residents from taking charge of the project at certain points. One great example of this, which occurred during the Community Trials Project, was the "Pregnant Pause" community awareness campaign initiated by residents (Holder et al., 1997). Initially, researchers had had little interest in addressing rates of alcohol-related birth defects, primarily because the incidence was too low to be captured statistically and compared with other communities. Community members themselves cared a great deal about this issue, and decided to take the initiative in creating Pregnant Pause. Researchers initially worried that this campaign would detract from the other goals of the intervention, as Pregnant Pause used both Community Trials resources and personnel. Researchers agreed to let community members and organizers take the helm and this strategy would pay off handsomely. As it turned out, the Pregnant Pause campaign solicited participation from local bar and restaurant owners who, in exchange for their participation in getting the word out about alcohol-related pregnancy complications, received free publicity. These bar and restaurant owners were thus primed about the nature of the Community Trials project through their participation in the community-led Pregnant Pause. Researchers in this case were simply facilitators for community-level prevention organizing. This early engagement from bar and restaurant owners also proved fruitful for later stages of the intervention, as the "responsible beverage service" component (which provided training and store-structuring recommendations to business owners), consequently appeared to local store owners as a mere extension of their previous participation as opposed to some random burden with no context (Holder et al., 1997).

All of this activity, and this interplay and partnership between researcher interest and community interest, may certainly embolden the sense of territoriality discussed by Newman (1972). There is yet another aspect of one's territory or community that might also be addressed—advertising. Corporations and small businesses advertise as a way of persuading customers to buy products. From the point of view of the advertiser, human consumers are mere symbolically manipulable subjects equipped with a very coveted resource (cash); very often, little to no corporate attention is paid to whether or not a product's prevalence in a community causes any harm. Get the product out and make sure sales are high. Any other consequences (such as alcohol-related pregnancy defects, alcohol-related crime, or underage drinking) are simply business "externalities" to be shouldered by the community.

As chapter 3 showed, alcohol advertising often has very specific, and statistically discernible, harmful consequences. Numerous other studies have found dose-dependent effects of exposure to alcohol advertising, and some have linked exposure to alcohol advertising to violence, though our study was perhaps the first to find *specific* effects of advertising by ethnicity. Nevertheless, other studies have shown that young boys who report high levels of exposure to alcohol advertising, either through media and entertainment or magazines, consume more alcohol than others who were less exposed (e.g., Connolly et al., 1994; see also Anderson et al., 2009). The alcohol industry itself frequently claims that their primary objective for aggressive advertising campaigns is to simply switch consumers' brand allegiance and *not* to encourage excess drinking or violence. Certainly, the alcohol industry is free to claim this, but they are not entitled to their own reality. In fact, exposure to alcohol advertising not only increases the amount of alcohol young people consume, it also increases the amount of anti-social aggression exhibited. One study, for example, found that young males who reported both a personal affinity for alcohol advertisements (i.e., thought them humorous or amusing) as well as a personal brand allegiance to some alcohol company, consumed more alcohol on average and were more likely to be involved in drunken physical altercations and disputes (Casswell & Zhang, 1998). A possible facilitating link between alcohol advertising, drinking, and aggression is the childishly macho nature of some of the ads, which appear to be selling male camaraderie and defiant machismo more than alcohol (e.g., Casswell & Zhang, 1998; see also Anderson et al., 2009 for a review of studies).

It perhaps is not obvious that businesses do more than sell products. In order to sell a product, the customer must be sold on what the product represents, or on how the product might be useful or enjoyable. This process of selling and promoting the product is akin to an informational campaign—here is the product, here's what it can do, now buy it! Alcohol companies are, however, in no way beholden to any accurate representation of the product or, indeed, to a representation of it at all. Much alcohol advertising today sells a lifestyle, or a desirable disposition, such as having many friends or being sexually desirable. Obviously, the alcohol itself will glean neither of these enviable dispositions, but one's implicit association between the product and some vague sense of contentment and enjoyment has proven more than sufficient to sell alcohol in consistently high quantities (Hill & Casswell, 2004).

Consequently, one of the primary and most prevalent educational resources for young people to learn about alcohol is alcohol advertising itself. This advertising is obviously biased toward industry desires for increased sales, of course, and completely unconcerned with educating the populace about the dangers of consumption. Indeed, content analyses of alcohol advertisements have shown that consequences to health and risk of aggression and violence are almost never portrayed in the advertisements themselves (Anderson et al., 2009). The alcohol industry, through its advertisements, "educates" its consumers about the mythical and fantastic goodies that comes one's way upon consumption (i.e., friendship, romance, memories, status) while intentionally and insidiously obscuring the side effects and risks of consumption. Perhaps "drink responsibly" is just vague enough not to hurt business. The Federal Trade Commission (FTC) continues to allow such advertising to be "self-regulated" by the alcohol industry, despite frequent FTC reports of code violations and of illegal attempts to target minors (Hill & Casswell, 2009).

As Hill and Casswell (2009) point out, alcohol advertising strategies were built off of cigarette-promoting tactics after the fad of smoking began to fade. Alcohol advertising in and around sporting events increased dramatically in 1970, the year smoking ads were banned. Conveniently, tobacco company Phillip Morris, sensing a downturn in demand, took the helm of Miller Breweries, which, at the time, just happened to be the sponsor of the Atlanta Braves. Tactics that had proved successful in selling cigarettes were immediately applied to alcohol advertising. Just as promoting a lavish or high-status, contented lifestyle had sold cigarettes, so it also began to sell booze. Taking a page from Miller's playbook, Coors and Anheuser-Busch also began to roll out lifestyle and sex appeal–oriented advertisements to sell their alcohol products as well (Hill & Casswell, 2009).

Does the alcohol industry *know* that their advertisements are causing underage youth (and adults) to drink excessively and become violent? One way to explore this question is to look at magazines that youth (under the legal drinking age of twenty-one) tend to read and to determine whether or not these publications appear to be targeted by the alcohol industry. As it turns out, targeting seems likely. A study by

Garfield and colleagues (2003), published in the *Journal of the American Medical Association*, found that beer advertising increased progressively as a magazine's youth readership increased. The authors write,

> To our knowledge, this study is the first to use advertisement placement frequency to statistically examine the association between alcohol industry magazine advertising and adolescent readership. We found that after adjustment for age, sex, race, and household income of magazine readers, as well as year, frequency of publication, and cost per advertisement, both beer and distilled liquor advertisements appeared more frequently in magazines with higher adolescent readership from 1997 through 2001. This relationship was nearly log linear, with the frequency of advertising increasing exponentially as adolescent readership increased. (Garfield et al., 2003: 2427)

Additionally, this targeting of young adolescent males with specifically beer and hard liquor is consistent with consumption demographics (young males tend to prefer the consumption of beer and hard liquor over wine), another indicator that alcohol advertisements are specifically tailored to underage drinkers. If this apparent targeting of underage drinkers was simply accidental, why didn't the proportion of wine advertisements *also* increase with adolescent readership? Alcohol industry marketing teams have access to the same demographic and consumption data as criminologists and sociologists; if *we* know potential young male alcohol consumers are reading these magazines, presumably so do they. No watertight case can be made that industry insiders are directly intending to market to underage drinkers. Yet, if criminologists are aware of the link between youth-targeted advertising, consumption, and potential aggression, what possible excuse remains for industry denials and evasions?

Given this firm foundation for arguing that alcohol produces harm in terms of violent crime, what should we do about this? Once again, it requires no great philosophical, methodological, or statistical leap of faith to argue that we should try and reduce this harm by utilizing a well-defined and practiced framework for alcohol control that dozens and dozens of political national states have built during the last two centuries. Specifically, what are the implications of the research presented in the previous chapters for local policy? If we accept the findings presented here, what should we do?

Some would argue that it is not the place of researchers like us to draw policy implications from our findings. We reject the notion most emphatically; we argue instead that it is irresponsible for researchers to act as if their findings have no implications for policy, and/or it is not the researcher's place to argue for the policy implications of their findings. Others will, inevitably, take such findings and make of them what they will, not always in honesty or from goodwill, but to let that be the only source of analysis of the implications of this research would border on criminal neglect in our view. An infamous example involves the California law governing prison policy, three strikes; a prominent expert produced a report prior to the enactment of three strikes which was used by its proponents to justify its passage, even through the report itself argued that three strikes was much less effective than other, more preventative alternatives. The original report did not sufficiently emphasize these alternatives, and was used effectively to convince voters that three strikes would be effective; the researcher later claimed he was misunderstood. However, if the original report had been more direct and emphatic about the weaknesses of three strikes relative to the alternatives, it would have been more difficult to claim the authority of the original report as supportive of this disastrous policy (see Greenwood et al., 1994; Parker, 2012 for discussion of this case). Despite what others may do with our results, we want to be up front and specific about what we think communities can and should do to reduce and prevent alcohol-related violence based on our research findings as reported here.

The first policy imperative is to lower consumption at the local level. In chapter 1, we show that consumption places one not only at risk for criminal victimization, but also at risk for injuries resulting from those victimizations. Less drinking in this context would lead to fewer victims and to fewer injured victims. Second, and equally important or more so, several of the chapters have shown how we can reduce youth involvement in violence by reducing youth access to alcohol; chapters 2, 3, 4, 7, 9, and 10 all show in various ways that reducing access to alcohol for youth has preventative and positive effects. Thus policies designed to reduce youth access to alcohol are also imperative. This is a very easy policy prescription, as we already have on the books a minimum drinking age, and we already make effects, some more, some less effective, to enforce this law.

Chapter 3, which reports the results of the advertising with sexually commodifying and ethnically targeted models, could be a strong impetus to take some action at the local level to ban or reduce the impact of such ads. Under the 1973 US Supreme Court case *Miller v. California*, some of the ads shown in chapter 3 certainly pass all three tests required by the Court in that landmark case, namely that a) the material depicted, taken as a whole, appeals to prurient interest; b) that the work depicts in a patently offensive manner, sexual conduct as defined by the state; and c) that the work has no literary, political, artistic, or scientific value. These tests are not to be applied by experts, policy analysts, or industry representatives, but by the community members themselves. If community members are offended by the nature of that depicted in these ads, local standards can be applied and would be upheld in court in our view. We offer this view not as legal experts, which we are not, but in terms of local community values; not all communities would agree with us, but we suspect that many communities would. The exciting thing about this finding from a policy point of view is that sexual assault is one of the most difficult crimes to prevent; if local communities could gain some leverage based on restricted certain kinds of alcohol ads in local liquor outlets, this would be a significant benefit for young women and cause no real pain to the stores or the industry—the latter can still plaster their stores with all kinds of ads, just not ones that also encourage sexual assault.

Chapter 4 contains much that is speculative and uncertain, but the results of our attempt to investigate alcohol's role in violence among those aged seven to nine years old reminds us that we should not ignore these very young children, or pretend that they are too young to be impacted by alcohol. Schools and parents should be vigilant to make sure that any children having exposure to alcohol get the interventions that are needed at these very young ages if necessary. The findings from chapter 5 remind us that the problem of alcohol-related violence and its links to gender structures and interaction patterns in the family, the home, and the workplace are not limited to one country or culture. These finds and those from chapter 3 remind us that alcohol and violence are not an isolated problem in society, but that alcohol is integrated into society, and interacts in specific and preventable ways with other institutions and characteristics of society, like gender interaction and the workplace. This means that we should take action to enhance and create new initiatives in prevention involving these interactions and institutions as well.

The results reported in the second half of this book, which focus on interventions, intentional or unintentional, and their impacts on alcohol-related violence, constitute a "to do" list for any community concerned about harm reduction. In most of these cases, nothing drastic happened to the alcohol industry's ability to sell alcohol, or to the retailer's ability to make profits. Minor changes in availability, in youth access, and in responsible service practices, the latter especially based on laws and regulations already in existence, resulted in reduced harm in terms of violence in the community. The major exception is the Barrow, Alaska, case, reported in chapter 8. If a community in an isolated area like Barrow, or on an Indian Reservation in South Dakota (see Williams, 2012), wants to take the drastic step of trying prohibition to prevent large-scale harm to their community, should the right of an industry to profit from that harm overshadow the right of the people to self-determination? Once again, no great harm to the alcohol industry would result if one isolated community gave up buying alcohol; the choice should be up to the community in any case. Chapters 7, 8, 9, and 10 show that community-based policies and practices can change the link between alcohol and violence, so in addition to reducing consumption, reducing availability, limiting youth access, and training servers to follow existing reasonable standards for whom and when and how to serve alcohol are just prudent common sense and good local practice to reduce harm from alcohol and to enhance its safe enjoyment by the community at large. Once again, no harm is done to the industry and to the retailers who sell alcohol, so why not act to reduce harm and prevent alcohol-related violence?

We can and should call for replication of the research in this volume, but in the larger sense this replication has been and is being done in multiple places by many scholars and researchers all over the developed world, and, increasing, in nations outside the traditionally wealthy, western, and northern countries as you read this. Waiting in the face of overwhelming evidence before acting is no virtue at all. Some will read this as an attack on business, but this is a false dichotomy. No one wants a business, no matter how profitable and how many jobs it would produce, that creates large-scale harm to the workers and customers and nearby residents from byproducts of the business. This is also not an all-or-nothing proposition, another kind of false dichotomy that is often offered up in the face of increasing pressure to act to reduce alcohol-related harm. No one is on a slippery slope from booze flowing like water to prohibition; there is no slope, slippery or otherwise. There is a space to have a reasonable discussion informed by the evidence which suggests that some significant regulation on the availability and sales practices of those who make a living by selling alcohol is necessary if we are to reduce the kinds of harms so well illustrated in the research discussed here.

We have shown here, along with many others working in this research and policy field, that we can reduce the harm from alcohol-related violence, without severely restricting the ability to consume alcohol for enjoyment and pleasure. We urgently need to act on that conclusion, as the result will be a safer and better society for everyone, including the industry, the seller, the drinker, and the non-drinker alike.

References

Abbott, P. J. (1996). American Indian and Alaska native aboriginal use of alcohol in the United States. *American Indian and Alaska Native Mental Health Research Online, 7*(2), 1–13.

Abel, E. L. (1987). Drugs and homicide in Erie County, New York. *Substance Use & Misuse, 22*(2), 195–200.

Akers, R. L. (1977). *Deviant behavior: A social learning approach.* Wadsworth Publishing Company.

Akers, R. L. (2009). *Social learning and social structure: A general theory of crime and deviance.* Piscataway, NJ: Transaction Pub.

Akers, R. L. & Jensen, G. F. (2006). The empirical status of social learning theory of crime and deviance: The past, present, and future. *Taking stock: the status of criminological theory.* New Brunswick, NJ: Transaction Publishers, 15, 37–76.

Alaniz, M. L, Cartmill, R. S., & Parker, R. N. (1998). Immigrants and violence: The importance of neighborhood context. *Hispanic Journal of Behavioral Sciences, 20*(2), 155–174.

Alaniz, M. L, Treno, A. J., & Saltz, R. F. (1999). Gender, acculturation, and alcohol consumption among Mexican Americans. *Substance use & misuse, 34*(10), 1407–1426.

Alaniz, M.L, & Wilkes, C. (1995). Reinterpreting Latino Culture in the Commodity Form: The Case of Alcohol Advertising in the Mexican American Community. *Hispanic Journal of Behavioral Sciences, 17*(4), 430–451. doi:10.1177/07399863950174002.

Alaniz, M. L. (1998a). Alcohol availability and targeted advertising in racial/ethnic minority communities. *Alcohol Health & Research World, 22*(4), 286–289.

Alaniz, M. L., Cartmill, R. S., & Parker, R. N. (1998). Immigrants and violence: The importance of neighborhood context. *Hispanic Journal of Behavioral Sciences, 20*(2), 155–174. doi:10.1177/07399863980202002.

Albrecht, E. (1984). Alcohol: Availability and abuse. *Circumpolar Health, 84,* 327–331.

Altheimer, I. (2008). Social support, ethnic heterogeneity, and homicide: A cross-national approach. *Journal of Criminal Justice, 36*(2), 103–114.

American Medical Association. (2002). *Alcohol Policy, Prevention Model*. Retrieved from www. alcoholpolicymd.com/alcohol_policy/effects_ep.htm.

Ammerman, R. T., Ott, P. J., & Tarter, R. E. (1999). *Prevention and societal impact of drug and alcohol abuse*. New York: Taylor & Francis.

Anda, R. F., Williamson, D. F., & Remington, P. L. (1988). Alcohol and fatal injuries among US adults: Findings from the NHANES I epidemiologic follow-up study. *JAMA: The Journal of the American Medical Association, 260*(17), 2529–2532. doi:10.1001/jama.1988.03410170077037.

Anderson, J. F. (2007). Screening and brief intervention for hazardous alcohol use within Indigenous populations: Potential solution or impossible dream? *Addiction Research & Theory, 15*(5), 439–448.

Anderson, P., de Bruijn, A., Angus, K., Gordon, R., & Hastings, G. (2009). Impact of alcohol advertising and media exposure on adolescent alcohol use: A systematic review of longitudinal studies. *Alcohol and Alcoholism, 44*: 229–243.

Angel, S. & University of California, B. (1968). Discouraging crime through city planning. *No.: WP-75*, 41.

Apel, R. & Kaukinen, C. (2008). On the relationship between family structure and antisocial behavior: Parental cohabitation and blended household. *Criminology, 46*(1), 35–70. doi:10.1111/j.1745-9125.2008.00107.x.

Archer, D. & Gartner, R. (1987). *Violence and crime in cross-national perspective*. New Haven: Yale University Press.

Armyr, G., Elmer, A., & Herz, U. (1982). *Alcohol in the world of the 80s: Habits, attitudes, preventive policies and voluntary efforts*. Stockholm: Sober Forglas AB.

Bachman, R. & Statistics, U. S. B. of J. (1994). *Violence and theft in the workplace*. US Department of Justice, Office of Justice Programs, Bureau of Justice Statistics.

Bailey, D. S., Leonard, K. E., Cranston, J. W., & Taylor, S. P. (1983). Effects of alcohol and self-awareness on human physical aggression. *Personality and Social Psychology Bulletin, 9*(2), 289–295.

Bailey, W. C. (1984). Poverty, inequality, and city homicide rates. *Criminology, 22*(4), 531–550.

Bailey, W. C. (1990). Murder, capital punishment, and television: Execution publicity and homicide rates. *American Sociological Review, 55*(5), 628–633. doi:10.2307/2095860.

Bailey, W. C. & Peterson, R. D. (1989). Murder and capital punishment: A monthly time-series analysis of execution publicity. *American Sociological Review, 54*(5), 722–743. doi:10.2307/2117750.

Balkwell, J. W. (1990). Ethnic inequality and the rate of homicide. *Social Forces, 69*(1), 53–70. doi:10.1093/sf/69.1.53.

Bandura, A. (1973). *Aggression: A social learning analysis*. Oxford: Prentice-Hall.

Barclay, G. A., Barbour, J., Stewart, S., Day, C. P., & Gilvarry, E. (2008). Adverse physical effects of alcohol misuse. *Advances in Psychiatric Treatment, 14*(2), 139–151. doi:10.1192/apt.bp.105.001263.

Barr, K. E., Farrell, M. P., Barnes, G. M., & Welte, J. W. (1993). Race, class, and gender differences in substance abuse: evidence of middle-class/underclass polarization among black males. *Soc. Probs., 40*, 314.

Bart, P. & Moran, E. G. (1993). *Violence against women: The bloody footprints*. New York: Sage.

Bean, F. D. & Cushing, R. G. (1971). Criminal homicide, punishment, and deterrence: Methodological and substantive reconsiderations. Retrieved from www.eric.ed.gov/ERIC-WebPortal/detail?accno=EJ049661.

Beaulieu, M. & Messner, S. F. (2010). Assessing changes in the effect of divorce rates on homicide rates across large US cities, 1960–2000: Revisiting the Chicago school. *Homicide Studies, 14*(1), 24–51.

Beck, K. H., Thombs, D. L., Mahoney, C. A., & Fingar, K. M. (1995). Social context and sensation seeking: Gender differences in college student drinking motivations. *Substance Use & Misuse, 30*(9), 1101–1115.

Bègue, L., & Subra, B. (2008). Alcohol and aggression: Perspectives on controlled and uncontrolled social information processing. *Social and Personality Psychology Compass, 2*(1), 511–538.

Bègue, L., Subra, B., Arvers, P., Muller, D., Bricout, V., & Zorman, M. (2009). A message in a bottle: Extrapharmacological effects of alcohol on aggression. *Journal of Experimental Social Psychology, 45*(1), 137–142. doi:10.1016/j.jesp.2008.07.018.

Bellenir, K. (Ed.). (1996). *Substance abuse sourcebook*. Detroit, MI: Omnigraphics.

Berk, R. A. (1983). An introduction to sample selection bias in sociological data. *American Sociological Review, 48*(3), 386–398. doi:10.2307/2095230.

Berreman, G. D. (1956). Drinking patterns of the Aleuts. *Quarterly Journal of Studies on Alcohol, 17*, 503–514.

Blumstein, A. (1995). Youth violence, guns, and the illicit-drug industry. *J. Crim. L. & Criminology, 86*, 10.

Block, C. R. (1987). *Homicide in Chicago*. Chicago: Loyola University Center for Urban Policy.

Bondy, S. (1995). Alcohol availability and alcoholism. *Journal of the American Medical Association, 274*, 1832.

Boswell, A. A., & Spade, J. Z. (1996). Fraternities and college rape culture: Why are some fraternities more dangerous places for women? *Gender & Society, 10*(2), 133–147. doi:10.1177/089124396010002003.

Boudouris, J. (1971). Homicide and the family. *Journal of Marriage and Family, 33*(4), 667–676. doi:10.2307/349440.

Bowers, W. J., Pierce, G. L., & McDevitt, J. F. (1984). *Legal homicide: Death as punishment in America, 1864–1982*. Boston: Northeastern University Press.

Box, G. E. P. & Jenkins, G. M. (1976). *Time series analysis: Forecasting and control*. San Francisco, CA: Holden Day.

Brent, D. A., Perper, J. A., & Allman, C. J. (1987). Alcohol, firearms, and suicide among youth: temporal trends in Allegheny County, Pennsylvania, 1960 to 1983. *JAMA: The Journal of the American Medical Association, 257*(24), 3369–3372. doi:10.1001/jama.1987.03390240075026.

Broidy, L. M., Daday, J. K., Crandall, C. S., Sklar, D. P., & Jost, P. F. (2006). Exploring demographic, structural, and behavioral overlap among homicide offenders and victims. *Homicide Studies, 10*(3), 155–180.

Browne, A. & Williams, K. R. (1989). Exploring the effect of resource availability and the likelihood of female-perpetrated homicides. *Law & Society Review, 23*, 75.

Browne, A., Strom, K. J., Barrick, K., Williams, K. R., & Parker, R. N. (2010). *Anticipating the future based on an analysis of the past: Intercity variation in youth homicide, 1984–2006* (Final Report). National Institute of Justice.

Bureau of Justice Statistics. (n.d. -a). *Alcohol and crime: Data from 2002–2008*. Retrieved from http://bjs.ojp.usdoj.gov/content/acf/29_prisoners_and_alcoholuse.cfm.

Bureau of Justice Statistics. (n.d.-b). *Homicide trends in the US 1975–2005: Trends by gender*. Retrieved from http://bjs.ojp.usdoj.gov/content/homicide/gender.cfm.

Bye, E. K. (2008). Alcohol and homicide in Eastern Europe A time series analysis of six countries. *Homicide Studies, 12*(1), 7–27.

Callanan, V. J., Parker, R. N., Saltz, R. F., & Cartmill, R. S. (1997). *The role of alcohol in violent victimization: a comparison of alcohol use by victims and non-victims* (Unpublished Report). Robert Presley Center for Crime and Justice Studies: University of California, Riverside.

Campbell, D. T., Stanley, J. C., & Gage, N. L. (1963). *Experimental and quasi-experimental designs for research.* Boston: Houghton Mifflin.

Campbell, J. C., Webster, D., Koziol-McLain, J., Block, C., Campbell, D., Curry, M. A., Gary, F., et al. (2003). Risk factors for femicide in abusive relationships: Results from a multisite case control study. *Journal Information, 93*(7).

Campbell, J. C., Glass, N., Sharps, P. W., Laughon, K., & Bloom, T. (2007). Intimate partner homicide review and implications of research and policy. *Trauma, Violence, & Abuse,* (8), 246–249.

Carroll, L. & Jackson, P. I. (1983). Inequality, opportunity, and crime rates in central cities. *Criminology, 21*(2), 178–194. doi:10.1111/j.1745-9125.1983.tb00257.x.

Casswell, S. & Zhang, J-F. (1998). Impact of liking for advertising and brand allegiance on drinking and alcohol-related aggression: a longitudinal study. *Addiction, 93*,1209–1217.

Center on Alcohol Marketing and Youth. (2003). *Exposure of hispanic youth to alcohol advertising: Executive summary.* Washington, DC: Georgetown University.

Chaloupka, F. J., Grossman, M., & Saffer, H. (2002). The effects of price on alcohol consumption and alcohol-related problems. *Alcohol Research and Health, 26*(1), 22–34.

Chiu, A. Y., Perez, P. E., & Parker, R. N. (1997). Impact of banning alcohol on outpatient visits in Barrow, Alaska. *JAMA: The Journal of the American Medical Association, 278*(21), 1775–1777. doi:10.1001/jama.1997.03550210073042.

Clarke, R. V. G. (1995). Situational crime prevention. *Crime & Just., 19,* 91.

Clarke, R. V. G. (1997). *Situational crime prevention.* Criminal Justice Press.

Clarke, R. V. G. & Felson, M. (1993). *Routine activity and rational choice.* New Brunswick, NJ: Transaction Publishers.

Clarke, R. V. G. (1989). Theoretical background to crime prevention through environmental design (CPTED) and situational prevention. In S. Geason & P.R. Wilson (Eds.), *Designing out crime: Crime prevention through environmental design* (pp. 13–21). Proceedings of the Australian Institute of Criminology and NRMA Insurance.

Cohen, L. E. & Felson, M. (1979). Social change and crime rate trends: A routine activity approach. *American Sociological Review, 44*(4), 588–608. doi:10.2307/2094589.

Cohen, L. E., Kluegel, J. R., & Land, K. C. (1981). Social inequality and predatory criminal victimization: An exposition and test of a formal theory. *American Sociological Review, 46*(5), 505–24. doi:10.2307/2094935.

Collins, J. J., Gottheil, E., & Druley, K. (1983). Alcohol use and expressive interpersonal violence: A proposed explanatory model. *Alcohol, Drug Abuse and Aggression,* 5–25.

Collins, J. J. & Wolfgang, M. E. (1981). *Drinking and crime: Perspectives on the relationships between alcohol consumption and criminal behavior.* London: Tavistock Publications.

Collins, J. J., Jr. (1989). Alcohol and interpersonal violence: Less than meets the eye. *Pathways to Criminal Violence.* Thousand Oaks, CA: Sage Publications.

Collins, J., Research Triangle Institute, & National Institute of Justice (US). Center for the Study of Crime Correlates and Criminal Behavior. (1980). *Alcohol use and criminal behavior an empirical, theoretical and methodological overview.* Research Triangle Park, NC: RTI.

Comstock et al. (1975). *Television and human behavior: The key studies.* Publications Department, The Rand Corporation. 1700 Main Street, Santa Monica, California 90406 ($10.00). Retrieved from www.eric.ed.gov/ERICWebPortal/detail?accno=ED116674.

Connolly, G. M., Casswell, S., Zhang, J.-F., & Silva, P. A. (1994). Alcohol in the mass media and drinking by adolescents. *Addiction, 89*, 1255–1263.

Cook, P. J. & Tauchen, G. (1982). The effect of liquor taxes on heavy drinking. *The Bell Journal of Economics*, 379–390.

Cook, P. J. & Tauchen, G. (1984). The effects of minimum drinking age legislation on youthful auto fatalities, 1970–1977. *Journal of Legal Studies, 13*, 169–190.

Crutchfield, R. D. (1995). Ethnicity, labor markets, and crime. In D. F. Hawkins (Ed.), *Ethnicity, race and crime: Perspectives across time and place* (pp. 194–211). Albany, NY: SUNY Press.

Crutchfield, R. D. (1989). Labor stratification and violent crime. *Social Forces, 68*(2), 489–512. doi:10.1093/sf/68.2.489.

Crutchfield, R. D., Geerken, M. R., & Gove, W. R. (1982). Crime rate and social integration: The impact of metropolitan mobility. *Criminology, 20*(3–4), 467–478. doi:10.1111/j.1745-9125.1982.tb00472.x

Darke, S., Duflou, J., & Torok, M. (2009). Drugs and violent death: Comparative toxicology of homicide and non-substance toxicity suicide victims. *Addiction, 104*(6), 1000–1005.

Dearden, J., Payne, J., & Criminology, A. I. of. (2009). Alcohol and homicide in Australia.

DeKeseredy, W. S. (1997). Measuring sexual abuse in Canadian University/college dating relationships. In M. D. Schwartz (Ed.), *Researching sexual violence against women: methodological and personal perspectives.* Thousand Oaks, CA: Sage Publications.

De La Rosa, M., Sanchez, M., Dillon, F., Ruffin, B., Blackson, T., & Schwartz, S. (2012). Alcohol use among Latinos: A comparison of pre-immigration, post-immigration, and US born Latinos. *Journal of Immigrant and Minority Health, 14*(3), 371–378. doi:10.1007/s10903-011-9498-x.

DeFronzo, J. (1983). Economic assistance to impoverished Americans: Relationship to incidence of crime. *Criminology, 21*, 119.

Donziger, S. R. (1996). The real war on crime: The report of the National Criminal Justice Commission. *No.: ISBN 0-06-095165-6*, 336.

Dowrick, S. & Akmal, M. (2005). Contradictory trends in global income inequality: A tale of two biases. *Review of Income and Wealth, 51*(2), 201–29.

Dugan, L., Nagin, D. S., & Rosenfeld, R. (1999). Explaining the decline in intimate partner homicide: The effects of changing domesticity, women's status, and domestic violence resources. *Homicide Studies, 3*(3), 187–214.

DuMouchel, W., Williams, A. F., & Zador, P. (1987). Raising the alcohol purchase age: Its effects on fatal motor vehicle crashes in twenty-six states. *J. Legal Stud., 16*, 249.

Duncan, S. C., Duncan, T. E., & Strycker, L. A. (2002). A multilevel analysis of neighborhood context and youth alcohol and drug problems. *Prevention Science, 3*(2), 125–133.

Eckhardt, C. I. & Crane, C. (2008). Effects of alcohol intoxication and aggressivity on aggressive verbalizations during anger arousal. *Aggressive Behavior, 34*(4), 428–436. doi:10.1002/ab.20249.

Edgerton, R. B. & C. MacAndrew. (1969). *Drunken comportment: A social explanation.* New York: Aldine Press.

Ehlers, C. L., Gilder, D. A., Criado, J. R., & Caetano, R. (2009). Acculturation stress, anxiety disorders, and alcohol dependence in a select population of young adult Mexican Americans. *Journal of Addiction Medicine, 3*(4), 227–233. doi:10.1097/ADM.0b013e3181ab6db7.

Ehrlich, I. (1975). The deterrent effect of capital punishment: A question of life and death. *The American Economic Review, 65*(3), 397–417.

Ellickson, P. L., Collins, R. L., Hambarsoomians, K., & McCaffrey, D. F. (2005). Does alcohol advertising promote adolescent drinking? Results from a longitudinal assessment. *Addiction, 100*(2), 235–246.

Ellis, L. (1989). *Theories of rape: Inquiries into the causes of sexual aggression.* New York: Taylor & Francis.

England, P., Farkas, G., Kilbourne, B. S., & Dou, T. (1988). Explaining occupational sex segregation and wages: Findings from a model with fixed effects. *American Sociological Review*, 544–558.

Ennett, S. T., Tobler, N. S., Ringwalt, C. L., & Flewelling, R. L. (1994). How effective is drug abuse resistance education? A meta-analysis of Project DARE outcome evaluations. *American Journal of Public Health, 84*(9), 1394–1401.

Estrada, A., Rabow, J., & Watts, R. K. (1982). Alcohol use among Hispanic adolescents: A preliminary report. *Hispanic Journal of Behavioral Sciences, 4*(3), 339–351. doi:10.1177/07399863820043004.

Fagan, J., Piper, E. S., & Cheng, Y.-T. (1987). Contributions of victimization to delinquency in inner cities. *The Journal of Criminal Law and Criminology (1973–), 78*(3), 586–613. doi:10.2307/1143570.

Fagan, J. (1990). Intoxication and aggression. In M. Torny & J. Q. Wilson (Eds.), *Drugs and crime, crime and justice: A review of research, 13* (pp. 241–320). Chicago: University of Chicago Press.

Fawole, O. I. (2008). Economic violence to women and girls is it receiving the necessary attention? *Trauma, Violence, & Abuse, 9*(3), 167–177. doi:10.1177/1524838008319255.

Federal Bureau of Investigation. (1987). *Supplemental Homicide Report, 1976–1983.*

Federal Bureau of Investigation. (2010). *Uniform Crime Report.* Retrieved from http://bjs.ojp.usdoj.gov.

Felson, R. B., & Staff, J. (2010). The effects of alcohol intoxication on violent versus other offending. *Criminal Justice and Behavior, 37*(12), 1343–1360.

Felson, M. (1986). Routine activities, social controls, rational decisions, and criminal outcomes. In D. Cornish & R.V.G. Clarke (Eds.), *The Reasoning Criminal.* New York, NY: Springer-Verlag.

Felson, M. (1995). Those who discourage crime. In J. E. Eck & D. Weisburd (Eds.), *Crime and Place.* Monsey, NY: Criminal Justice Press.

Fendrich, M., Mackesy-Amiti, M. E., Goldstein, P., Spunt, B., & Brownstein, H. (1995). Substance involvement among juvenile murderers: comparisons with older offenders based on interviews with prison inmates. *Substance Use & Misuse, 30*(11), 1363–1382.

Fiala, R., & LaFree, G. (1988). Cross-national determinants of child homicide. *American Sociological Review, 53*(3), 432–445. doi:10.2307/2095650.

Firebaugh, G. (2006). *The new geography of global income inequality.* Cambridge: Harvard University Press.

Flanagan, F. J. & Maguire, K. (Eds.). (1990). *Sourcebook of Criminal Justice Statistics, 1989.* Washington, DC: Bureau of Justice Statistics.

Fradella, H. F. (2006). Why judges should admit expert testimony on the unreliability of eyewitness testimony. *Federal Courts Law Review.*

Garfield, C. F., Chung, P. J., & Rathouz, P. J. (2003). Alcohol advertising in magazines and adolescent readership. *Journal of the American Medical Association, 289*: 2424–2429.

Garriott, J. C. (1993). Drug use among homicide victims: Changing patterns. *The American Journal of Forensic Medicine and Pathology, 14*(3), 234–237.

Gartner, R. & Parker, R. N. (1990). Cross-national evidence on homicide and the age structure of the population. *Social Forces, 69*(2), 351–371.

Gartner, R. (1990). The victims of homicide: A temporal and cross-national comparison. *American Sociological Review, 55*(1), 92–106. doi:10.2307/2095705.

Gartner, R., Baker, K., & Pampel, F. C. (1990). Gender stratification and the gender gap in homicide victimization. *Social Problems, 37*, 593.

Gerson, L. W. & Preston, D. A. (1979). Alcohol consumption and the incidence of violent crime. *Journal of Studies on Alcohol, 40*(3), 307–312.

Ghose, A. K. (2004). Global inequality and international trade. *Cambridge Journal of Economics, 28*(2), 229–252.

Giancola, P. R. (2004). Difficult temperament, acute alcohol intoxication, and aggressive behavior. *Drug and Alcohol Dependence, 74*(2), 135–145. doi:10.1016/j.drugalcdep.2003.11.013.

Giesbrecht, N. & Pederson, A. (1992). Focusing on the drinking environment or the high-risk drinker in prevention projects: Limitations and opportunities. In H. D. Holder & J. M. Howard (Eds.), *Community prevention trials for alcohol problems: Methodological issues* (pp. 97–112). Westport, CT: Praeger.

Gilbert, M. J. & Cervantes, R. C. (1986). Patterns and practices of alcohol use among Mexican Americans: A comprehensive review. *Hispanic Journal of Behavioral Sciences, 8*(1), 1–60. doi:10.1177/07399863860081001.

Godlaski, A. J. & Giancola, P. R. (2009). Executive functioning, irritability, and alcohol-related aggression. *Psychology of Addictive Behaviors, 23*(3), 391–403. doi:10.1037/a0016582.

Golden, R. M. & Messner, S. F. (1987). Dimensions of racial inequality and rates of violent crime. *Criminology, 25*(3), 525–542. doi:10.1111/j.1745-9125.1987.tb00809.x.

Goldstein, P. J., Brownstein, H. H., & Ryan, P. J. (1992). Drug-related homicide in New York: 1984 and 1988. *Crime & Delinquency, 38*(4), 459–476. doi:10.1177/0011128792038004004.

Goodman, R. A., Mercy, J. A., Loya, F., Rosenberg, M. L., Smith, J. C., Allen, N. H., Vargas, L., et al. (1986). Alcohol use and interpersonal violence: Alcohol detected in homicide victims. *American Journal of Public Health, 76*(2), 144–149.

Gottfredson, M. R. & Office, G.-B. H. (1984). *Victims of crime: The dimensions of risk.* HM Stationery Office.

Gover, A. R. (2004). Risky lifestyles and dating violence: A theoretical test of violent victimization. *Journal of Criminal Justice, 32*(2), 171–180. doi:10.1016/j.jcrimjus.2003.12.007.

Greene, W. (2011). *Econometrics* (7th ed.). New York: Prentice-Hall.

Greene, W. (n.d.). *Econometric analysis.* New York: Macmillan.

Greenwood, P. W., Rydell, C. P., Abrahamse, A., Caulkins, J. P., Chiesa, J., Model, K. and Klein, S. P. (1994). *Three strikes and you're out: Estimated benefits and costs of California's new mandatory-sentencing law.* Los Angeles, CA: Rand Corporation, pp. 87.

Grekin, E. R., Sher, K. J., & Larkins, J. M. (2004). The role of behavioral undercontrol in the relation between alcohol use and partner aggression. *Journal of Studies on Alcohol, 65*(5), 658–662.

Grube, J. W. (1997). Preventing sales of alcohol to minors: Results from a community trial. *Addiction, 92*, S251–S260. doi:10.1111/j.1360-0443.1997.tb02995.x.

Gruenewald, P. J., Millar, A. B., Treno, A. J., Yang, Z., Ponicki, W. R., & Roeper, P. (1996). The geography of availability and driving after drinking. *Addiction, 91*(7), 967–984.

Guilamo-Ramos, V., Jaccard, J., Johansson, M., & Tunisi, R. (2004). Binge drinking among Latino youth: Role of acculturation-related variables. *Psychology of Addictive Behaviors, 18*(2), 135–142. doi:10.1037/0893-164X.18.2.135.

Gursoy, D., Chi, C. G., & Rutherford, D. G. (2011). Alcohol-service liability: Consequences of guest intoxication. *International Journal of Hospitality Management.*

Gusfield, J. R. (1986). *Symbolic crusade: Status politics and the American temperance movement.* Champaign: University of Illinois Press.

Haberman, P. W. (1987). Alcohol and alcoholism in traffic and other accidental deaths. *The American Journal of Drug and Alcohol Abuse, 13*(4), 475–484.

Hagan J., Albonetti, C., Alwin, D., Gillis, A. R., Hewitt, J., Palloni, A., Parker, P., et al. (1989). *Structural Criminology.* New Brunswick: Rutger University Press.

Hansen, J. P. (1985). Criminal homicide in Greenland. *Arctic Medical Research, 40*, 61–64.

Hawley, A. (1950). *Human ecology: A theory of community structure.* New York: Ronald.

Hedayati Marzbali, M., Abdullah, A., Razak, N. A., & Maghsoodi Tilaki, M. J. (2012). The influence of crime prevention through environmental design on victimization and fear of crime. *Journal of Environmental Psychology.*

Hepburn, J. & Voss, H. L. (2006). Patterns of criminal homicide: A comparison of Chicago and Philadelphia. *Criminology, 8*(1), 21–45. doi:10.1111/j.1745-9125.1970.tb00727.x.

Hill, L. & Casswell, S. (2004). Alcohol advertising and sponsorship: Commercial freedom or control in the public interest? In N. Heather & T. Stockwell (Eds.), *The essential handbook of treatment and prevention of alcohol problems.* New Jersey: Wiley & Sons.

Hindelang, M. J., Gottfredson, M. R., & Garofalo, J. (1978). *Victims of personal crime: An empirical foundation for a theory of personal victimization.* Ballinger Cambridge, MA.

Hingson, R., McGovern, T., Howland, J., Heeren, T., Winter, M., & Zakocs, R. (1996). Reducing alcohol-impaired driving in Massachusetts: The saving lives program. *American Journal of Public Health, 86*(6), 791–797.

Hingson, R. & Howland, J. (1987). Alcohol as a risk factor for injury or death resulting from accidental falls: A review of the literature. *Journal of Studies on Alcohol, 48*(3), 212–219.

Hipp, J. R., & Yates, D. K. (2011). Ghettos, thresholds, and crime: Does concentrated poverty really have an accelerating increasing effect on crime? *Criminology, 49*(4), 955–990.

Hirschi, T. (2002). *Causes of delinquency.* Piscataway, NJ: Transaction Publishers.

Hirschi, T., Gottfredson, M., Paternoster, R., & R. Bachman. (2001). Self-control theory. *Explaining Crime and Criminals* (pp. 81–96). Los Angeles, CA: Roxbury Press.

Hlady, W. G. & Middaugh, J. P. (1988). Suicides in Alaska: Firearms and alcohol. *American Journal of Public Health, 78*(2), 179–180. doi:10.2105/AJPH.78.2.179.

Holder, H. D. (1988). Review of Research Opportunities and Issues in the Regulation of Alcohol Availability, A. *Contemp. Drug Probs., 15*, 47.

Holder, H. D. (2000). Community prevention of alcohol problems. *Addictive Behaviors, 25*(6), 843–859.

Holder, H. D., Gruenewald, P. J., Ponicki, W. R., Treno, A. J., Grube, J. W., Saltz, R. F., Voas, R. B., Reynolds, R., Davis, J., Sanchez, L., Gaumont, G., & Roeper, P. (2000). Effect of community-based interventions on high-risk drinking and alcohol-related injuries. *Journal of the American Medical Association, 284*, 2341–2347.

Holder, H. D., Saltz, R. F., Grube, J. W., Treno, A. J., Reynolds, R. I., Voas, R. B., & Gruenewald, P. J. (1997). Summing up: Lessons from a comprehensive community trial. *Addiction, 92*: 293–302.

Holder, H. D. & Reynolds, R. I. (1997). Application of local policy to prevent alcohol problems: experiences from a community trial. *Addiction, 92*(6s1), 285–292.

Holder, H. D., Saltz, R. F., Grube, J. W., Voas, R. B., Gruenewald, P. J., & Treno, A. J. (1997). A community prevention trial to reduce alcohol-involved accidental injury and death: Overview. *Addiction, 92*(6s1), 155–172.

Holder, H. D. & Treno, A. J. (1997). Media advocacy in community prevention: news as a means to advance policy change. *Addiction, 92*, S189–S199.

Holder, H. D. & Wagenaar, A. C. (1990). Effects of the elimination of a state monopoly on distilled spirits' retail sales: a time-series analysis of Iowa. *British Journal of Addiction, 85*(12), 1615–1625.

Howland, J. & Hingson, R. (1987). Alcohol as a risk factor for injuries or death due to fires and burns: review of the literature. *Public Health Reports, 102*(5), 475–483.

Howland, J. & Hingson, R. (1988a). Alcohol as a risk factor for drownings: A review of the literature (1950–1985). *Accident Analysis & Prevention, 20*(1), 19–25. doi:10.1016/0001-4575(88)90011-5.

Howland, J. & Hingson, R. (1988b). Issues in research on alcohol in nonvehicular Unintentional injuries. *Contemporary Drug Problems, 15*, 95.

Huff-Corzine, L., Corzine, J., & Moore, D. C. (1991). Deadly connections: Culture, poverty, and the direction of lethal violence. *Social Forces, 69*(3), 715–732.

Hull, J. G. (1981). A self-awareness model of the causes and effects of alcohol consumption. *Journal of Abnormal Psychology, 90*(6), 586.

Hull, J. G., Levenson, R. W., Young, R. D., & Sher, K. J. (1983). Self-awareness-reducing effects of alcohol consumption. *Journal of Personality and Social Psychology, 44*(3), 461.

Hurd, N., Zimmerman, M., & Xue, Y. (2009). Negative adult influences and the protective effects of role models: A study with urban adolescents. *Journal of Youth and Adolescence, 38*(6), 777–789. doi:10.1007/s10964-008-9296-5.

International Labor Office. (1977). *Yearbook of labour statistics*. Geneva: International Labor Office.

Ito, T. A., Miller, N., & Pollock, V. E. (1996). Alcohol and aggression: A meta-analysis on the moderating effects of inhibitory cues, triggering events, and self-focused attention. *Psychological Bulletin, 120*(1), 60.

Jackson, A., Gilliland, K., & Veneziano, L. (2006). Routine activity theory and sexual deviance among male college students. *Journal of Family Violence, 21*(7), 449–460. doi:10.1007/s10896-006-9040-4.

Jacobs, J. (1961). *The death and life of great American cities*. New York: Vintage.

Janes, K. & Gruenewald, P. J. (1991). The role of formal law in alcohol control systems: A comparison among states. *The American Journal of Drug and Alcohol Abuse*.

Jeffery, C. R. (1971). *Crime prevention through environmental design*. Beverly Hills: Sage Publications.

Jeffery, C. R. (1999). CPTED: Past, present and future. *4th Annual International CPTED Association Conference*. Mississauga, Ontario (pp. 20–22).

Jeffery, C. R. & Zahm, D. L. (1993). Crime prevention through environmental design, opportunity theory, and rational choice models. In R. V. G. Clarke & M. Felson (Eds.),

Routine Activity and Rational Choice: Advances in Criminological Theory (pp. 323–350). New Brunswick, NJ: Transaction Publishers.

Johnston, J. (1972). *Econometric Methods*. New York: McGraw-Hill.

Johnson C. C., Myers, L., Webber, L. S., & Hunter, S. M. (n.d.). Alcohol federal bureau of investigation consumption among adolescents and young adults: The Bogalusa Heart Study 1981–1991. *American Journal of Public Health*, (85), 979–982.

Johnson, P. B. (1982). Sex differences, women's roles and alcohol use: Preliminary national data. *Journal of Social Issues*, *38*(2), 93–116.

Jones, N. E., Pieper, C. F., & Robertson, L. S. (1992). The effect of legal drinking age on fatal injuries of adolescents and young adults. *American Journal of Public Health*, *82*(1), 112–115.

Kellermann, A. L., Mercy, J. A., et al. (1992). Men, women, and murder: gender-specific differences in rates of fatal violence and victimization. *The Journal of Trauma*, *33*(1), 1.

Kelly-Weeder, S., Phillips, K., & Rounseville, S. (2011). Effectiveness of public health programs for decreasing alcohol consumption. *Patient Intelligence*, 29. doi:10.2147/PI.S12431.

Kelso, D. & Dubay, W. (1985). Alaskan natives and alcohol: A sociocultural and epidemiological review. Presented at the Conference for Epidemiology of Alcohol Use and Abuse Among US Ethnic Minority Groups, Bethesda, MD.

Kerr, W. C., Greenfield, T. K., Bond, J., Ye, Y., & Rehm, J. (2004). Age, period and cohort influences on beer, wine and spirits consumption trends in the US National Alcohol Surveys. *Addiction*, *99*(9), 1111–1120.

Klaus, M., Room, R., Single, E., Sulkunen, P., & Walsh, B. (1981). *Alcohol, society and the State* (vol. 1). Toronto: Addiction Research Foundation.

Kmenta, J. (1985). *Elements of Econometrics* (2nd ed.). New York: Macmillan.

Kohn, M. L. (1987). Cross-national research as an analytic strategy: American Sociological Association, 1987 Presidential Address. *American Sociological Review*, *52*(6), 713–731. doi:10.2307/2095831.

Krahn, H., Hartnagel, T. F., & Gartrell, J. W. (1986). Income inequality and homicide rates: Cross-national data and criminological theories. *Criminology*, *24*(2), 269–294. doi:10.1111/j.1745-9125.1986.tb01496.x.

Kratcoski, P. C. (1990). Circumstances surrounding homicides by older offenders. *Criminal Justice and Behavior*, *17*(4), 420–430. doi:10.1177/0093854890017004003.

Kuhns, J. B., Wilson, D. B., Clodfelter, T. A., Maguire, E. R., & Ainsworth, S. A. (2011). A meta-analysis of alcohol toxicology study findings among homicide victims. *Addiction*, *106*(1), 62–72.

Kuhns, J. B., Wilson, D. B., Maguire, E. R., Ainsworth, S. A., & Clodfelter, T. A. (2009). A meta-analysis of marijuana, cocaine and opiate toxicology study findings among homicide victims. *Addiction*, *104*(7), 1122–1131.

Lenke, L. (1982). Alcohol and crimes of violence: A causal analysis. *Contemporary Drug Problems, 11*, 355–66.

Lenke, L. (1987). Alcohol and crimes of violence in France and Sweden: A comparative time series analysis. Presented at the International Conference on Alcohol Abuse, Aix-en Provence.

Lenke, L. (1990). *Alcohol and criminal violence: Time series analyses in a comparative perspective.* Stockholm: Almquist & Wiskell.

La, S. & Dr, F. (2009). The effect of alcohol advertising, marketing and portrayal on drinking behaviour in young people: systematic review of prospective cohort studies. *BMC Public Health*, *9*, 51.

Landau, S. F. & Pfeffermann, D. (1988). A time series analysis of violent crime and its relation to prolonged states of warfare: The Israeli Case. *Criminology, 26*(3), 489–504. doi:10.1111/j.1745-9125.1988.tb00852.x.

Lauritsen, J. L, Sampson, R. J., & Laub, J. H. (1991). The link between offending and victimization among adolescents. *Criminology, 29*(2), 265–292. doi:10.1111/j.1745-9125.1991.tb01067.x.

Lin, M.-J. (2008). Does unemployment increase crime? Evidence from U.S. Data 1974–2000. *Journal of Human Resources, 43*(2), 413–436. doi:10.3368/jhr.43.2.413.

Lindqvist, P. (1986). Criminal homicide in Northern Sweden 1970–1981: Alcohol intoxication, alcohol abuse, and mental disease. *International Journal of Law and Psychiatry, 8,* 19–37.

Lipsey, M. W., Wilson, D. B., Cohen, M. A., & Derzon, J. H. (1997). Is there a causal relationship between alcohol use and violence? A synthesis of evidence. *Recent Developments in Alcoholism, 13* (pp. 245–282). New York: Plenum Press.

Livingston, M. (2008). Alcohol outlet density and assault: a spatial analysis. *Addiction, 103*(4), 619–628. doi:10.1111/j.1360-0443.2008.02136.x.

Loftin, C. & McDowall, D. (1982). The police, crime, and economic theory: An assessment. *American Sociological Review*, 393–401.

Loftin, C., & Hill, R. H. (1974). Regional subculture and homicide: An examination of the Gastil-Hackney thesis. *American Sociological Review, 39*(5), 714–724. doi:10.2307/2094316.

Losoya, S. H., Knight, G. P., Chassin, L., Little, M., Vargas-Chanes, D., Mauricio, A., & Piquero, A. (2008). Trajectories of acculturation and enculturation in relation to heavy episodic drinking and marijuana use in a sample of Mexican American serious juvenile offenders. *Journal of Drug Issues, 38*(1), 171–198.

Luckenbill, D. F. (1977). Criminal homicide as a situated transaction. *Social Problems*, 176–186.

Lw, G. (1978). Alcohol-related acts of violence: who was drinking and where the acts occurred. *Journal of Studies on Alcohol, 39*(7), 1294.

MacDonald, J. M. & Gover, A. R. (2005). Concentrated disadvantage and youth-on-youth homicide assessing the structural covariates over time. *Homicide Studies, 9*(1), 30–54.

Maddala, G. S. (1971). The use of variance components models in pooling cross section and time series data. *Econometrica: Journal of the Econometric Society*, 341–358. doi:10.2307/1913349.

Maguire, K. & A.L. Pastore (Eds.). (1997). *Sourcebook of criminal justice statistics.* Retrieved from www.albany.edu/sourcebook.

Maldonado-Molina, M. M., Reingle, J. M., Tobler, A. L., & Komro, K. A. (2010). Effects of beverage-specific alcohol consumption on drinking behaviors among urban youth. *Journal of Drug Education, 40*(3), 265–280.

Males, M. A. (1986). The minimum purchase age for alcohol and young-driver fatal crashes: A long-term view. *The Journal of Legal studies, 15*(1), 181–211.

Markus, G. B. (1988). The impact of personal and national economic conditions on the presidential vote: A pooled cross-sectional analysis. *American Journal of Political Science*, 137–154.

Martinez, R., Jr. (1996). Latinos and lethal violence: The impact of poverty and inequality. *Soc. Probs., 43,* 131.

Martinez, R. & Lee, M. T. (1998). Immigration and the ethnic distribution of homicide in Miami, 1985–1995. *Homicide Studies, 2*(3), 291–304. doi:10.1177/1088767998002003009.

Maxfield, M. G. (1987). Lifestyle and routine activity theories of crime: Empirical studies of victimization, delinquency, and offender decision-making. *Journal of Quantitative Criminology, 3*(4), 275–282. doi:10.1007/BF01066831.

McCleary, R., Hay, R., Meidinger, E. E., McDowall, D., & Land, K. C. (1980). *Applied time series analysis for the social sciences.* Beverly Hills, CA: Sage Publications.

McDowall, D. (1980). *Interrupted time series analysis.* Beverly Hills, CA: Sage Publications.

McKinney, C. M., Caetano, R., Harris, T. R., & Ebama, M. S. (2009). Alcohol availability and intimate partner violence among US couples. *Alcoholism: Clinical and Experimental Research, 33*(1), 169–176. doi:10.1111/j.1530-0277.2008.00825.x.

Messman-Moore, T. L., Coates, A. A., Gaffey, K. J., & Johnson, C. F. (2008). Sexuality, substance use, and susceptibility to victimization risk for rape and sexual coercion in a prospective study of college women. *Journal of Interpersonal Violence, 23*(12), 1730–1746. doi:10.1177/0886260508314336

Messner, S. F, Raffalovich, L. E., & Sutton, G. M. (2010). Poverty, infant mortality, and homicide rates in cross-national perspective: Assessments of criterion and construct validity. *Criminology, 48*(2), 30, 509–537.

Messner, S. F. & Sampson, R. J. (1991). The sex ratio, family disruption, and rates of violent crime: The paradox of demographic structure. *Social Forces, 69*(3), 693–713.

Messner, S. F. (1982). Poverty, inequality, and the urban homicide rate: Some unexpected findings. *Criminology, 20*(1), 103–114. doi:10.1111/j.1745-9125.1982.tb00450.x.

Messner, S. F. (1983). Regional differences in the economic correlates of the urban homicide rate. *Criminology, 21*(4), 477–488. doi:10.1111/j.1745-9125.1983.tb00275.x.

Messner, S. F. & Golden, R. M. (1992). Racial inequality and racially disaggregated homicide rates: An assessment of alternative theoretical explanations. *Criminology, 30*, 421.

Messner, S. F. & Tardiff, K. (1986). Economic inequality and levels of homicide: An analysis of urban neighborhoods. *Criminology, 24*(2), 297–316. doi:10.1111/j.1745-9125.1986.tb01497.x.

Messner, S. F. (1989). Economic discrimination and societal homicide rates: Further evidence on the cost of inequality. *American Sociological Review, 54*(4), 597–611. doi:10.2307/2095881.

Miethe, T. D., Stafford, M. C., & Long, J. S. (1987). Social differentiation in criminal victimization: A test of routine activities/lifestyle theories. *American Sociological Review, 52*(2), 184–194. doi:10.2307/2095447.

Miron, J. A. & Tetelbaum, E. (2009). Does the minimum legal drinking age save lives? *Economic Inquiry, 47*(2), 317–336.

Miron, J. A. & Zwiebel, J. (1991). Alcohol consumption during prohibition. *National Bureau of Economic Research Working Paper Series, 3675*. Retrieved from www.nber.org/papers/w3675.

Moffitt, T. E. (1993). Adolescence-limited and life-course-persistent antisocial behavior: a developmental taxonomy. *Psychological Review; Psychological Review, 100*(4), 674.

Moss, A. C. & Albery, I. P. (2009). A dual-process model of the alcohol–behavior link for social drinking. *Psychological Bulletin, 135*(4), 516–530. doi:10.1037/a0015991.

Mundlak, Y. (1978). On the pooling of time series and cross section data. *Econometrica, 46*(1), 69–85. doi:10.2307/1913646.

Murdoch, D. D. & Pihl, R. O. (1988). The influence of beverage type on aggression in males in the natural setting. *Aggressive Behavior, 14*(5), 325–335.

Murdoch, D. & Ross, D. (1990). Alcohol and crimes of violence: Present issues. *Substance Use & Misuse, 25*(9), 1065–1081.

National Institute of Alcohol Abuse and Alcoholism. (1990). *9th Special report to the US Congress on alcohol and health: Highlights from current research*. Washington, DC: US Government Printing Office.

National Institute of Alcohol Abuse and Alcoholism. (2000). *10th special report to the US Congress on alcohol and health: Highlights from current research*. Washington, DC: US Government Printing Office.

National Institute of Alcohol Abuse and Alcoholism. (2007). *Apparent per capita ethanol consumption for the United States, 1850–2004*. Retrieved from www.niaaa.nih.gov/Resources/DatabaseResource /QuickFacts/AlcoholSales/consum01.

National Institute on Alcohol Abuse and Alcoholism. (2002). *Alcohol alert: Alcohol and minorities, 55*. Retrieved from www.ehd.org/health_alcohol_13.php.

National Research Council. (1993). *Understanding and preventing violence*.

Nelson, J. P. (2006). Alcohol advertising in magazines: Do beer, wine, and spirits ads target youth? *Contemporary Economic Policy, 24*(3), 357–369. doi:10.1093/cep/byj036.

Nerlove, M. (1971). A note on error components models. *Econometrica: Journal of the Econometric Society*, 383–396.

Newman, O. (1972). *Defensible space: Crime prevention through urban design*. New York: Macmillan.

Norberg, K. E., Bierut, L. J., & Grucza, R. A. (2009). Long-term effects of minimum drinking age laws on past-year alcohol and drug use disorders. *Alcoholism: Clinical and Experimental Research, 33*(12), 2180–2190.

Nutt, D. J., King, L. A., & Phillips, L. D. (2010). Drug harms in the UK: A multicritera decision analysis. *The Lancet, 376*, 1558–1565.

O, E. & Jr, L. R. (1985). Influence of acute alcohol intoxication on the outcome of severe non-neurologic trauma. *Acta chirurgica Scandinavica, 151*(4), 305.

O'Malley, P. M., Wagenaar, A. C., et al. (1991). Effects of minimum drinking age laws on alcohol use, related behaviors and traffic crash involvement among American youth: 1976–1987. *Journal of studies on Alcohol, 52*(5), 478.

Organization for Economic and Cooperative Development. (2012). *Inequality by country*. Retrieved from http://stats.oecd.org/Index.aspx?QueryId=26067&Lang=en.

Ornstein, S. I., & Hanssens, D. M. (1985). Alcohol control laws and the consumption of distilled spirits and beer. *Journal of Consumer Research*, 200–213.

Parker, K. D., Weaver, G., & Calhoun, T. (1995). Predictors of alcohol and drug use: A multiethnic comparison. *The Journal of social psychology, 135*(5), 581–590.

Parker, K. F. & Reckdenwald, A. (2008). Concentrated disadvantage, traditional male rold models and African-American juvenile violence. *Criminology, 46*(3), 711–735. doi:10.1111/j.1745-9125.2008.00119.x.

Parker, R. N. (1989). Poverty, subculture of violence, and type of homicide. *Social Forces, 67*(4), 983–1007.

Parker, R. N. (1998). Alcohol, homicide, and cultural context: A cross-national analysis of gender-specific homicide victimization. *Homicide Studies, 2*(1), 6–30.

Parker, R. N. (2012). Why California's three strikes fails as crime and economic policy, and what to do. California Journal of Politics and Policy.

Parker, R. N, McCaffree, K. J., & Skiles, D. (2011). The impact of retail practices on violence: The case of single serve alcohol beverage containers. *Drug and Alcohol Review, 30*(5), 496–504.

Parker, R. N, & Smith, M. D. (1979). Deterrence, poverty, and type of homicide. *American Journal of Sociology*, 614–624.

Parker, R. N, Williams, K. R., McCaffree, K. J., Acensio, E. K., Browne, A., Strom, K. J., & Barrick, K. (2011). Alcohol availability and youth homicide in the 91 largest US cities, 1984–2006. *Drug and Alcohol Review*, *30*(5), 505–514.

Parker, Robert N., & Toth, A. M. (1990). Family, intimacy, and homicide: A macro-social approach. *Violence and Victims*, *5*(3), 195–210.

Parker, Robert Nash. (1989). Poverty, subculture of violence, and type of homicide. *Social Forces*, *67*(4), 983–1007. doi:10.1093/sf/67.4.983

Parker, Robert Nash. (1993). The effects of context on alcohol and violence. *Alcohol Health & Research World*, *17*(2), 117–122.

Parker, Robert Nash. (1995). Bringing "booze" back in: The relationship between alcohol and homicide. *Journal of Research in Crime and Delinquency*, *32*(1), 3–38. doi:10.1177/00224 27895032001001.

Parker, Robert Nash, Mccaffree, K. J., & Skiles, D. (2011). The impact of retail practices on violence: The case of single serve alcohol beverage containers. *Drug and Alcohol Review*, *30*(5), 496–504. doi:10.1111/j.1465-3362.2011.00318.x.

Parker, R. N. & Rebhun, L.-A. (1995). *Alcohol & homicide*. Albany, NY: SUNY Press.

Parker, R. N. & Smith, M. D. (1979). Deterrence, poverty, and type of homicide. *American Journal of Sociology*, *85*(3), 614–624.

Parker, R. N. (1992). Alcohol, homicide, and cultural context: A cross-national analysis of gender-specific homicide victimization. *Kettil Bruun Society*. Presented at the 18th Annual Alcohol Epidemiology Symposium, Toronto.

Parker, R. N. (1993). Alcohol and theories of homicide. In F. Adler & W. Laufer (Eds.), *New Direction in Criminological Theory* (pp. 113–144). Piscataway, NJ: Transaction Publishers.

Parker, R.N. (n.d.). Violent crime. In J. F. Sheley (Ed.), *Criminology: A Contemporary Handbook* (pp. 143–160). Belmont, CA: Wadsworth Publishing Company.

Parker, R. N. & D. Anderson-Facile. (2000). Violent crime trends. In J. F. Sheley (Ed.), *A Handbook of Criminology* (pp. 191–213). Belmont, CA: Wadsworth Publishing Company.

Parker, R. N. & E. K. Ascensio. (2008). *GIS and spatial analysis for the social sciences: Coding, mapping, modeling*. New York: Routledge.

Parker, R. N. & Auerhahn, K. (n.d.). Alcohol, drugs and violence. In John Hagan (Ed.), *Annual Review of Sociology*, 24. Palo Alto, CA: Annual Review Press.

Parsai, M., Voisine, S., Marsiglia, F. F., Kulis, S., & Nieri, T. (2009). The protective and risk effects of parents and peers on substance use, attitudes, and behaviors of Mexican and Mexican American female and male adolescents. *Youth & Society*, *40*(3), 353–376. doi:10.1177/0044118X08318117.

Pedersen, W. C., Aviles, F. E., Ito, T. A., Miller, N., & Pollock, V. E. (2002). Psychological experimentation on alcohol-induced human aggression. *Aggression and Violent Behavior*, *7*(3), 293–312. doi:10.1016/S1359-1789(01)00044-1.

Peralta, R., & Cruz, J. (2006). Conferring meaning onto alcohol-related violence: An Analysis of alcohol use and gender in a sample of college youth. *The Journal of Men's Studies*, *14*(1), 109–125. doi:10.3149/jms.1401.109.

Pernanen, K. (1991). *Alcohol in human violence*. The Guilford substance abuse series. New York: Guilford Press.

Pernanen, K. (1976). Alcohol and crimes of violence. In B. Kissin & H. Begleiter (Eds.), *The Biology of Alcoholism, Social Aspects of Alcoholism, 4* (pp. 351–444). New York: Plenum Press.

Pernanen, K. (1981). Theoretical aspects of the relationship between alcohol consumption and criminal behavior. In J. J. Collins Jr. (Ed.), *Drinking and crime: Perspectives on the rela-*

tionship between alcohol consumption and criminal behavior (pp. 1–69). New York: Guilford Press.

Pernanen, K. (1989). Causal inferences about the role of alcohol in accidents, poisoning and violence. In N. Giesbrecht, R. Gonzales, M. Grant, E. Osterberg, R. Room, I. Rootman, & L. Towle (Eds.), *Drinking and Casualties* (pp. 158–171). New York: Tavistock/Routledge.

Perry, C. L., Williams, C. L., Veblen-Mortenson, S., Toomey, T. L., Komro, K. A., Anstine, P. S., McGovern, P. G., et al. (1996). Project Northland: Outcomes of a communitywide alcohol use prevention program during early adolescence. *American Journal of Public Health, 86*(7), 956–965.

Peterson, J. B., Rothfleisch, J., Zelazo, P. D., & Pihl, R. O. (1990). Acute alcohol intoxication and cognitive functioning. *Journal of Studies on Alcohol; Journal of Studies on Alcohol.*

Peterson, R. D., & Bailey, W. C. (1992). Rape and dimensions of gender socioeconomic inequality in U.S. metropolitan areas. *Journal of Research in Crime and Delinquency, 29*(2), 162–177. doi:10.1177/0022427892029002004.

Petticrew, M., Cummins, S., Ferrell, C., Findlay, A., Higgins, C., Hoy, C., Kearns, A., et al. (2005). Natural experiments: An underused tool for public health? *Public health, 119*(9), 751–757.

Pettigrew, T. F. & Spier, R. B. (1962). The ecological structure of Negro homicide. *American Journal of Sociology, 67*(6), 621–629.

Pihl, R. O., Peterson, J. B., & Lau, M. A. (1993). A biosocial model of the alcohol-aggression relationship. *Journal of Studies on Alcohol, Suppl 11*, 128–139.

Pizarro, J. M., DeJong, C., & McGarrell, E. F. (2010). An examination of the covariates of female homicide victimization and offending. *Feminist Criminology, 5*(1), 51–72.

Pokorny, A. D. (1965). A comparison of homicides in two cities. *The Journal of Criminal Law, Criminology, and Police Science, 56*(4), 479–487.

Ponicki, W. R. & Gruenewald, P. J. (2005). *S3: Spatial Statistical System (version 5.2)*. Berkeley, CA: Prevention Research Center.

Ponicki, W. (1990). *The price and income elasticities of the demand for alcohol: A review of the literature*. Berkeley, CA: Prevention Research Center.

Pratt, T. C. & Cullen, F. T. (2005). Assessing macro-level predictors and theories of crime: A meta-analysis. *Crime and Justice, 32*, 373–450.

Price, J. A. (1975). An applied analysis of North American Indian drinking patterns. *Human Organization, 34*(1), 17–26.

Pridemore, W. A. (2011). Poverty matters: A reassessment of the inequality–homicide relationship in cross-national studies. *British Journal of Criminology, 51*(5), 739–772.

Pridemore, W. A. & Grubesic, T. H. (2011). Alcohol outlets and community levels of interpersonal violence: Spatial density, outlet type, and seriousness of assault. *Journal of Research in Crime and Delinquency.*

Radford, J. & Stanko, E. A. (1994). The contradictions of patriarchal crime control. *Peace Review, 6*(2), 149–158.

Reiss, A. J., Roth, J. A., & Miczek, K. A. (1993). *Understanding and preventing violence: Social influences, 3*. Washington, DC: National Academy Press.

Reiss, A. J., Jr., & Nelson, J. P. (1988). Economic and legal determinants of alcoholic beverage consumption in the U.S.: A Bayesian approach. University Park, PA: Department of Economics, Pennsylvania.

Reuter, P. (2009). Systemic violence in drug markets. *Crime, law and social change, 52*(3), 275–284.

Reynolds, R. I., Holder, H. D., & Gruenewald, P. J. (1997). Community prevention and alcohol retail access. *Addiction, 92*(6s1), 261–272.

Riedel, M., Zahn, M. A., Mock, L. F., (US), N. I. of J., & Crime, S. I. U. (System). C. for the S. of. (1985). *The nature and patterns of American homicide.* US Department of Justice, National Institute of Justice Washington, DC.

Robinson, R.B. (n.d.). The theoretical development of CPTED: 25 years of responses to C. Ray Jeffery. In W. Laufer & F. Adler (Eds.), *The Criminology of Criminal Law: Advances in Criminological Theory, 8* (pp. 427–462). New Brunswick, NJ: Transaction Publishers.

Rogers, R. G. (1992). Living and dying in the USA: Sociodemographic determinants of death among blacks and whites. *Demography, 29*(2), 287–303.

Roncek, D. W. & Maier, P. A. (1991). Bars, blocks, and crimes revisited: Linking the theory of routine activities to the empiricism of "hot spots." *Criminology, 29*(4), 725–753. doi:10.1111/j.1745-9125.1991.tb01086.x.

Room, R., Collins, G., Abuse, N. I. on A., Branch, A. (US). N. R. C., & University of California, B. S. of P. H. S. R. G. (1983). *Alcohol and disinhibition: Nature and meaning of the link.* US Department of Health and Human Services, Public Health Service, Alcohol, Drug Abuse, and Mental Health Administration, National Institute on Alcohol Abuse and Alcoholism.

Room, R. (1976). Ambivalence as a sociological explanation: The case of cultural explanations of alcohol problems. *American Sociological Review, 41*(6), 1047–1065. doi:10.2307/2094802

Room, R. (1972). Relations between ethnic and cross-national comparisons. *Drinking and Drug Practices Surveyor, 5*(12).

Room, R. (1989). Responses to alcohol-related problems in an international perspective: Characterizing and explaining cultural wetness and dryness. Presented at the La ricera Italiana sulle bevande alcoiche nel confronto internazionale, Santo Stefano Belbo, Italy.

Room, R. & Collins, G. (Eds.). (1983). *Alcohol and disinhibition: Nature and meaning of the link.* Washington, DC: National Institute on Alcohol Abuse and Alcoholism.

Roussos, S. T., & Fawcett, S. B. (2000). A review of collaborative partnerships as a strategy for improving community health. *Annual Review of Public Health, 21*(1), 369–402.

Saffer, H. & Grossman, M. (1987). Drinking age laws and highway mortality rates: Cause and effect. *Economic Inquiry, 25*(3), 403–417.

Saltz, R. F. & Stanghetta, P. (1997). A community-wide responsible beverage service program in three communities: Early findings. *Addiction, 92*(6s1), 237–250.

Sampson, R. J. & Lauritsen, J. L. (1990). Deviant lifestyles, proximity to crime, and the offender-victim link in personal violence. *Journal of Research in Crime and Delinquency, 27*(2), 110–139.

Sampson, R. J. (1985). Neighborhood and crime: The structural determinants of personal victimization. *Journal of Research in Crime and Delinquency, 22*(1), 7–40. doi:10.1177/00 22427885022001002.

Sampson, R. J. (1987). Urban African American violence: The effect of male joblessness and family disruption. *American Journal of Sociology, 93*(2), 348–382.

Sampson, R. J. & Raudenbush, S. W. (1999). Systematic social observation of public spaces: A new look at disorder in urban neighborhoods. *American Journal of Sociology, 105*(3), 603–651.

Sampson, Robert J., & Wooldredge, J. D. (1987). Linking the micro- and macro-level dimensions of lifestyle-routine activity and opportunity models of predatory victimization. *Journal of Quantitative Criminology, 3*(4), 371–393. doi:10.1007/BF01066837

Sampson, R. J. (1986). Neighborhood family structure and the risk of personal victimization. In J. M. Byrne & R. J. Sampson (Eds.), *The Social Ecology of Crime* (pp. 25–46). New York: Springer-Verlag.

Sampson, R. J. & W. J. Wilson. (n.d.). Toward a theory of race, crime and urban inequality. In J. Hagan & R. D. Peterson (Eds.), *Crime and Inequality* (pp. 37–54). Stanford: Stanford University Press.

Sanday, P. R. (1997). *A woman scorned: Acquaintance rape on trial.* Berkeley: University of California Press.

Savage, J., Bennett, R. R., & Danner, M. (2008). Economic assistance and crime: A cross-national investigation. *European Journal of Criminology, 5*(2), 217–238.

Savolainen, J. (2000). Inequality, welfare state, and homicide: Further support for the institutional anomie theory. *Criminology, 38*(4), 1021–1042.

Schreck, C. J. & Fisher, B. S. (2004). Specifying the influence of family and peers on violent victimization: Extending routine activities and lifestyle theories. *Journal of Interpersonal Violence, 19*(9), 1021–1041.

Schwartz, M. D. & Pitts, V. L. (1995). Exploring a feminist routine activities approach to explaining sexual assault. *Justice Quarterly, 12*(1), 9–31.

Schwartz, M. D. & DeKeseredy, W. S. (1997). *Sexual assault on the college campus: The role of male peer support.* Thousand Oaks, CA: Sage Publications.

Scribner, R. A., Cohen, D. A., & Fisher, W. (2000). Evidence of a structural effect for alcohol outlet density: a multilevel analysis. *Alcoholism: Clinical and Experimental Research, 24*(2), 188–195.

Scribner, R. A., MacKinnon, D. P., & Dwyer, J. H. (1995). The risk of assaultive violence and alcohol availability in Los Angeles County. *American Journal of Public Health, 85*(3), 335–340. doi:10.2105/AJPH.85.3.335.

Seale, J. P., Seale, J. D., Alvarado, M., Vogel, R. L., & Terry, N. E. (2002). Prevalence of problem drinking in a Venezuelan Native American population. *Alcohol and Alcoholism, 37*(2), 198–204.

Seale, J. P., Shellenberger, S., Rodriguez, C., Seale, J. D., & Alvarado, M. (2002). Alcohol use and cultural change in an indigenous population: a case study from Venezuela. *Alcohol and Alcoholism, 37*(6), 603–608.

Sherman, L. W., Gartin, P. R., & Buerger, M. E. (1989). Hot spots of predatory crime: Routine activities and the criminology of place. *Criminology, 27*(1), 27–56. doi:10.1111/j.1745-9125.1989.tb00862.x.

Short, B., ph, J. I., & Willenbring, M. L. (2000). Alcohol home delivery services: A source of alcohol for underage drinkers. *Journal of Studies on Alcohol, 61*(1), 81–84.

Silverman, R. A. & Kennedy, L. W. (1987). Relational distance and homicide: The role of the stranger. *J. Crim. L. & Criminology, 78,* 272.

Silverman, R. A., & Kennedy, L. W. (1988). Women who kill their children. *Violence and Victims, 3*(2), 113–127.

Skog, O. (1986). Trends in alcohol consumption and violent deaths. *British Journal of Addiction, 81*(3), 365–379. doi:10.1111/j.1360-0443.1986.tb00343.x.

Skog, O. (1989). Trends in alcohol consumption and violent death. In N. Giesbrecht, R. Gonzales, M. Grant, E. Osterberg, R. Room, I. Rootman, & L. Towle (Eds.), *Drinking and Casualties* (pp. 319–342). New York: Tavistock/Routledge.

Small, M., Singer, J. D., & Bennett, R. (1982). *Resort to arms: International and civil wars, 1816–1980, 4.* Beverly Hills: Sage Publications.

Smart, R. G. & Mann, R. E. (1987). Large decreases in alcohol-related problems following a slight reduction in alcohol consumption in Ontario 1975–83. *British Journal of Addiction*, *82*(3), 285–291. doi:10.1111/j.1360-0443.1987.tb01482.x

Smart, R. G. (1977). The relationship of availability of alcoholic beverages to per capita consumption and alcoholism rates. *Journal of Studies on Alcohol*, *38*, 891–896.

Smith, D. A. & Jarjoura, G. R. (1988). Social structure and criminal victimization. *Journal of Research in Crime and Delinquency*, *25*(1), 27–52. doi:10.1177/0022427888025001003.

Smith, M. D. & Parker, R. N. (1980). Type of homicide and variation in regional rates. *Social Forces*, *59*(1), 136–147.

Smith, M. & Bennett, N. (1985). Poverty, inequality, and theories of forcible rape. *Crime & Delinquency*, *31*(2), 295–305. doi:10.1177/0011128785031002008.

Snyder, L. B., Milici, F. F., Slater, M., Sun, H., & Strizhakova, Y. (2006). Effects of alcohol advertising exposure on drinking among youth. *Archives of Pediatrics and Adolescent Medicine*, *160*(1), 18.

Spano, R. & Nagy, S. (2005). Social guardianship and social isolation: An application and extension of lifestyle/routine activities theory to rural adolescents. *Rural Sociology*, *70*(3), 414–437. doi:10.1526/0036011054831189.

Spunt, B., Brownstein, H., Goldstein, P., Fendrich, M., & Liberty, H. J. (1995). Drug use by homicide offenders. *Journal of Psychoactive Drugs*, *27*(2), 125–134. doi:10.1080/0279107 2.1995.10471681.

Spunt, B., Goldstein, P., Brownstein, H., Fendrich, M., & et al. (1994). Alcohol and homicide: Interviews with prison inmates. *Journal of Drug Issues*, *24*(1-2), 143–163.

Steele, C. M. & Josephs, R. A. (1990). Alcohol myopia: Its prized and dangerous effects. *American Psychologist*, *45*(8), 921.

Stein, J. L. (2007). Peer educators and close friends as predictors of male college students' willingness to prevent rape. *Journal of College Student Development*, *48*(1), 75–89. doi:10.1353/csd.2007.0008.

Stets, J. E. (1990). Verbal and physical aggression in marriage. *Journal of Marriage and Family*, *52*(2), 501–514. doi:10.2307/353043.

Stevens, B. R., Smith, T. R., Fein, K. R., Gottschalk, M., & Howard, G. J. (2011). A deadly mix? An international investigation of handgun availability, drinking culture, and homicide. *International Journal of Comparative and Applied Criminal Justice*, *35*(1), 39–51.

Stimson, J. A. (1985). Regression in space and time: A statistical essay. *American Journal of Political Science*, *29*(4), 914–947. doi:10.2307/2111187.

Strom, K. J. & MacDonald, J. M. (2007). The influence of social and economic disadvantage on racial patterns in youth homicide over time. *Homicide Studies*, *11*(1), 50–69.

Suarez, E. & Gadalla, T. M. (2010). Stop blaming the victim: A meta-analysis on rape myths. *Journal of Interpersonal Violence*, *25*(11), 2010–2035. doi:10.1177/0886260509354503.

Sugarmann, J. (2010, January 26). Pennsylvania leads nation in black homicide victimization. *Huffington Post*. Retrieved from www.huffingtonpost.com/josh-sugarmann/pennsylvania-leads-nation_b_437049.html.

Tardiff, K., Marzuk, P. M., Leon, A. C., Hirsch, C. S., Stajic, M., Portera, L., & Hartwell, N. (1995). Cocaine, opiates, and ethanol in homicides in New York City: 1990 and 1991. *Journal of Forensic Sciences*, *40*(3), 387.

Taylor, C. L. & Hudson, M. (1972). *World handbook of political and social indicators*. New Haven: Yale University Press.

Tcherni, M. (2011). Structural determinants of homicide: The big three. *Journal of Quantitative Criminology*, 1–22.

Testa, M. & Livingston, J. A. (2009). Alcohol consumption and women's vulnerability to sexual victimization: Can reducing women's drinking prevent rape? *Substance Use & Misuse*, *44*(9-10), 1349–1376. doi:10.1080/10826080902961468.

Thompson, M. P., Koss, M. P., Kingree, J. B., Goree, J., & Rice, J. (2011). A prospective mediational model of sexual aggression among college men. *Journal of Interpersonal Violence*, *26*(13), 2716–2734. doi:10.1177/0886260510388285.

Treno, A. J. & Lee, J. P. (2002). Approaching alcohol problems through local environmental interventions. *Alcohol Research and Health*, *26*(1), 35–41.

Treno, A. J., Parker, R. N., Holder, H. D., et al. (1993). Understanding US alcohol consumption with social and economic factors: a multivariate time series analysis, 1950–1986. *Journal of Studies on Alcohol*, *54*(2), 146–157.

Treno, A. & Parker, R. N. (1994). Economic indicators, routine activity, age structure and alcohol beverage type: A multivariate time series analysis. Presented at the Annual Meeting of American Sociological Association, Los Angeles, CA.

US Bureau of the Census, Census of the Population. (1993). *Summary file STF3, block-group summary*. Washington, DC: U.S. Government Printing Office.

US Department of Labor. (1997). *National Census of fatal occupational injuries, 1996*. Washington, DC: Bureau of Labor Statistics.

United Nations. (1951). *Demographic yearbook*. New York.

United Nations. (1985). *Social development questions: Capital punishment* (#85-12176). Economic and Social Council.

US Department of Justice, Office of Juvenile Justice and Delinquency Prevention. (n.d.). *juveniles as offenders*. Retrieved from www.ojjdp.gov/ojstatbb/offenders/qa03105.asp?qaDate=2009.

Valdez, A., Kaplan, C. D., & Curtis, R. L., Jr. (2007). Aggressive crime, alcohol and drug use, and concentrated poverty in 24 US urban areas. *The American Journal of Drug and Alcohol Abuse*, *33*(4), 595–603.

Vieraitis, L. M., Britto, S., & Morris, R. G. (2011). Assessing the impact of changes in gender equality on female homicide victimization, 1980–2000. *Crime & Delinquency*.

Vingilis, E. R. & De Genova, K. (1984). Youth and the forbidden fruit: Experiences with changes in legal drinking age in North America. *Journal of Criminal Justice*, *12*(2), 161–172.

Violence Policy Center. (2010). *Black homicide victimization in the US*. Washington, DC Retrieved from www.vpc.org/studies/blackhomicide10.pdf.

Voas, R. B., Holder, H. D., & Gruenewald, P. J. (1997). The effect of drinking and driving interventions on alcohol-involved traffic crashes within a comprehensive community trial. *Addiction*, *92*, S221–S236.

Voas, R. B., Tippetts, A. S., & Fell, J. C. (2003). Assessing the effectiveness of minimum legal drinking age and zero tolerance laws in the United States. *Accident Analysis & Prevention*, *35*(4), 579–587.

Voisine, S., Parsai, M., Marsiglia, F. F., Kulis, S., & Nieri, T. (2008). Effects of parental monitoring, permissiveness, and injunctive norms on substance use among Mexican and Mexican American adolescents. *Families in Society: The Journal of Contemporary Human Services*, *89*(2), 264–273. doi:10.1606/1044-3894.3742.

Volkow, N. D., Ma, Y., Zhu, W., Fowler, J. S., Li, J., Rao, M., Mueller, K., et al. (2008). Moderate doses of alcohol disrupt the functional organization of the human brain. *Psychiatry Research: Neuroimaging*, *162*(3), 205–213.

Voss, H. L., Hepburn, J. R., Northwestern University 357 East Chicago Avenue Chicago IL 60611, & Williams and Wilkins Co 428 East Preston Street Baltimore MD 21202. (1968). Patterns in Criminal Homicide in Chicago (IL). *Journal of Criminal Law, 59*(4), 499–508.

Wade, R. H. (2004). Is globalization reducing poverty and inequality? *World Development, 32*(4), 567–589.

Wagenaar, A. C. (1983). *Alcohol, young drivers and traffic accidents: Effects of minimum age laws.* Lexington, MA: D.C. Heath and Co.

Wagenaar, A. C., Finnegan, J. R., Wolfson, M., Anstine, P. S., Williams, C. L., & Perry, C. L. (1993). Where and how adolescents obtain alcoholic beverages. *Public Health Reports, 108*(4), 459.

Wagenaar, A. C., Holder, H. D., & others. (1991). A change from public to private sale of wine: results from natural experiments in Iowa and West Virginia. *Journal of Studies on Alcohol, 52*(2), 162–173.

Wagenaar, A. C., & Toomey, T. L. (2002). Effects of minimum drinking age laws: review and analyses of the literature from 1960 to 2000. *Journal of Studies on Alcohol and Drugs,* (14), 206.

Warner, T. D., Fishbein, D. H., & Krebs, C. P. (2010). The risk of assimilating? Alcohol use among immigrant and U.S.-born Mexican youth. *Social Science Research, 39*(1), 176–186. doi:10.1016/j.ssresearch.2009.07.001.

Watts, R. K. & Rabow, J. (1983). Alcohol availability and alcohol-related problems in 213 California cities. *Alcoholism: Clinical and Experimental Research, 7*(1), 47–58. doi:10.1111/j.1530-0277.1983.tb05410.x.

Weatherburn, D. J. (2008). The role of drug and alcohol policy in reducing Indigenous over-representation in prison. *Drug and Alcohol Review, 27*(1), 91–94.

Weatherby, N., Nam, C., & Isaac, L. (1983). Development, inequality, health care, and mortality at the older ages: a cross-national analysis. *Demography, 20*(1), 27–43. doi:10.2307/2060899.

Welte, J. W., Abel, E. L., & Wieczorek, W. (1988). The role of alcohol in suicides in Erie County, NY, 1972–1984. *Public Health Reports, 103*, 648–652.

Welte, J. W. & Abel, E. L. (1989). Homicide: Drinking by the victim. *Journal of Studies on Alcohol, 50*(3), 197–201.

White, H. R., Brick, J., & Hansell, S. (1993). A longitudinal investigation of alcohol use and aggression in adolescence. *Journal of Studies on Alcohol, Suppl 11*, 62–77.

White, H. Raskin, Pandina, R. J., & LaGrange, R. L. (2006). Longitudinal predictors of serious substance use and delinquency. *Criminology, 25*(3), 715–740 doi:10.1111/j.1745-9125.1987.tb00816.x.

Wieczorek, W. F, Welte, J. W., & Abel, E. L. (1990). Alcohol, drugs and murder: A study of convicted homicide offenders. *Journal of Criminal Justice, 18*(3), 217–227. doi:10.1016/0047-2352(90)90002-S.

Williams, K. R. (1984). Economic sources of homicide: Reestimating the effects of poverty and inequality. *American Sociological Review, 49*(2), 283–289. doi:10.2307/2095577

Williams, K. R. & Flewelling, R. L. (1988). The social production of criminal homicide: A comparative study of disaggregated rates in American cities. *American Sociological Review,* 421–431. doi:10.2307/2095649.

Williams, T. (2012, 4 April). Indian beer bill stalls: Industry money flows. *New York Times.*

Wilsnack, R. W., Wilsnack, S. C., Kristjanson, A. F., Vogeltanz-Holm, N. D., & Gmel, G. (2009). Gender and alcohol consumption: patterns from the multinational GENACIS project. *Addiction, 104*(9), 1487–1500.

Wilson, W. J. (1987). *The truly disadvantaged: The inner city, the underclass, and public policy.* Chicago: University of Chicago Press.

Wolfgang, M. E. (1958). *Patterns in criminal homicide.* Philadelphia: University of Pennsylvania.

Wolfgang, M. E. & F. Ferracuti. (1967). *The subculture of violence: Towards an integrated theory in criminology.* New York: Tavistock Publications.

Wood, E. (1961). *Housing design: A social theory.* Citizens' Housing and Planning Council of New York.

Wood, J. B. (1996). *The Barrow reclamation.* Barrow, AL: North Slope Borough Department of Public Safety.

World Health Organization. (1951). *World Health Statistics Annual: Vital Statistics and Causes of Death.* Geneva.

Worrall, J. L. (2009). Social support and homicide. *Homicide Studies, 13*(2), 124–143.

Wortley, R. (2001). A classification of techniques for controlling situational precipitators of crime. *Security Journal, 14*(4), 63–82.

Zhu, L., Gorman, D. M., & Horel, S. (2004). Alcohol outlet density and violence: a geospatial analysis. *Alcohol and Alcoholism, 39*(4), 369–375.

Index

Abbott, P. J., 127
aboriginal peoples, 126–27, 168–69
acculturation stress, 32
advertising, 6, 37, 172; cars, motorcycles, and sexual availability in, 44, *47*, *48*; cigarette industry, 173; cultural and historical icons used, 40–44, *43*, *44*, 55; ethnic targeting and content, 40, 42–50, 55, *58*, 59; Latina models in, 40–41, *42*, *45–50*, 55; non-drinkers affected by, 98; outlet density and, 40, 53, 55, 59–60; sexual availability portrayed, 40, 44, *46–50*, 175; sexual violence and, 39–60, *57*, *58*; sporting events, 8, 173; underage drinkers targeted, 173–74
African Americans, 54; Florence, South Carolina, 159; historic discrimination, 8, 112–13, 115, 120; poverty and economic inequality, 31, 104–5, 108, 111–13, 115, 120, 149; Union City, California, *148*, 149; victimization rates, 104–5, 108; youth homicide, 114–16, *115*
Alaniz, M. L., 53–54
Alaskan Natives, 126
alcohol: acute vs. chronic use, 62; as biochemically "hard" drug, 13; biphasic structure of intoxication, 17; consumption rates, 1, 107; costs to society, 62; ethanol, 35, 37, 64; homicide, role in, 1; as precursor to aggressive acts, 62; types consumed, 110–11, 113, 122; as variable, 13; youth consumption rates, 111
Alcohol and Beverage Control (ABC) agencies, 34, 157
"Alcohol and Health" (NIAAA, 2000), 3–4
Alcohol and Homicide: A Deadly Combination of Two American Traditions (Parker and Rebhun), 4
"Alcohol and Interpersonal Violence: Less than Meets the Eye" (Collins), 2–3
alcohol industry, 2, 6, 144; isolated communities and, 168–69, 176; minorities targeted by, 31, 37, 40–41; political lobbying, 168–69; youth, position toward, 39. *See also* outlet density
alcohol myopia, 63, 167
"Alcohol Outlet Density and Mexican American Youth Violence" (California Wellness Foundation), 32–33
Alcohol Research and Health, 3

About the Authors

Robert Nash Parker is professor of sociology and director of the Presley Center for Crime and Justice Studies at the University of California, Riverside. He received his PhD in sociology from Duke University, his MA in sociology from Indiana University, and his AB in quantitative methods in the social sciences, a major of his own design, from Brown University. He has held appointments at the University of Akron, Rutgers University, and the University of Iowa and was also a senior research scientist and study director at the Prevention Research Center in Berkeley, California, a unit of the Pacific Institute for Research and Evaluation (PIRE). For most of the last two decades, Parker's research has been focused on the alcohol and violence relationship and on the development of and application to social science research of Geographic Information Systems and Geospatial Statistical Models. Author of two earlier books, *Alcohol and Homicide: A Deadly Combination of Two American Traditions* (1995) and *GIS and Spatial Analysis for the Social Sciences* (2008), he has also published articles recently in the *Drug and Alcohol Review*, *Contemporary Drug Problems*, the *American Journal of Community Psychology*, and the *California Journal of Politics and Policy*.

Kevin J. McCaffree is a doctoral student at the University of California, Riverside. He has thus far copublished an extensive, cross-cultural review of the literature on alcohol and human experience, along with two articles, coauthored with Robert Nash Parker, that have appeared in the journal *Drug and Alcohol Review*. Kevin has been and continues to be a research assistant on multiple projects at UC Riverside. These projects have more recently included public policy work on alcohol and violence at the local city level as well as work on a cross-national, interdisciplinary research grant to study human morality across its sociological, psychological, economic, and philosophical dimensions. Kevin is currently working on a dissertation that provides a perception-based theory of the cultural evolution of morality across various technological and scientific stages of society.

Maria Luisa Alaniz, PhD, is professor and former chair of the Social Science Department and director of Social Science Teacher Education at San Jose State University. Maria received a BA, MA, and Pupil Personnel Credential from San Jose State University, an EdS in educational evaluation, and a PhD in sociology of education from Stanford University. She conducted research on alcohol outlet density and youth violence in Mexican American communities at the Prevention Research Center in Berkeley from 1991 to 2000. Maria was the coprincipal investigator of studies funded by NIH, the California Wellness Foundation, and the California Endowment Foundation. Her numerous articles on alcohol use among Mexican Americans, ethnic and gender specific–targeted advertising and drinking patterns among women have been published in national and international journals in the alcohol field.

Valery J. Callanan, PhD, is an associate professor of sociology at the University of Akron. She received her PhD in 2001 from the University of California, Riverside, and her dissertation was published in 2005 by LFB Scholarly Publishing, under the title, "Feeding the Fear of Crime: Crime-Related Media and Support for Three Strikes." Her most recent research has appeared in *Suicide and Life-Threatening Behavior* and *Feminist Criminology*.

Randi S. Cartmill, MS, is a researcher working at the Center for Quality and Productivity Improvement at the University of Wisconsin-Madison. Her research interests include gender, health and healthcare, aging, and technology implementation.

Deborah M. Plechner, PhD, received her doctorate from the University of California, Riverside. She teaches feminist theory in the Women's Studies Department, University of Minnesota, Duluth.

Robert Saltz, PhD (sociology), is a senior scientist at the Prevention Research Center, a unit of Pacific Institute for Research & Evaluation in Berkeley, California. The Center is one the national research centers funded by the National Institute on Alcohol Abuse and Alcoholism. Dr. Saltz's work has centered on ways in which drinking contexts may influence the risk of subsequent injury or death, with special emphasis on drinking in licensed commercial outlets and on college campuses. His research topics have included alcohol-impaired driving, responsible beverage service in retail businesses, and the design and implementation of comprehensive community prevention interventions to reduce alcohol-involved trauma. He is currently the principal investigator of a multi-campus college prevention randomized trial funded by NIAAA, and another community-level randomized trial funded by the Substance Abuse and Mental Health Services Administration (SAMHSA) aimed at reducing excessive drinking among youth and young adults. Among his professional activities,

Dr. Saltz has served on several NIAAA, CDC, and NIH review committees, served as a board member for the Society for Prevention Research, has served on several committees for the Research Society on Alcoholism, and served as a reviewer for many academic journals. He also served on the Surgeon General's Workshop on Drunk Driving as well as NIAAA's Task Force on College Drinking.